CRANSWICK ON
CAMARO

1967-1981

Marc Cranswick • Foreword by John Schinella

Contents

Foreword
Generation I Camaro
by John Schinella

Before getting into one of my favorite first Camaro history stories, I should tell you a little about myself.

I was born in 1939, in Concord New Hampshire to two great parents, John and Mable Schinella. My mother was a registered nurse and my father was a foreman for the Book Binding Division of the Rumford Press Printing Company. In his off time, Dad raced motorcycles, with Mom close by in attendance.

My education began at University of New Hampshire and the New England School of Art and Design, located in Boston Massachusetts. I was also influenced in design through my father and his family, their Italian heritage, and their work in marble and granite.

While in Boston, I was approached by General Motors design staff about a new program they were starting. It involved recruiting creative people that did not attend the more prominent automotive design universities. Diversity was their goal.

They interviewed over 40 promising students to be part of this new program. Wow, I was one of four. Only four were chosen. When they called I packed my bags and hit the road to Michigan. The work was not easy, and on top of this new stress it was entirely probationary. But I learned, and finally three of us were accepted into General Motors' production design studios.

My first assignment was at the Cadillac studio to work on the new 1965 Cadillacs. I worked on all models. I worked 24/7 for the first year. Finally, the design was right, whew.

Because of my achievements at the Cadillac studio, I was assigned to Vice President William Mitchell's secret warehouse studio. Under the head of the studio, Larry Shinoda, I was part of the team that worked on the first mid-engine Chevrolet Chaparral race car and the Mako Shark II. The Mako Shark II turned out to be the theme car for the 3rd Generation 1968 Corvette. All work in the secret studio was extremely hush hush!

At this time, the Chevrolet I exterior design studio was overflowing with future and production assignments. The Chief Designer of this studio,

Irv Rybicki, felt it was necessary to add a second Exterior and an Interior Chevrolet studio, and got the okay from Mitchell to do this. Under Irv Rybicki, Hank Haga, his assistant, was promoted to Chief Designer of the new Chevrolet II studio. Because of my design accomplishments, I was assigned to the new studio and joined Hank. What a great dream. We were to design sporty cars like the Corvette. In the studio, we felt that we should work on a small, fast, tight, four-seat sports car.

The scuttle butt in the air had many automotive companies hedging their bets that something was about to explode on the market. It turned out to be the new Ford Mustang.

Just before the Ford introduction, GM in 1963, was creating a vehicle very similar called the Super Nova. At the 1964 New York Auto Show, we debuted the Super Nova. This was ahead of Ford's Mustang introduction. Ford's execs were nervous when they reviewed our Super Nova. The competition was obvious. Ford, to add even more confusion to the market, introduced a new mid-engine race car called the GT40. Wow! What a significant machine it turned out to be.

The Super Nova received a positive reception, and we thought we would get the green light to move to production. Bunkie Knudsen, General Manager of Chevrolet division, while cognisant of the fact that many car models were in different stages of production (including the New 1965 Corvair) still was pushing hard to see that the Super Nova got there. Unfortunately, Vice President Jack Gordon put the red light on the project. Everyone in the studio, including Bill Mitchell, was disappointed at this news. At the same time, Ford released the new Ford Mustang for production. Mustang's sales went through the roof.

Overnight we got the green light to create a competitive answer. With many designs already in scale models and drawings, we began our pursuit of a pure sport version of the Super Nova. We worked on simplicity of shape and form, with less chrome. The Mustang used a more angular, large car design, shrunk down to a smaller size. Ford overly did the chrome on this Mustang. They did have great proportions with a long nose and short deck. Mustang hit a home run that no company had achieved at this time. General Motors management put us on a crash course 'push' to produce a sporty car for a September 1966 introduction.

Chevrolet II studio was small, but charged with explosive energy to create a successful sports car. This new studio provided an opportunity for other personnel to be rotated in and out of other studios. The assignments to design more sports-orientated vehicles constituted a different focus than the current family sedans. We had very talented designers, like Don Wood, Dave Stollery, Phil Garcia, and Graham Bell. We also had talented engineers and sculptors that contributed to our team.

This studio had full support from Bill Mitchell, Chuck Jordan, and Bunkie Knudsen. Believe me, it helps when management backs your horse.

During the evolution of our new sports car, while in full size clay, Bunkie visited many times. Bunkie's visions were always directed to the younger consumer. Not unlike what he did for Pontiac Motor Division.

The overall design of our new unnamed sports car was taking shape, with a sharp peak throughout the body, front-to-rear. This was similar to many Chevy design features. A full-width design for the front grill and headlight was sculpted to be in keeping with authentic race cars. Wheel orientation was very important, with a stretched skin covering the overall structure and theme. We took the car to Texas in scale model form, and conducted a wind tunnel test for a week. The two Chevrolet engineers that joined us were excited about the successful test. Each day of that week we made many changes, and were able to improve front cooling and downforce on the front and rear, for ground hugging performance.

During the development of this sports car, while working on the project, Hank Haga calmly walked over to me and let me know that I had been promoted to Assistant Chief Designer. When your nose is to the grind stone you don't have time to think about these matters, but I was very proud to receive this endorsement.

While in the studio Bunkie saw a unique sketch on my desk with hidden headlights. With great energy and support, we got this feature into production on the Rally Sport option.

Before we cover interior, I would like to introduce the man that would eventually handle this assignment, George Angersbach.

George joined me in the Mitchell secret warehouse studio to design front- and mid-engine Corvettes. While there, we were also assigned to 'clean-up' the 1963 Corvette for 1965 sales. This was done by eliminating the fake scoops on the hood and rear-quarter panel. Prior to this, we had learned that consumer reaction to the Corvette was poor. They did not care for this fake ornamentation. Corvette buyers have a strong emotional relationship to this model. We designed functional front fender scoops and air extractor vents for the rear-quarter panel, and I personally designed a new wheel cover that reflected an aluminum cast wheel design. When I saw a 1965 Corvette in the dealership, however, the wheel cover looked like a chrome pie plate. Seeing this cut-rate execution of my design got me so enraged that I went straight to Irv Rybicki. Agreeing with me, he contacted Chevrolet to find out what happened. It was discovered that Chevy eliminated the cast aluminum wheel cover design and color finish to save money. It was unfortunate that Chevy did not communicate this to the design staff prior to production.

George and I were assigned back to the main building to the new Chevrolet II exterior and interior studios. Bill Mitchell expressed that he wanted someone with gasoline in their blood, who could direct a sporty interior to support the exterior of the still unnamed sports coupe. This was a big change, going from exterior design to interior design. So to set up the tone, George mounted a multi-speed shifter to his design chair, and while entering the new Chevrolet II interior studio he shouted loud race car sounds. He had arrived. George was then, and always has been, a great friend and comrade.

Because of the intensity of working on the exterior, I was not close to the overall interior minute design details. It was clear to me that George and the interior design team did a great job by creating an overall 'aircraft' feeling, similar to the 1965 Corvair and the up and coming 1968 Corvette.

After much consternation over many submitted names for this car, Camaro was chosen. The name Camaro means 'a friend.'

In 1967, the first year, total production reported by Chevrolet was 220,906 cars sold.

My achievements and time as a Junior Designer then Assistant Chief Designer, in the secret warehouse studio and later the Chevy II exterior studio, formed the most significant, memorable and enthusiastic design experience in my life.

The amazing leadership and talent of Bill Mitchell, Chuck Jordan, Hank Haga, Jack Humbert and Stan Wilen definitely helped shape my focus and vision in life.

These moments and years slipped by so fast that we all barely had time to sit back and enjoy those unbelievable, beautiful cars. However, now, when we attend car shows, cruises and especially the famous Woodward Cruise, we thank the real heroes, those who have purchased and restored and drive these iconic cars, and make them a living history.

Thank you,

John R Schinella

Introduction
Camaro – GM's Prowling Panther

"See the USA in your Chevrolet." That's what Dinah Shore sang in the TV commercials, and it was sound advice. Indeed, with a Chevrolet you had a well made, durable vehicle, that embodied the latest industry innovations, from a company that was number one in the sales race. If you needed a car, chances are Chevrolet made it. This included America's only volume-produced sports car, the Corvette, and even the car-based pickup known as El Camino. Both weremostly powered by 'The Hot One,' Chevrolet's efficient small block V8, released in 1955. However, in 1964 there arose a problem. Some guy at Ford came up with a car called the Mustang; maybe you've heard of it? But not to worry, Chevrolet had a solution called Camaro.

In racing, where you are on lap one isn't nearly as important as your position when the checkered flag falls. By 1981, Camaro was so far in front of Mustang, Henry needed binoculars to see the Z28's tail-lights! Long before that, Camaro was part of the speed shop brigade, and made into special big block versions by the most famous names of the muscle car era. And whether it involved racing on a road course or drag strip, Chevrolet's pony left no stone unturned inside and outside America.

With the fuel crisis, insurance premiums, and inflation, America sought a new kind of sporty machine, and Camaro could oblige. The Bowtie coupe even outsold Mustang in the process, with the Camaro Z28 350 firmly possessing the upper hand in the Chevrolet versus Ford rivalry during 1973-81. There wasn't even a shadow of a contest. Chevrolet's dedicated coupe outfoxed Ford's sedan-based Mustang, even when the new third generation Fairmont-based cars came. Today, the pre-1982 'Hugger' & 'Super Hugger' era Camaros are acknowledged classics. If the Corvette is the King of American sports cars, then the Chevrolet Camaro must be the Prince of Ponies!

Marc Cranswick

CHAPTER
One

Chevrolet Camaro – The Original (1967-69)

Between 1904 and 1979, the United States of America led the world in volume automobile production. In addition, for the majority of this period, such production came from American companies. In the postwar era Volkswagen was the only foreign company to begin making cars in the USA, with VW Rabbits issuing forth from a former Chrysler plant in Westmoreland, Pennsylvania from 1978. However, for the most part it was the Big Three, and 'lil AMC, with 85.2 per cent of the American auto market as late as 1976.[1]

After the once equally dominant Ford Model T ran out of gas, for the majority of the 20th century it was mighty Chevrolet that accounted for a large part of the nation's output of cars. More often than not, Chevrolet was number one in the auto industry, and for a fair share of those post WWII times, the Chevrolet Impala was America's number one selling car. So, if you were looking for some kind of car or truck, or truck car (El Camino), Chevrolet had you covered. The year 1964 was no exception, almost ...

On the small sized end of the scale, Chevrolet had two players: the Corvair and Chevy II. To meet a late '50s small import car tidal wave, in the wake of a major recession, Detroit cooked up three new 'compact' cars to deal with those pesky imports that mostly hailed from Europe. The Chevrolet Corvair, Ford Falcon and Plymouth Valiant largely foiled those small, foreign space invaders. Together with Rambler American and the Studebaker Lark, imported Renaults, Fiats and Dafs returned to their shade tree mechanics, where they lingered mostly unseen from 1960. Can you say Dauphine?! A wider dealer network, greater durability, and the more attuned nature of the compacts to US driving conditions won the practicality vote.

Of course, there was one small import that survived: the VW Beetle. It was said Beetle that Chevrolet targeted with its Corvair. Like the German machine, the Corvair went with a rear-engined, rear-drive small sedan format, with an air-cooled

The iconic '57 Chevrolet family car helped make Chevrolet No 1 in the auto industry.
(Courtesy Mac's Shortbread Company)

The Monza version of the rear-engined Corvair with four on the floor and bucket seats was a sales success that inspired the Ford Mustang. (Courtesy GM Archives)

boxer motor. With both cars, four-wheel independent suspension came along for the ride. This was all radical thinking on GM's part. Naturally, the Corvair was larger than the Beetle, and came with flat-six punch. Very soon buyers could specify factory-fitted air-conditioning on Corvair. The Bug didn't get a/c until later. Unlike the VW, Chevrolet engineers set up their Corvair as a determined understeerer. Most automotive critics were agreed on this point, as long as the correct tire pressures were maintained.

It soon transpired that the public warmed more towards the Falcon and Valiant. In addition, it seemed the Big Three had guessed a little too small with their compacts. The public also wanted something more conventional than a four-cylinder Pontiac Tempest with a bent driveshaft. So it was that the larger, front-engined Chevy II drove into Detroit and studied Ford's Falcon more closely than Dr Porsche's creation. However, during development of the intermediate-sized Chevelle, Chevrolet management had considered dropping the Chevy II.

The theory was that the sporty Monza version had kick-started Corvair sales satisfactorily. Although the public didn't buy the concept of the flat-six Chevrolet as a new small family car, they did take to it as a two-passenger sports runabout. The

Monza was an early indicator of a burgeoning youth market. Indeed, with Corvair's revised suspension, of standard front swaybar and transverse leaf spring, plus an extra 19 cubes for the turbo flat-six, *Popular Mechanics* was moved to describe Chevrolet's littlest machine as " ... an off-the-shelf fun car ... " [2]

Yes, this was the Corvair viewpoint, in such enlightened pre-Nader times. Between said Corvair and the new Chevelle, Chevrolet felt there was insufficient size gap or sales need for the Chevy II. Chevrolet division's 1955 family car, which introduced 'The Hot One' small block V8 to the masses, had been one of the most popular GM cars to date. Chevelle followed in this earlier car's tire tracks as the happy medium. With 195in length, and the refinement of four coil-spring suspension, product planners were confident Chevelle would be a good fit for most families. Smaller, easier to maneuver, cheaper to buy and run. Yes, Chevelle made good horsepower and sense, and also looked good!

The surprise for Chevrolet was the Chevy II model's rampant spring '63 sales. It made for an approximate 225,000 unit sales bedrock. So, Chevy II had earned its right to stay. This proved fortuitous for a future sporty bow-tie wearer: the Camaro.

However, in the present, the truly sporty Chevrolet, and America's only volume-produced sports car, was the Corvette. Sitting on a 98in wheelbase, the C2 Corvette was in its second year. This already-revered car wouldn't get its four-wheel disk brakes until 1965, but had already deep-sixed its split rear window, and did offer a 375 horse, Ramjet fuel-injected 327 V8.

Chevrolet certainly had the hardware, and even the Chevy II gained a 195bhp 283 V8 option for the '64 model year. When combined with the factory supplied four-speed and heavy-duty suspension, it made for one of the sportiest family cars in the world. More mechanical options, but fewer model versions, made for reduced dealer inventories.

Putting aside sales performance, sporty performance of the Chevy II V8 was compromised by nose-heavy weight distribution. It induced wheelspin from not being able to get the power down. This was part of the motivation for developing the front-drive 1966 Oldsmobile Toronado V8. Putting the engine over the driving wheels to get traction made that Olds the 1966 Pikes Peak hillclimb winner.

Regardless of the above, the number one selling car in the country was the Impala. This full-size Chevrolet, sitting on a 119in wheelbase with 209in overall length, was a six-seater family car. The full-size segment was the biggest sales sector, and where most of the engineering time and budget went. And just like you could specify a four-speed Corvette V8 drivetrain for the El Camino, power trips could be taken with the family Impala also.

Corvette couldn't have a big block in 1964, but the Impala could. With the possibility of an 11:1 comp ratio 409 V8, fed by dual four-barrel carbs and backed by four on the floor, family vacations would be slower by Boeing 707! In such halcyon days, the optioning permutations were legion. It didn't seem to worry Chevrolet or GM that no one would specify a car in such a manner. The engineers had deemed it possible. So, if you could dream it, and finance it, they would build it!

It was enough to make the Beach Boys sing, and they did with their tune *409*, "She's real fine my 409." It was a tribute to a 409 V8-powered hot rod. The single last appeared on their 1963 album *Little Deuce Coupe*. The irony of that Ford connection, would prove telling for Chevrolet in 1964. At the other extreme, the Corvair yielded the Greenbrier family van. This was a snazzier, more powerful equivalent of a VW Microbus. There was no question that Chevrolet and GM left no stone unturned in the quest for sales. Anything that hinted at being popular was tried. However, there was one thing they missed.

Chevrolet had left the 'low cost three' days behind, with its cars offering power and luxury high enough to worry upscale brands, which lacked the giant's budget. At the same time, it had watched the sales phenomenon that was VW, and responded to the funny looking foreign cars with some style. However, a certain gentleman over at the Ford Motor Company thought it might prove fruitful to wrap the plain Falcon in a new wrapper. Introduced mid-way through the 1964 model year, this coupe, called Mustang, garnered a fair few sales. It also got the public and Detroit thinking small and sporty.

Chevrolet's stealthy panther

It was a time when GM's Pontiac division turned the humble Tempest into the GTO, formally starting the muscle car move. The GTO made it to 32,450 sales in 1964, but Henry's horse, although a much cheaper ride, scored very nearly four times that total in half the time. Someone had created something genuinely new, from a marketing angle, since under that exciting body still lay a plain Falcon. However, the public were fooled, smitten, and buying. FoMoCo's rivals were worried, with 121,538 Mustang units sold in just half a model year. It seemed a Grand Canyon's worth of potential sales had opened up, out of nowhere. To the drawing boards post-haste!

Historically, the term pony car has been attributed to *Car Life* magazine's former editor Dennis Shattuck. The title of first pony car, or sport compact given the size class, could be awarded to the Chevrolet Corvair Monza. The Monza coupe's front buckets, and four on the floor were all part of a sales success that inspired Ford's Mustang. The revised second generation Chevrolet Corvair of 1965 achieved the sporty compact nameplate's peak sales of 235,528 units. *Car and Driver* called the Corvair's 1965 restyle "The best of established foreign and domestic coachwork." [3]

Ford saw such sporty fare, sales and great handling, and tried the formula at Dearborn. The writings of Ralph Nader, and the Mustang's 271hp K code 289 V8, plus rumors of a new pony car challenger from Chevrolet, slowed Corvair sales appreciably. The Turbo Monza's 180bhp just couldn't compete. More historical pony car precedent came in the form of the Plymouth Barracuda. The Barracuda was a fastback styled pony, beating Mustang to the showroom punch by two weeks.

Although Mopar's drag racing image was enviable, and the Barracuda came with a raucous 273 small block V8 option, Ford's pony outsold it ten to one! Therein lay the importance of styling. The homely looking 1964-66 Barracuda had a little too much plain vanilla envelope Valiant aesthetic to ring the public's bell. With pony cars it was wise to spend more on styling

Chevrolet wasn't there in that April 1964 showroom. With Corvair's sales dropping to 103,743 units in 1966, a decision was made to halt development of the rear-engined machine. Chevrolet decided it was easier to put its eggs in the front-engined V8 coupe basket. Straight line performance was easier to achieve via this route, and the V8 horsepower war was building. So it was that by mid-1965 rumors were abound concerning Chevrolet's Panther project. The matter was broached with the press in a most cryptic fashion.

On June 21 1966, around 200 journalists received a GM telegram advising them to reserve noon of June 28 for a SEPAW meeting. The communiqué added "Hope you can be on hand to help scratch a cat." The strange message came from Chevrolet public relations man John L Cutter. If all that wasn't confusing enough, the next day saw a further telegram from SEPAW (Society for the Eradication of Panthers from the Automotive World). It came from the SEPAW secretary, John L Cutter, and indicated that the 28th would be the first and last meeting of the society.

This meet to end all meets was held at the Detroit Statler Hilton Hotel. It proved a first for live press conferences, in that 14 cities were connected via telephone. The event was hosted by Chevrolet's general manager Pete Estes. Estes had raised some corporate hell earlier, working with John Z DeLorean and ad man extraordinaire Jim Wangers to circumvent GM's anti performance policy, and get the Pontiac GTO on the road. This time he informed all attendees that they were charter members of SEPAW. He also said that the new XP-836 project vehicle, would have a 'C' prefix letter like other Chevrolets.

Getting the right nameplate was even more crucial in the 1960s. Pete Estes said the new moniker " ... suggests the comradeship of good friends as a personal car should be to its owner, and that to us the name means just what we think the car will do ... go." Of course, the name in question was Camaro. During the development stage it had

Chevrolet had a response to Ford's Mustang ... the 1967 Camaro! (Courtesy Marc Cranswick)

gone by Panther, but to fit in with Chevrolet practice, a name beginning with 'C' was necessary. With some jocularity, Chevrolet product planners told the assembled press that Camaro was a small, vicious animal that ate Mustangs. This was similar to the naming idea behind the DeTomaso Mangusta. That is, a mongoose that devours cobras!

In truth, the Camaro name appears to have originated from a consulted French/English dictionary. It seemed that Chevrolet merchandising manager Bob Lund, and GM Vice President Ed Rollett, had seen the book. Therein a word was found that was a derivation of camarade or comrade. This new pony car amigo was first shown to the press on September 12 1966 in Detroit. A Los Angeles show and tell was held on September 19. The Camaro's public introduction occurred on September 26. The car went on sale on the 29th of the same month, as a 1967 model year ride.

The Camaro's arrival came not a moment too soon. Pony car sales were still in the ascendancy. With Corvair about to enter its eighth production year, the newness had worn off, and the coupe was in sales decline. In addition, Plymouth was about to release a much more sexily styled A-body Barracuda. Camaro's F-body sibling, the Pontiac Firebird, would be on the scene soon. Plus, American Motors would join the pony car craze with the Javelin in 1968. So, the time for sales action was most certainly, now. Now for the public came in the form of early Camaro TV commercials, and the relatively recent arrival of color TV was timely.

The '67 TV ad voice-over proudly declared "Fiery new creation from Chevrolet." A new Camaro SS350 was then shown emerging from a volcano!

By the early '60s Chevrolet thought it had the market covered. The Camaro fixed one omission ... pony cars! From the Camaro's first year, this 1967 ragtop was purchased as a 327 V8-powered Powerglide automatic. The bumblebee nose stripe decal was associated with the SS (Super Sports) package. (Courtesy www.smokymountaintraders.com)

Mention was made of GM's newly designed energy absorbing steering column, Camaro's optional fold down rear seats, and also optional auxiliary console gauges. There was no mention of Corvette in this particular ad, but others did.

Camaro engineering

The Camaro had a major advantage over the Mustang, and it was called the Corvette. Often referred to as the F-body's big brother, in an hierarchical sports fashion if not in physical size, having the Corvette as a sports mentor was a good thing in this era. If there was a sports direction in terms of handling, engines or general hardware, Chevrolet engineers had explored such routes earlier with the so-called Plastic Fantastic. Observing the early Camaro Z28s, one would find a number of mechanical parts of Corvette origin.

The Camaro hailed from an era when cars had more ashtrays than seatbelts. However, it came with a contemporary padded dash, and its small size (184.6in length) made it plenty maneuverable. (Courtesy www.smokymountaintraders.com)

Originally the 350 V8 added to this ragtop was rated at 295 ponies. However, this mill makes more thanks to a Weiand aluminum intake and 600cfm Edelbrock four-bbl carb. (Courtesy www.smokymountaintraders.com)

Further upgrades for this 1967 convertible include a Turbo Hydramatic 350 automatic, four-wheel power disk brakes, and full dual exhaust system using Flow Master mufflers. (Courtesy www.smokymountaintraders.com)

Due to feared rollover safety tests that never came, a factory F-body ragtop wouldn't return until the late third gen. (Courtesy www.smokymountaintraders.com)

This beneficial relationship could be mutual at times.

The 1982 Corvette's L83 Crossfire V8 motor, utilized a cross-ram intake manifold, influenced by an homologation intake from the first gen Camaro Z28's SCCA Trans Am days. For the '80s the Corvette engineers had mostly just substituted two TBI (Throttle Body Injection) fuel-injectors, for the aforementioned Z28's dual four-barrel carburetion. That said, it should be noted that the redesigned second gen Corvair's IRS (independent rear suspension) was similar to the setup on the contemporary C2 Corvette. The Camaro didn't get IRS until the fifth gen models of 2010.

Cost omissions aside, Camaro had a lot to draw upon. In contrast, the Thunderbird was of little help to the Mustang, except for occasionally bestowing big block V8s. Since the early two-seater Thunderbirds, Ford's personal sports machine originally aimed at Corvette, became a larger and larger four-seater pleasure dome. It was nice for comfort, but of little benefit to the Mustang, which mostly took over the high-performance mantle at Ford, tenuously drawing on that Cobra connection as it did so. In contrast, the Camaro had the Corvette, Chevy II, and a computer in its corner. Being a corporate giant, Chevrolet had a resource pool of designers and computers, not available to smaller

This '67 Camaro RS (Rally Sport) included hideaway headlamps as standard. By coincidence, Firestone's high performance tire was called the Wide Oval Super Sports (SS). Just perfect for a Camaro SS to burn rubber with!
(Courtesy Cragar)

firms. Chevrolet said that with the new Camaro, computer technology was utilized to a greater degree than with any previous GM car.

Camaro followed Chevy II in a looser sense than the Mustang being Falcon-based. However, like the

A '67 Camaro ragtop, featured with Firestone's Wide Oval tire. Wide Ovals were the default sporty car choice until Goodyear's Polyglas took over in popularity from its Bluestreaks. All icons of those bias-belted, kidney-punching days!
(Courtesy Firestone)

Mustang/Falcon interchange, some Chevy II chassis components were held in common with the Camaro. Just like Chevy II, the Camaro relied on a partial unibody. Both cars were of unitary construction up to the firewall, with a subframe supporting engine, gearbox, front suspension and steering thereafter. Said subframe was joined to the unibody, by using heavy bolts bushed with rubber. There were two mounting points per side, with the connection under the seat riser and cowl base. The four rubber mounts were described as being like 'double biscuits' in nature.

The part unibody construction attempted, and largely succeeded, in producing the best of both worlds in chassis design. Full frame cars were great at reducing NVH (noise, vibration and harshness), but were heavy. Full frame also didn't allow for a deep footwell area, since the frame was under

An early range topper, this 1967 Camaro SS350 RS coupe came with the early top motor, sports (SS) and appearance (RS) packs, plus a vinyl roof. It was enough to make the dealership and Allstate insurance men sing! (Courtesy GM Archives)

the body. By the mid to late '60s there was also a growing general consensus that full frame cars compromised on passive safety. With a body perched on a frame, such cars lacked a crumple zone to absorb shock, and a rigid center to protect occupants. Full unibody designs were lighter, and rigid, but tended to have interiors that drummed loudly and trapped all kinds of rattles and squeaks.

Chevrolet engineers experimented with the partial frame concept, using Chevy II-based test mules, before settling on what was dubbed the 'wheelbarrow' arrangement. Aside from the part unibody concept, the Camaro was a very conventional car in looks and engineering. Front suspension was Chevelle-like, and similar to many domestics, with a short/long arm independent arrangement. Coil springs lived between the two arms, with telescopic shock absorbers within said springs. A front 0.687in swaybar was standard equipment. Out back lived the ubiquitous live axle, single leaf springs and more telescopic shocks.

The single leaf springs were in the style of Chevy II, but were shortened to 56in in Camaro's case.

Single leaf springs raised eyebrows in autoland. They were okay on a six shooter economy car, but on a V8-powered pony, what about axle wind up? Well, there had never been a reported Chevy II case of a broken rear spring, and in fact everything was very scientific. The engineers had consulted a computer, and, even for the Firebird 400 sibling, the answer was single leaf springs. Computer simulation programs had been consulted for all aspects of ride, handling and suspension hardware, producing the end result.

Camaro chassis engineers had fed into the computer the views of private buyers and professional racing drivers concerning what constituted sports car character. The electronic brain saved a lot of permutation work, and Camaro was in a hurry to hit the street and challenge that Mustang. The powerplant was set almost directly over the front end center line, with a Chevy II-fashioned single piece axle housing to the rear. The Chevrolet computer had a lot to say on suspension. Based on supplied inputs, it provided the subframe's parameters, and pulled all elements together. Spring rates, rubber bushing stiffness, the vertical placement

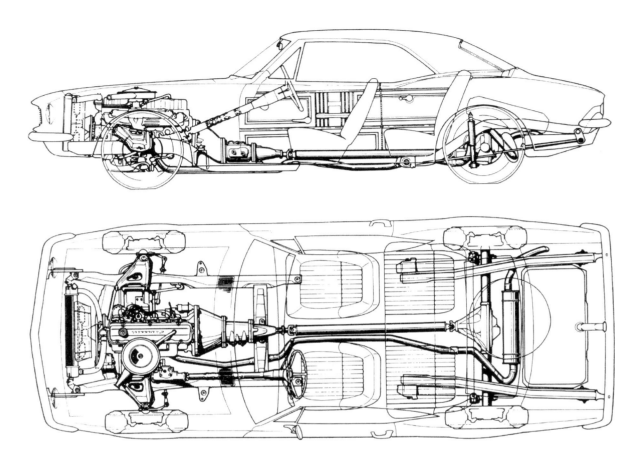

If you had Superman's X-ray vision it was plain to see six-cylinder Camaros were in the minority on Mainstreet USA. Many questioned the computer selection of single leaf rear springs for all '67 Camaros ... and Firebirds! (Courtesy GM Archives)

of rear shocks and rear spring angle that enabled a large gas tank: these were all computer evaluated.

One concession to taming that rear live axle was a single traction bar on the right side of all Camaro V8s with four on the floor. The computer suggested that, too! Indeed, Chevrolet's engineering director Alex C Mair disclosed that, late in the development stage, computer modeling resulted in the rear track being widened to improve directional stability. On a base '67 Camaro six, front and rear tracks were 59in and 58.9in respectively. Early on, only small block V8 power was available for the Camaro. However, Chevrolet engineers anticipated that speed shop dealerships and drag racers would be slotting in some big block 427 action, with an eye to Super Stock. So, unlike the post fuel crisis era, an extra margin of body strength was designed into Camaro.

Like its rivals, the '67 Camaro also played it safe concerning pending mandatory federal regulations. This concerned the collapsible steering column and dual circuit braking system. Regardless of disk or drum brakes specified, all Camaros had a dual circuit, hydraulic braking set up, with tandem master cylinders. If one circuit failed, the majority of the car's braking capability would still be maintained. Camaro's standard brakes themselves were held in common with pony car rivals, and were unexceptional. They involved four-wheel drums sized 9.5 x 2.5 in front and 9.5 x 2.0 in at the rear. Total swept braking area was 268.6 square inches.

The drums were sized the same as Chevrolet's Corvair, Chevy II and Chevelle. Such four-wheel drums were even what the buyer got with the hi-po Camaro SS350. For $37, metallic linings could be

If the Firebird could snag the Goat's 400, then Camaro was entitled to the Chevelle SS396's big block. Similarly, the Firebird 400 and Camaro SS396 were both alloted the THM 400 automatic. (Courtesy GM Archives)

Camaro had something for everyone, even the little lady. Naturally, a Camaro SS396 convertible was out front, and that's where Chevrolet was in the industry. (Courtesy GM Archives)

specified for such self adjusting drums, and were a wisely chosen option over standard. They were okay for everyday driving and cruising, but owners that habitually did mountain road driving were prudent if they optioned the $79 front disk brakes. At the time pony cars, and most domestics, came with four-wheel drums as standard. The Camaro's disk/drum set up permitted straight line, fade free multiple stops, and avoided the inconsistent, swerving car behavior of overheated drums.

The disk brake option brought 11in ventilated disk rotors, gripped by four-piston fixed calipers. The rear drums got upsized to 9.5 x 2.25in, and total swept area was a much improved 332.4 square inches. Drag racers preferred drums, they brought less drag wind resistance, for a swifter $1/4$ mile pass. If the Camaro owner had aftermarket spoked mag wheels fitted, it provided an opportunity to paint

the brake drums to match the car's exterior color! It made for a visual treat, and was seen on four-wheel drum braked rides from muscle cars to VW Bugs. If the Camaro prospect was looking at the disk brake option, metallic drum linings option, or both, the $42 servo assisted power brake option was essential.

Disk brakes don't have the natural regenerating braking effect associated with drums. Then too, all drum set ups with metallic linings also need a heck of a lot of pedal pressure to stop a car. So even on a small, light, 3000lb compact, power brakes were practically mandatory. The reduced pedal feel and easy chance of lock up being necessary evils. The same applied to the option of power steering, and Camaro was no exception. A manual recirculating ball steering system had less kickback than rack and pinion set ups. The Camaro's manual steering had some feel, but was slow at four turns lock-to-lock.

The obvious solution was Camaro's power steering, that reduced turns lock-to-lock to just three. However, domestic power steering was more attuned to parking than driving. Power steering and power brakes, even on a sporty domestic, tended to lack feel, although Mopar cars seemed worse when it came to over assisted steering. The solution was to combine the power steering's fast ratio, with the non-power steering to create fast manual steering. This was a $16 option on 1967 Camaros. Chevrolet had a fast manual for its sporty car, when many didn't.

It was thought that using a fast ratio with non-boosted steering would make things too heavy. However, when TV's *Dream Car Garage* host Peter Klutt tried a first gen COPO Camaro 427, he said Camaro's power steering never really felt quite right. On the other hand, the fast manual of the car he was driving had more feel, and wasn't overly heavy. GM had to consider a wider range of buyers than those looking at the European imports. The lumberjack may have been okay with his Camaro in a parking lot, but not his wife.

Horsepower to the people

In the job of having something for everyone, you can't go past Detroit's engines. Domestic cars commonly offered many choices, and this was certainly the case with pony cars. *Cars* magazine's Fred Mackerodt outlined GM's policy in the March 1967 issue. In common with the Big Three, the plan was to share bodies, and allow each division to supply its own powerplant designs, " ... each car line is as distinct as its powerplants, and this can be quite a distinction." The statement explained the difficulty various GM divisions would have, when the shared family engine policy started in the 1980s.

What makes your version special? It wasn't a problem in the '60s. Chevrolet had worthy sixes and iconic V8s to draw upon. Six-cylinder Camaros came in two engine sizes, a 230 cube edition making 140 horses at 4400rpm and a 250ci big brother with 155bhp at 4200rpm. These overhead valve inline motors both had one-barrel carburetion, and a modest regular swigging 8.5:1 compression ratio. That said, the sixes did have seven main bearings for durability and smoothness. Ford's equivalent entry level 200ci six had 120bhp, with Barracuda's 225 slant six on 145 horsies.

An easy way to tell a first year Camaro, or Firebird, is the presence of quarter vent windows. Only the '67s had 'em! (Courtesy Randall Accardo)

Originally a six-cylinder coupe, this Camaro completed a full rotisserie restoration by 2014. Procar seats were part of the build. (Courtesy Randall Accardo)

Chevrolet's sixes were entry level fare. High performance implied a V8, and this modified 350 crate motor is just that. A 750 CFM dual-feed Holley provides the juice. (Courtesy Randall Accardo)

Chevrolet's 250ci six cost an extra $26.35, and was a sensible upgrade.

As with fellow Big Three intermediates and full-size cars, the entry level sixes were just that. Secretary specials for ponies, the fleet market and the budget buyer who couldn't get 'em basic enough. Performance-wise, more could be done with them, but automakers didn't because that's what V8s were for. When it came to V8s, Chevrolet had a real duesey with its small block. Since 1955 the Chevrolet small block V8 had become an industry standard for power, durability and even fuel efficiency. However, cars were getting bigger, and the public's desire for more power wouldn't quit, so the small block moved with the times.

The 265 and 283ci small block V8s were familiar to many. However, Chevrolet engineers reckoned the 283 was too small to serve duty as the starter Camaro V8. The 283 had been a rebored and recored 265, but now a newly cast block allowed greater displacements to be safely attained, while giving owners a chance to do their overbores when wear and tear arose. So there were new sizes of 327 and 350 cubes, with the latter starting out as a Camaro exclusive. In 1968 the new C3 Corvette had the 327 V8 in 300 and 350 horsepower guises, but had to wait for 1969 to get the new 350. Camaro's newest motor was titled '350 Turbo Fire V8' on debut.

The 327 had bore and stroke dimensions of 4.00 x 3.25in, making 210bhp at 4600rpm and 320lb/ft at 2400rpm on an 8.75:1 comp with one two-barrel carb. It proved enough for most folks. The 350 stroked matters to 3.48in, added one four-barrel carb and used a 10.25:1 CR, which made premium gas mandatory. The vital stats for the 350 V8 were 295bhp at 4800rpm and 380lb/ft at 3200rpm. With either V8 it was a hydraulic lifter scenario, implying no need to adjust valve clearances. Most American car buyers wanted quiet cars, with maintenance routines kept to a minimum. Hence the single four-barrel carb.

The moderately hi-po 350 V8 had intake and exhaust valves sized 1.94in and 1.50in respectively. Lift for intake and exhaust sides were a respective 0.390in and 0.410in. Camshaft profile duration on intake and exhaust sides were 310 and 320 degrees respectively. A goodly engine indeed, but autofans wanted more. The next step was the big block. From 1958 to 1965 Chevrolet put mechanical Ramjet 'Doghouse' fuel-injection, as an option, on its cars. The highest profile Ramjet exponent being Corvette,

naturally. However, it was an expensive option, sometimes temperamental, and with gas being as cheap as it was, bigger was better, right?

The Corvette led the way for Camaro. 1965's Ramjet 327 had given way to the 427 four-bbl for 1966. The regular Camaro wouldn't get the 427, but would receive the 'porcupine' semi-hemi 396 four-bbl V8. Chevrolet's latest big blocks replaced the externally larger and heavier W series 348/409s, which had arrived in 1958. In the Camaro application, the 396 had a 10.25:1 CR, and one Rochester four-barrel. It put out 325 gross ponies at a tractable 4800rpm.

An engine large enough to propel a 30-passenger bus, with over 300 gross horses, seemed like just enough to carry two adults and a little luggage in comfort. Such was life during '60s hedonism. As with any pony car, the rear seats were just for kids. The driveshaft was low enough, and the rear bench flat enough, to permit three humans to sit back there, in theory.

You didn't even really need a big block to push an intermediate, but when the Tempest borrowed the Catalina's big motor, rivals had to do likewise. Then the idea got traction ... why not place said big block in a compact? Shelby had big inch Mustangs, but they were pricey. So FoMoCo fans eagerly anticipated the coming of a factory Mustang 390 for 1967. Utilizing the Fairlane's FE series V8, this Mustang 390 didn't really pack the pep for the price that Ford fans had been hoping for. It seemed like all that Ford big block did was raise the sticker price and the rear wheels off the deck!

Over in camp Mopar the reworked A-body Plymouth Barracuda was packing 280 horses worth of big block 383 V8. The fancy fish had the styling and big inch bliss, but some things were missing. You couldn't have a good set of headers, there was no room at the inn. Space constraints also dictated against power steering and a/c. The Valiant-derived Barracuda just wasn't designed for a big block and the creature comforts in the one machine. Those engineering refinements would have to wait for the new 1970 E body 'Cuda.

Naturally, power steering, a/c and some decent headers could all be had on a '67 Camaro SS396, with the first two coming factory delivered. That it could get it all together so early on was another sign of Chevrolet's size and budget. However, there was one hot pony, more than any other, that prompted the Camaro SS396 with THM 400 autobox to be

The rear end features a Positraction lsd with 3.73 gears, and this '67 coupe has been mini tubbed.
(Courtesy Randall Accardo)

This modified '67 Camaro was featured at the 2019 July 13 Slam'D & Cam'D Indoor Car Show.
(Courtesy Randall Accardo)

a factory reality ... the Pontiac Firebird 400. In the March 1967 issue of *Motor Trend*, John Ethridge speculated that this was indeed the case.

Mustang's upscale partner in crime was the Mercury Cougar. Well, if FoMoCo had Cougar, then one of the GM divisions would have to provide a Camaro cousin, and John Z DeLorean had an angle. Pontiac would win out over Oldsmobile and Buick. Pontiac had risen to number three in the sacred sales race by going for a young, racy image.

DeLorean had a cunning plan, by delivering the XP-833 sports car to top GM brass as a fait accompli. You see, he knew full well that management would never green-light another two-seat sports car to rival Corvette. Then again, as GM's rising star, what better compensation for passing on XP-833, than letting Pontiac build that upscale F-body Camaro cousin called Firebird?

Both F bodies had to kind of honor GM's anti-racing policy, and rule that, with the exception of the

Left pics: It's the '67 Camaro with the mostest, a SS396 RS convertible! Would you believe 325 horse at 4800rpm? Well, what about 350bhp and a small burro? It was more like 400 ponies, but the Allstate insurance man believed GM, so why worry?
The Super Sport package was designated RPO (Regular Production Order) Z27, with Rally Sport called RPO Z22. Both are present.
You couldn't get a regular Camaro 427. However, various speed shop dealers offered a 427 as a Camaro SS396 replacement motor. (Courtesy Erik)

Main pic: Camaro SS396 replacement motor. In the mix & match optioning game, this 1968 Camaro was originally a 327 RS hardtop coupe. (Courtesy Jim Council)

Corvette, no new sporty car could beat ten pounds per horsepower when it came to power to weight ratio. So, the Camaro SS396 made 325 horses at 4800rpm, and so did Firebird 400, precisely. Plainly specified hardtop coupes came in at a lithe 3250lb. Both big powerplants easily made more power at higher rpm, but such ratings kept the AMA (American Manufacturers Association) and the insurance companies at bay. It was worth considering engine weight, and front-to-rear weight distribution.

Back in the days when the tires were skinny and the racing drivers were portly, how much weight a car carried up front really impacted understeer and getting that power to terra firma. For the Camaro six it was 54.9/45.1 per cent front-to-rear. Small block Camaros took respective matters on to 57.5/42.5 per cent, with the Camaro big block V8s sitting at 59.3/40.7 per cent nose-to-tail. Chevrolet's small block V8 was around 550lb, with the inline six at 200lb under, and the big block at 200lb over. This would suggest the small block-powered Camaro, as representing the happy medium.

The gearbox choices for the various powerplants, were immense. All manual transmissions were fully synchronized in all forward gears, but matters started simply with a manual three on the tree. This was the standard gearbox for sixes, and the 327/350 V8 motors, too. Ratios for sixes were 2.85 (1st), 1.68 (2nd), and direct top. For the 327/350 motors it was 2.54 (1st), 1.50 (2nd), and direct top. The HD (Heavy-duty) three-speed manual was only available as a floor shift, and 2.41 (1st), 1.57 (2nd) and 1.00 (3rd) were your HD ratios. This HD box could only be had with the SS350, and when it arrived, SS396 Camaro.

Four on the floor was available to all, and was the only way to get a four-speed, but ratios varied. For six-cylinder Camaros, the story went 3.11 (1st), 2.20 (2nd), 1.47 (3rd) and 1.00 (4th). With all V8s, including SS396, 1st and 2nd ratios changed to 2.52 and 1.88 respectively. Then there was the four-speed reserved for Chevrolet's 302 and 396 V8s. Ratios were now 2.20 (1st), 1.64 (2nd), 1.27 (3rd) and direct top 1:1. For shiftless driving Camaro owners could count on the venerable two-speed Powerglide for all engines bar the 302 and 396 V8s. Powerglide was famous for its smoothness and durability. Many a powerful V8 has sat in front of a 'Glide.' Ratios were 1.76 for low, and 1.00 with high, but the torque converter ratio varied. It was 2.40:1 with sixes, and 2.10:1 on V8s.

It's 1968, and that meant Astro flow through ventilation on all GM F bodies. This '68 Camaro adds aftermarket Pro Comp gauges. A GM Muncie M21 four-speed is connected to a 10-bolt Positraction lsd, with highway-friendly 3.55 rear gears. (Courtesy Jim Council)

The hi-po street moxie comes courtesy of a 1984 350 V8 with four-bolt mains and big Thumper cam. A Holley 650 supplies the juice, with spark aid from a Pro Billet distributor and MSD ignition box. (Courtesy Jim Council)

The powerhouse 396 V8 was the only first generation Camaro specifiable with the Turbo Hydra Matic 400 automatic. Its ratios were 2.48 (1st), 1.48 (2nd), with a direct top. Torque converter amplification was the same as per other V8s. However, in a car as light as the Camaro or Corvette, the humble 327 V8/Powerglide combination could get one moving in style with minimal fuss. Left to its own automatic devices, a Camaro 327 could reach

A '68 Camaro 350 can be seen as a robbery getaway vehicle in the 1977 movie *In Hot Pursuit*, between the 50 minute and 1 hour and 10 minute time marks, driven by the Watson brothers: https://www.youtube.com/watch?v=LODc-bwHB34 (Courtesy Jim Council)

60mph in first. Around 115-120mph would come up in top with the 2.73:1 final drive ratio. No need to manually shift since pedal to the metal would produce an upshift from low to high at 4900rpm, a mere 100rpm shy of redline.

In December 1966 *Motor Trend* achieved 0-60mph in 10.7 seconds, and the 1/4 mile in 18.2 seconds at 77mph. Its Camaro 327 RS with Powerglide had done the talking. More importantly, the 50-70mph passing time was a neat 6.6 seconds. These figures would improve with the GM Muncie four-speed to hand. *Motor Trend* tested a Camaro SS350 RS four-speed at the same time, long before the Camaro's showroom debut. At the GM test track

This restomod 1968 Camaro brings the upgrades that many add in such a build. This SEMA-featured coupe is a showstopper! (Courtesy Chris & RKMotorsCharlotte.com)

it did 0-60mph in 8 seconds flat, with the 1/4 mile in 15.4 seconds at 90mph. A sensible coupe with highway friendly 3.31 gears and a mere 2500rpm at 56mph in top gear.

In March 1967, *Car Life* got 120mph out of a similar machine with shorter 3.55 rear gears. Fuel economy, if you had to ask, and not many did in 1967, was in the 16 to 17mpg zone. This all produced a range of around 350 miles with the shorter gearing. How short could a Camaro SS350 go? Try 4.88:1!! It was enough to win any traffic light grand prix or send you deaf, whichever came first. It might even have pulled you out in front of those pesky VWs with mountain master first gears. Or you could play it cool with a relatively sleepy 3.07:1. Either way in that 'GO' era, you weren't really swinging unless you had a four-speed. Some option packages wouldn't hurt either.

SS & RS option packs

For $211 the SS350 package was a quick and complete set menu to high-performance. The pack included the high output 350 V8 with 295bhp, and functional along with cosmetic items. Coming or going you knew it was a Super Sport, with that SS badge smack dab in the middle of the grille, along with a tethered rear circular gas cap that read SS350. The front fascia bumblebee stripe was hard to miss, with space for 'SS' signage midway up the front fender stripe. Faux diecast trim hood louvers gave the impression your V8 was drawing in fresh air. Then there was the custom steering wheel with plastic chrome trim and center 'SS' insignia horn button.

The Camaro SS350 had handling covered thanks to wide, for the times, 14x6in Rally steel rims wrapped in Firestone Super Sports Wide Ovals. This all harmonized with the firmer shocks and springs of the standard heavy-duty suspension. It was an all-purpose fun machine. A four-speed and front disk brakes would have to be optioned separately. Ditto the $79 three-dial Special Instrumentation living just in front of the floorshift. From left-to-right it was gas and coolant temp in gauge one, a clock in the middle, and oil pressure plus battery charge on the right. Getting full instrumentation, as opposed to just idiot lights, wasn't that easy to achieve on sporty cars of the day. Those extra low down gauges weren't that large, or easy to scan, but were welcome nonetheless.

The RS (Rally Sport) pack was purely for appearance. There was RS badging on the leading edge of the front fenders, where it would normally say SS. Then there were RS letters on the rear central fascia gas cap, although, unlike SS, the filler cap wasn't tethered. The most prominent RS trick was concealed headlamps. Hideaway lights were a Detroit favorite, although their lack of reliability caused a few buyers to avoid them. With Camaro it was a case of concealing grille sliding doors that pivoted inwards when the headlights were activated. The standard parking lights were now relocated to the front valence under the bumper.

RS specified Camaros had solid red tail-lights surrounded by flat black trim outline, not the usual chrome. Back-up lamps were moved to the lower valence. The Rally Sport package cost $105.35 upon Camaro's 1967 debut. It could be applied to a base $2466 six-cylinder Sport Coupe, but was more mentally associated with V8 cars. RS could be combined with the performance SS350 package, and often was. If so, SS badging would take precedence over RS equivalents, in the usual locations.

Increasingly as the years went by buyers got more and more turned on by comfort. Even with sporty personal cars. The Camaro's optional deluxe interior pack provided a look and feel that most buyers would have wanted as standard. This $94.80 Custom Interior brought molded vinyl side paneling and integrated armrests, with door handles located in a depression for passive safety. Rear seat armrests even came with ashtrays! A coveted option of the era was the console: for looks, somewhere to rest your leg, and even just to show you could spring for those extra bucks! A console could tastefully wraparound a floor-mounted shifter and, on Camaro, included a rear courtesy light for folks in back. There was even a bonus ashtray. It was a real lucky strike! It may have been tight back there, but at least you didn't have to smoke in the dark. The courtesy light could be worked via the Camaro's door switches.

Styling the Camaro

Vehicular styling was right up there in importance with high-performance; perhaps even more so. After all, how else could dealers offload those plain Jane, six-cylinder pea shooter, secretary specials? You had to have the right look. For many the 1964 Barracuda was more functional than fun looking. They overlooked those Mopar mechanicals, and a car that could swallow a surfboard ... on the inside! No, the madding crowd beat a path to Henry's hacienda for a Mustang. So what would Chevrolet do with the Camaro? A good first move was to put the GM F-body in talented hands. To this end, the recently created Chevrolet 2 Studio was at hand. It was Chief Designer Hank Haga, with future Pontiac

The ubiquitous GM LS V8 in 6.0 form. Powerful enough with standard electronic fuel-injection and coil packs. However, a big Texas Speed & Performance cam makes things even more so. (Courtesy
Chris & RKMotorsCharlotte.com)

A Tremec six-speed stick controls the 6-liter V8. The Vintage Air a/c fitted was designed specifically for 1st gen F bodies. A Kenwood audio system and GPS sat nav bring things up to speed. (Courtesy
Chris & RKMotorsCharlotte.com)

Custom build additions include a color-matched D80 front spoiler and Stinger themed hood. However, trunk capacity remains an unmodified 8.3ft^3. (Courtesy Chris & RKMotorsCharlotte.com)

The rear fenders have been widened 4in and house Forgeline Grip Schism rims. Aftermarket rack and pinion steering and four-wheel Wilwood disk brakes keep this BASF/Glasurit burgundy beauty under control. (Courtesy Chris & RKMotorsCharlotte.com)

2 Studio head John Schinella as Assistant Chief Designer. Haga and Schinella had worked together on the Super Nova show car. This Super Nova was a starting point for Camaro styling.

Chevrolet public relations talk at the time said Camaro's basic styling commenced in the Corvette studio. No doubt given the reverence the Corvette was held in by this hour, PR folks wanted to work that Corvette-Camaro connection early on. Some similarity in general profile and curved fender lines can be discerned. The Coke bottle styling look was in vogue, but Camaro had a very different look to pony car rivals. Early journalistic comments surrounding the first four prototypes was of slender Chevy IIs, but this was a good Chevrolet ruse!

The 1967 Camaro had clean, muscular styling, and the PR folks once again added to the conversation that the short deck, long hood look in America, had been popularized by Corvette. Whereas the Mustang was very detailed, perhaps over-decorated, the Camaro went with simplicity. Some voices even said Camaro was a little bland, but there was much function to Camaro's style. To combat sidewinds, computers checked the shape all along the line. The scale model went to a wind tunnel in Dallas, Texas for evaluation. Computers saved many hours in refining the Camaro's shape. During final changes there were slight modifications to the under-bumper valence area, to reduce front end lift.

This attention to detail was pretty key because the C2 Corvette got very light at the front around 100mph, the accepted minimum speed for aerodynamic assessment. Zora Arkus Duntov had wanted to add hood openings to allow updrafts to escape, but he was overruled for fear of rain shorting out the electrics. The new Camaro had moved forward in technical development, compared to the C2 Corvette. It showed up the older design in 1967. The new C3 wasn't ready in time for '67 MY. Similarly, the new '82 Camaro made the final C3 Corvette's older design noticeable.

The original 1967 Camaro's shape was put on tape for a computer worked die cutting machine. Apart from saving time, Chevrolet GM Pete Estes said the end result was " … probably more perfect than can be done normally." The clay model then went to the wind tunnel. John Schinella, Assistant Chief Designer on Camaro and future Pontiac 2 Studio styling chief, said Chevrolet 2 Studio's work with the Camaro provided an invaluable starting point for creating F-body sibling the Pontiac Firebird.

Although muscle cars and pony cars oftentimes favor the round headlamp look, the RS's hideaway lamp look was a clean, functional alternative to fussy Mustang. The Camaro also marked a trend at GM away from external decoration. GM's sporty cars had been freed of extraneous faux vents, grille doors, scoops and badging. The center rear fascia

Kristy O'Connel posing with a restomod '69 Camaro, for South Africa's *SXdrv* magazine.
Chris Doyle & Richard Middleton's *SXdrv* magazine often features restomod classics. Their appeal is eternal.
(Courtesy SXdrv.com)

Originally, this '69 Camaro 327 RS had a Powerglide. However, power now comes from a worked LS1 V8.
Added cruise control and Vintage Air a/c make this a cool ride in more ways than one.
(Courtesy Shawn Byrd)

gas filler door meant clean fenders on both sides. Very realistic wire wheel covers had been done for the Corvair earlier, and the P02/N95 wire wheel cover option was available on Camaro. However, publicity shots liked to display the Rally wheel style, in keeping with the F-body's sporty nature.

For the ultimate in posing, you can't beat a convertible. The safety lobby had yet to muscle out this long running concept that buyers still loved in the late '60s. With that top up or down, Camaro convertible looked the part, and the price was right. The premium for fresh air fiends over a base Camaro was $238, with $2704 the list price for a six-cylinder ragtop. It drove well too. Chevrolet made engineering changes to the F-body, boosting rigidity and quelling NVH. There was a strengthened floorpan and side structure.

The double channel in the rocker sills got back lost rigidity. Four corner-located vibration dampers dealt with shock from the increased channel stiffness. Said dampers were an encased spring weight in an oil bath. The specter of rollover roof strength tests had yet to surface, so, for now, convertible fans could still breathe easy. The engineers had good things for Camaro passive safety. They worked-in front seatback latches that stopped the front seats tipping forward during heavy braking. There was also a safety wire stopping the seatback from striking the dashboard top.

Camaro model development & buyer reception

The 1967 Camaro's 220,906 total issued from GM plants in Norwood, Ohio and Van Nuys in California. However, 1st gen Camaros were built outside

This Camaro's original LF7 327 two-bbl V8 made 210 gross ponies. Now it's 430 net rear wheel horsepower, going through a GM 4L60 four-speed automatic.
Further modifications incorporated in this '69 Camaro RS include a CPP pro touring suspension and four-wheel disk brake conversion. Plus interior and headlamp lighting come from LEDs.
(Courtesy Shawn Byrd)

America, too. This move was to escape local import duties, with CKD assembling companies turning out a very small number of high priced Camaros, in a single specification, for wealthy customers looking for something a little more unique than a BMW or Mercedes coupe. With production numbers being small, quality was high. So the Philippines, Belgium, Venezuela, Peru and Switzerland, saw Camaro assembly outside the USA.

The Swiss operation in Biel was a good example of the single spec Camaro. It came as a 283 V8-powered hardtop coupe, with max power of 198bhp at 4800rpm and 285lb/ft at 2400rpm. Front disk brakes were standard, as was Positraction lsd and other safety equipment. A three-speed manual transmission wasn't even available, and Switzerland was stricter on emissions than other European countries. In a similar fashion, Karmann of Karmann Ghia fame, CKD assembled the AMC Javelin for

European sale. Local content to allow the cars to fit in with required tastes and law would include radial tires and better headlights.

On debut, big pronouncements were made concerning Camaro. Chevrolet GM Pete Estes said it's a " ... four-passenger package of excitement." Chevrolet's chief engineer for passenger cars, Donald H MacPherson, said in a press release, "Chevrolet's new Camaro, perhaps more than any other of today's cars, is a true product of the computer age." With the Z28 and big block V8 options pending, plus Chevrolet's resources, those statements were warranted. As a state of the art American pony, the Camaro largely made good on its promises. The Mustang had a fight on its hoofs! The first year of Camaro production saw some glitches, only to be expected of a newcomer. Not everything was perfect, and not everyone was okay with CAD (Computer Aided Design).

Popular Mechanics ran the results of a Camaro owner survey in July 1967. It picked up on the debut quality snafus concerning loose bolts, poorly adjusted doors, orange peel paint and wayward upholstery. However, by-and-by owners largely liked their Camaros, and sang its praises: "Good maneuverability for city driving," said an Iowa radio news director. "Fuel economy exceeded my expectations," added a Maryland electronics technician. "Just right for my needs," echoed an Ohio plasterer. Then, too, somewhat confirming 'secretary specials' folklore, "Fell in love with the looks of it," admitted a Delaware secretary! Well, the Camaro was a fine looking ride.

Priority for purchasing reasons nearly matched those of a Caddy Eldorado survey. Top reason for purchase was styling (65.3 per cent). It's unlikely that was the major motivation behind purchases of the Chevy Citation! Handling was reason two (62.9 per cent), and power came third on a relatively distant 29.8 per cent. For the Eldo, front-drive replaced handling as reason two. [4] The survey threw up results showing Camaro had import-like qualities behind its success, such as reasonable size and economy of operation.

At 184.6in long, 72.5in wide and 51in for height, the original '67 Camaro was a real compact car. It was closer in size to the early '60s compacts than the late '60s equivalents. It seems the public still dug that handy smaller size for parkability and roadability. There was also some concern over how such a small machine could accommodate. Powertrain and driveline were derived from larger

Other ponies could run but couldn't hide from the Camaro SS350's value for money. More than that, this Camaro was uprated to 300 horses for 1969! (Courtesy Mike)

domestic model lines. *Popular Mechanic's* survey also showed powerplant choices to be very "even steven," with 17.5 per cent selecting the 250 cube six, and exactly 16 per cent going for the 327 and 350 V8s respectively. Even during the musclecar era it seemed buyers were watching the pennies, and were pretty moderate souls.

Number one grievance was Camaro's rear suspension, in terms of axle wind up under power and a fuss budget ride over rough surfaces. Rear shock absorbers nearly vertical in nature and outboard of single leaf springs were the culprits. The computer said this was optimal to deal with washboard road surfaces and to allow a good cruising range size gas tank. However, buyers didn't much care for it. The flipside to all this was great handling, and it was commonly felt Detroit had trouble supplying good ride and handling in the one car. Solution? Have an Impala and a Camaro! Tight rear accommodation was also a sore point. Once again it seemed buyers were looking for a single, all-purpose car, and for that reason had considered imported makes. That said, such surveys showed owners were loyal Chevrolet folk, with 45.9 per cent of *Popular Mechanics'* Camaro owners also owning another car of the bow tie brand.

Something had to be done about that rear suspension for 1968, and was. Hi-po Camaros four-speed 327/350 and 396 V8 cars got multileaf rear springs and staggered shocks (and said shocks were now angled). Once again the GM computer was used to bring revisions to spring eyes, traction bars and shock absorber angle. Computers can get a bad

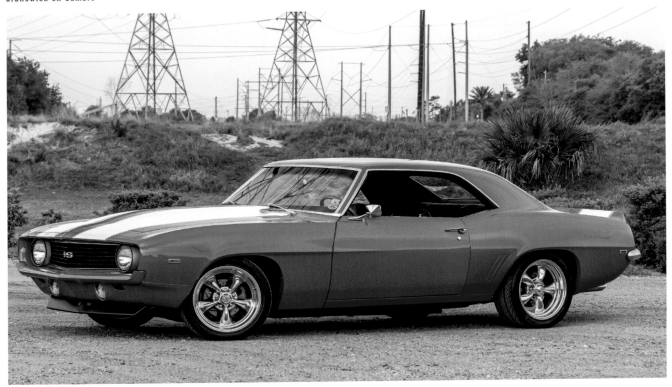

(This page and opposite) At a glance, it can be hard to tell a restomod 1st gen Camaro from a 5th gen Camaro. This '69 coupe has had a ground-up rebuild. A very serious ZZ502 V8 motor (8.2 liters) with March pulley system and Fitech fuel-injection send all that good stuff through a built GM 700R4 automatic. The 1969 Camaro ran beyond the existing '69 MY. It set a sales record that wouldn't be beat until 1978! For info and ergonomics, Autometer gauges and a Ididit steering column keep this Camaro on its flight path.
To stiffen the chassis, stock suspension has been combined with polyurethane bushings. Plus, the frame connectors joining the subframe to the unibody have been welded in.
(Courtesy Tim Biers & www.facebook.com/ RussMullerPhotography/)

rap, but can only work with inputs that are given. It seems Chevrolet's goals from 1967 needed some adjustment, too. Lo po Camaros stayed with their 1967 rear suspension, their limited power hadn't really troubled the Camaro chassis.

There was some slight restyling work for 1968. Most noticeable were the absence of quarter vent windows, and the addition of sidemarker lamps. The former went with the newly GM F-body introduced Astro Ventilation, and the latter was federally mandated. The sharp eyed might also have discerned a more pointed grille and divided tail-lights. Front running lights had also changed from circle to oval on non-RS spec Camaros. Big block Camaro SS396s carried a low gloss, black rear tail-light panel as a point of distinction.

On a humbler level, 1968 saw the introduction of Torque-Drive. This semi-automatic two-speed box was an inexpensive entry level avenue to clutchless driving. It was very similar to a Powerglide, but with

some hardware omitted to lower price. Items absent were automatic valve body, governor, vacuum modulator, high-speed downshift mechanism, and some other stuff. Chevrolet GM Pete Estes announced Torque-Drive and said it, " ... eliminates the clutch pedal, offers comparable economy to the regular three-speed manual, and has a list price of only $65." It also had built-in safety to stop overshooting from 'D' into neutral on the fly.

The Big Three still didn't like to openly acknowledge the existence of such a thing as an imported car selling in North America. However, GM, Ford and Chrysler were aware of any developments. Torque-Drive was GM's answer to the VW 1500's $135 option of Stick-Shift, which included semi-trailing arm rear suspension. In the Beetle's case it was an automated manual transmission, with floorshift, not a modified torque converter affair like Torque-Drive. *Motor Trend* reported on the $68.65 Torque-Drive when testing a Camaro 250 six in 1968's July issue.

By econocar standards the Torque-Drive Camaro was a spirited machine. A big 52mph was attained in low, and 96mph in high, plus an 18.7 second $1/4$ mile at 74.19mph recorded at Orange County International Raceway was pretty nifty indeed. The 17.5mpg wasn't bad either, given four-speed Bugs were in the mid 20s. Trouble was, once you had specified essential power steering, this Camaro was $800 over the semi-auto Bug. After a year of depreciation, both cars would be equal in value. It was something GM had to, and was, thinking about. In *Popular Mechanics*' survey 6.8 per cent of Camaro owners also owned Pontiacs and VWs. Quality, cost and service issues were making domestic buyers consider the imports.

In its August 1970 issue *Road Test* also did a survey of its first gen Camaro owners. Compared to *Popular Mechanics*' survey, the *Road Test* study covered ownership of all three first gen years, and owners were more enthusiast oriented. So, many survey cars were in SS and RS spec, or both. There weren't many plain Janes, and there was zero mention of Torque-Drive or Powerglide Camaros. The buyers were young, with over half being 25 or less, 51 per cent were single men, 25 per cent were women. Nine per cent were in the military. Chevrolet claimed this last stat was the highest reported figure for the domestic brands. Ninety-six per cent of the Camaros bought were purchased as new cars, and over 60 per cent owned at least one more car.

Once again purchases were influenced by Chevrolet and Ford loyalties, between Camaro and Mustang. However, said purchases were based on merit, and the buyer group was looking beyond just domestic brands. Many had checked out the Mustang/Cougar, with 49 per cent considering an import as a sports car, sedan or sports sedan. They were Bow Tie fans but they were also looking for their new daily driver, and many decided the Camaro provided the best overall deal. This included purchase price, size and handling, performance and more. Economy of ownership, even in the late '60s, was a factor for 52 per cent of owners. This encompassed price, gas mileage and maintenance.

There was no mention of insurance premiums at this stage, nor trade-in value. Owners praised the front disk brake package, liked the SS handling package, but one half of owners disliked the harsh ride. Camaro owners indicated that they followed SCCA road racing and drag racing, and that Donohue/Penske/Sunoco Trans Am magic seemed to have contributed to their decision to go Camaro. The consensus was that most owners loved their Camaros, and that they had mostly been reliable. Pollution controls had been responsible for indifferent running, but could still be 'tuned out,' as it were. This was code for "If I adjust the carb and ignition settings so it runs like God, and not the EPA, intended, then it works fine."

Road Test's survey brought up a number of buyer likes and dislikes, plus contemporary car ownership issues that would weigh heavy as the '60s became the '70s. If anything was steering Camaro owners away from home-designed it was the dealers. Oftentimes they took too long, overcharged, and/or didn't do the work properly. So owners increasingly favored independent shops, and tolerated dealers for warranty work. Quite a few times such work wasn't honored. Overall only 37 per cent of Camaro owners wouldn't buy another Camaro. However 72 per cent of this 37 per cent said they would select a different pony or musclecar. Perhaps a Chevelle SS396?

The remaining 28 per cent of the 37 per cent said they were willing to try an import. Mercedes and Volvo were specifically mentioned. This suggested the desire for a compact coupe (Mercedes W114 & Volvo 142S), with good brakes and moderate operating costs. Both brands had four-wheel disk brakes, and were thrifty on gas. Camaro owners at the time seemed to like such qualities. Four-wheel disks were a Camaro option concerning 1st gen cars. Although

Normally, big block '69 Camaros are SS cars with blacked-out rear fascias. However, there's nothing normal about this 502 cube car. A Mercedes red exterior and Z28 style skunk stripes keep you guessing! (Courtesy Tim Biers & www.facebook.com/RussMullerPhotography/)

This restomod rotisserie '69 Camaro rolls on ROH three-piece Modena rims, 18 x 8in front and 18 x 12in rear. The color is the original Inca Silver but in two-pack acrylic; not the original GM lacquer. (Courtesy Perth Street Car)

The basis was a Chevrolet 350 SB with 3.75in SCAT stroker crank and rods for 383ci. Claimer pistons and a big solid lifter Comp Cams cam, Demon 825 CFM four-bbl, MSD ignition and Hooker headers aid exhaling. An Edelbrock Victor Jr intake fits over 64cc aluminum Edelbrock Victor heads for 480bhp and 440lb/ft ... there's no cat! (Courtesy Perth Street Car)

there were no six banger Camaros in the survey, comments concerning the new 2nd gen Camaro were insightful. Current 1st gen Camaro owners weren't completely happy about the new Hugger being bigger, pricier and lacking small V8s. The 327 V8 had been the perfect compromise for many Chevrolet owners, and not just with the Camaro.

Comparing the long and short of it Road & Track tried a four-speed Camaro 327 RS in March 1967. A moderately specified car that achieved a 16.9 second $^1/_4$ mile at 87mph, 0-60mph in 9.1 seconds and 120mph flat out. All figures bettered the rival Mustang 289 four-bbl, also evaluated in the same test. The test trio's Barracuda was marginally outgunned but offered better gas mileage. On price the Camaro undercut FoMoCo and Mopar. In the Big Three tussle it was Camaro on $2707 versus Ford's $2960 Mustang and the $3020 Barracuda. Ford

priced the Mustang high to exploit its popularity. Even though the Barracuda 273 V8 was thrifty and quick, you seemed to get more pony for your buck at Chevrolet, and a more refined one, too.

Road & Track aired its usual domestic industry grievances of an American sedan in fancy dress, rather than the real sporting car, import style, that the magazine hankered for. However, this was selling the Camaro short, both in style and substance. There was a world of difference between a base Chevy II and a Camaro SS350. R&T had to concede that the Camaro was a stylish, nice handling coupe, even with standard suspension.

The journal felt the Mustang looked old-fashioned next to Camaro and Barracuda. However, it let out a "GM stylists have gone beserk" line in response to Camaro repeating the lower side of the Coke bottle styling with the rocker panel molding. Ditto those retractible RS headlamps. After all, by now even the VW Beetle was getting too ritzy for *R&T!* Of course, no one put a gun to your head to order that RS appearance pack.

Magazine road tests often said as much about the magazine as the cars under scrutiny. After the '70s everything started converging to a common viewpoint. To get from point A to B you really couldn't kick it any faster than a big block Camaro SS396 four-speed. *Car Life* tried one during the 1st gen Camaro's final year. Its May 1969 "Hugger Strip Tease" report had the numbers sports fans would be impressed with, mostly. This ZL-2 fresh air induction hood SS396 did 0-60mph in a scant 6.8 seconds, with the $1/4$ mile posted in 14.77 seconds at 98.72mph.

This purposeful looking bolide could do a 30-70mph passing maneuver in just 5.7 seconds. It could also manage a recorded top speed of 126mph. This was achieved with 3.73 rear gears, which proved a penalty for gas mileage and top speed.

The overall figure was 8.5mpg on premium gas. For comparison, not that a Chevrolet person would care, a '67 Shelby Mustang GT500 costing $4195 did 0-60 mph in 6.2 seconds, a 14.52 second $1/4$ mile at 101.35mph, and, with 3.50 final drive ratio, this four-speed machine maxed out at 120mph. According to *Motor Trend* it drank 11.1mpg overall. However, value for money had to be considered.

Two years later, and equipped with all the go fast goodies, *Car Life's* Camaro SS396 was $4294. It also came with 375bhp at 5600rpm and 415lb/ft at 3600rpm. The bigger engined 428-powered Shelby only came with a mere 355bhp and 420lb/ft from dual Holley four-barrels. The Camaro had just one Holley four-bbl. More than that, the Camaro's cold air induction opened at 80 per cent throttle as a smog concession. This machine was practically environmentally friendly! You really did get more coupe for your cash at Chevrolet.

The breakdown of those must have options at 1969 prices was $296 for the SS package. This now

A built GM THM 400 has a 3500rpm torque converter stall speed, with the action reaching an Illinois Strange Engineering 9in diff with 3.7:1 final drive ratioed Detroit Locker lsd. Caltracs traction bars control rear axle wind-up. (Courtesy Perth Street Car)

included power front disk brakes, along with HD suspension, 14 x 7 in Rally rims, and F70-14 tires. Add a further $316 and the big block 396 V8 mill came on board. And at $79 the new ZL-2 cold air induction hood was a steal. From a collector point of view, wise were the ones that bought such affordable options back in the day, that would eventually be worth gold.

The great thing about ZL-2 was that it actually worked. There's a good pressure area at the base of the windshield, and moving a scoop aperture further away from this location ain't functional. The

Cowl Induction lets in the air, and a full 3in dual exhaust system with mandrel bends delivers a warning to challengers. (Courtesy Perth Street Car)

the power to the ground was the problem. That 59.3/40.7 per cent front-to-rear weight distribution didn't help.

It was a similar situation with the biggest engined pony car of 1969, the Plymouth 'Cuda 440. Just like the Camaro big block, once you were rolling take-off traction wasn't an issue. Such coupes were unstoppable in a straight line. However, all that weight in the nose of a short car made for wheel hop on take-off, and axle tramp under braking. Which implied that go and whoa weren't what they should have been. Understeer would have to be tamed with the gas pedal, but it wasn't neat like a small block. Well, if it was struggling for traction on the street, it wasn't breaking a sweat in the showroom.

The sales keep coming!

Sales increased from 220,906 in 1967 to 235,147 in 1968, and there was a monster 243,085 in 1969! Chevrolet GM Pete Estes predicted that Camaro would overtake Mustang during 1969. However, as usual the best laid plans of mice and men can go awry. 1969 proved to be a very long model year for Camaro. The new 2nd gen F-body just wasn't ready in time, due to production problems. So, the 1st gen soldiered on into November 1969. Indeed, even though all 1969 first gen Camaros possessed 1969 VIN codes, GM literature called the late '69 Camaros … 1970 Camaros! Chevrolet's F-body was still riding the pony car wave, or at least getting conquest sales from Mustang. There was no resting on laurels, with genuine improvements for '69 MY to bolster brand loyalty.

Except for hood and trunklid, all sheetmetal was new for 1969. There was a V cant grille, with deep-set headlamps, along with new door skins and rear fenders and valence panel. The aforementioned ZL-2 cold air induction hood had been preceded by 1967's Z28 open element air cleaner. An optional cowl plenum duct delivered cold air to the side of the air cleaner housing. There was a new base V8 in the 307, and the refinement of a three-speed automatic for Camaros south of the SS396, bar the stick shift only Camaro Z28.

The non-hi-po 350 was rated at 255 horses, but the base Camaro still had four-wheel drum brakes. Press release info could be a little exaggerated, like Pete Estes' belief Camaro would exceed Mustang sales soon. The statement was released that Camaro SS rims could be 8in wide in 1969. Dimensionally, pony cars were getting bigger. For Camaro this implied 186in for length, 74in with width and 51.6in

enterprising could even jury rig the cold air induction to open prior to 80 per cent throttle. Keeping the engine hot by ingesting hot air was good for emissions, but not for power. Then again, that wasn't what was holding the 1st gen Camaro SS396 back. It could have gone faster than high 14s, but getting

on height. There was a drive in the industry to make ponies look like the money they cost. Plain Jane styling was out! So Camaro and Firebird puffed out a tad for '69, and the Mustang was in there with 'em. Mopar and AMC would join the class expansion in 1970 and 1971, respectively.

It was new outside and inside with Camaro. There was a new dashboard molding. Speedo and tach were now larger, less recessed and clearly visible. Auxiliary console gauges had changed for '68 MY. Four small trapezoidal gauge faces were now angled towards the driver. They looked like refugees from a sound recording studio. Well, Motown was named after the Motor City of Detroit. The gauges weren't exactly in plain sight, but info rather than idiot lights were always welcomed in this era. Overall, you would have to judge Camaro was pretty good, especially if you consider Mustang as a rival.

Car and Track took a gander at the '69 Mustang 428 Cobra Jet. During the exercise TV host Bud Lindemann had some comments, or ammunition for the Bow Tie Boys, to pass along. With the weight of that Ford FE big block, he had some concerns if the rear wheels were still on the ground. The dashboard warning lights were looked upon as possibly cheerful for the holiday season. As for handling, well, the only time one would see more plow would be on a farm! So, Chevrolet wasn't alone in trying to tame big block V8 weight distribution in a pony car. Speaking in general about this era, Dream Car Garage's Peter Klutt said Goodyear Polyglas GTs didn't exactly squeal going around corners, they just kind of sang!

Of course the devil was in the optioning, and high-output small block V8s combined with the right kind of suspension would satisfy souls looking for a Hugger that handled. Big block cars could get around a corner, but were strongest at highway running, challenging Chrondeks and the occasional stop light street grand prix. More importantly, Camaro was a success. It may have come after Mustang, but Chevrolet's Project Panther hit the ground running. The public and critics alike swooned over Camaro, and sales were gaining on Mustang by the minute. Chevrolet ads called Camaro an encore to Corvette, and there was truth in that. Hardware was shared, not just image.

With an inline six Camaro provided gas mileage not far from VW's ballpark, along with a lot more interior and trunk space. With the right V8 and HD suspension, it was truly the closest thing to the Plastic Fantastic on two lane blacktop. In the era of win on Sunday, sell on Monday, Donohue, Penske & Camaro were keeping sports fans happy. Mustang paced the field at The Brickyard on debut, but so too would Camaro. At the Indy 500, Chevrolet's big block-powered hardtop didn't miss a beat, and like the ad said, it was the heartbeat of America.

CHAPTER
Two
The Hugger Goes Pacing & Road Course Racing

ESSO

USAC

These championship races were conducted under the auspices of the United States Auto Club.

In the 1st gen Camaro's era, it was all about V8 power. Social motivations to save fossil fuel or the environment weren't exactly partners on anyone's dance card. From late 1969 model year, the 325bhp L35 396 V8 and its higher output, same-sized L78 cousin, with 375 horses, saw the 1st gen Camaro through to its conclusion. However, the humbler small blocks didn't stand still. The starter two-barrel LF7, 210 horse, 327 V8 continued up to mid '69 MY. It was then superseded by the smaller L14 two-barrel 307ci V8, which made an even 200 ponies.

In the middle to higher ground, the L30 four-barrel 327 with 275bhp survived through to the end of '68 MY. This 327 was effectively replaced by the LM1 350 with 255 horses for '69 MY. The LM1 350 gave way to the 250bhp L65 350 V8 by mid '69 MY. Then there was the hi-po L48 350, often seen in the Corvette. This V8 ran right through the 1st gen Camaro's life, but was re-rated upward from 295 to 300 ponies for '69 MY. Three hundred wild horses not enough, what about 400+? Chevrolet's publicity folks said, going into '69 MY, that they had an experimental Camaro with dual four-barrel carburetion that could exceed 150mph. However, remember Chevrolet's official line: "Chevrolet is not in racing."

The anti-racing pact struck between AMA Big Three players and AMC was getting very hard to believe; just try visiting any drag strip, or running of the Indy 500, even. FoMoCo's Mustang, on its debut, had paced the great race in 1964. Now the 1967 Camaro was doing likewise. At the Brickyard that year, one would see a suitably liveried Camaro SS396 convertible, with L35 396 and THM 400 power team, reliably pace the field. However, there was more afoot than meets the eye. The same went for the traditional bottle-of-milk race winner, AJ Foyt. The official line has been that 103 of the Ermine White 1967 Camaro SS350 convertible pace car replicas were made. It seems there were more, and they were more varied.

Most prominent were the three cars reserved for pace car duty. One to pace, one as back-up, plus the show quality finish version, to be presented to the winner of the Indianapolis 500. Then there were the 43 Festival Committee vehicles, along with 10 for the Speedway's VIPs and 25 so-called brass hat cars. This took the total to 81 cars. Complications came from Canadian Chevrolet dealers. They were a

1967 Indy 500 champ AJ Foyt ended up having a special Camaro SS396 pace car as a prize. Chevrolet made sure it had factory a/c and power top, just like he wanted! (Courtesy Exxon Mobil)

little salty over being left out of the Camaro pace car special edition loop. So, more cars were ordered by them, under the 80055 option code.

Within this additional Canadian run were 11 pace car replicas with 396 V8/THM 400 powertrains. Ten came with 350s and the Powerglide autobox. Ten of the small block replicas had 327s! Then there was AJ Foyt, who declined his prize car because it lacked a/c and a power top. Chevrolet obliged Foyt, with a special car built within the Canadian run.

There was also the Pacesetter promotional campaign to consider. This was a sales event commemorating the Camaro's pacing of the 1967 Indy 500. More Camaro pace cars could have been created and sold at this time. To get more showroom traffic, it was common for dealers to create special edition clones, and it was relatively easy to do so. Just order an Ermine White '67 SS350 RS or SS396 RS with stripe deleted, paint on the bumble bee stripe and add decals to serve … voila, an instant pace car replica!

In 1967 the Camaro emulated the Mustang by successfully pacing the Indianapolis 500 on debut. The publicity glow of the Brickyard couldn't be ignored. (Courtesy AmericanMuscleCar.com)

The Camaro ragtops that paced the Indy 500 had a L35 396/THM 400 power team. However, most replicas employed the SS350's L48 350 shown here. (Courtesy AmericanMuscleCar.com)

Lightning struck again in 1969, when the Camaro paced the Indy 500 once more. This time it was a Dover White Camaro SS convertible with RS appearance package. The cars had Hugger Orange Z28 style stripes, and a Custom Interior (code 720) in houndstooth cloth. The ZL-2 cowl induction hood was also present on every pace car. This time around Chevrolet took no chances with the race winner's pace car prize, and provided a convertible with a/c and power top.

Chevrolet also provided fleet support for the event, which included non-Camaro Chevrolets. As part of the fleet, 130 pace car replicas had their roles. There were 43 Festival Committee Camaro SS350 RS automatics. One came with a set of matching luggage for the Festival Queen. Seven cars were for speedway officials, five for USAC officials, and 75 pace cars for press and VIPs. Some of those 75 were Camaro SS396 RS four-speed convertibles. All pace cars attending race day were February-built cars, from the Norwood, Ohio factory.

The pace cars that did the actual pacing were Camaro SS396 RS automatics. They were ordered with L89 aluminum heads, and were sent to the GM Tech Center, where Chevrolet Engineering and Chevrolet Experimental Department prepared the convertibles for the rigors of pacing. These cars couldn't afford to fail! For durability and reliability, L78 cast-iron heads and a six-bolt COPO torque converter were fitted. JL8 four-wheel disks, 3.31 rear gears, HD battery and 61 amp alternator also made it through. Drive belts were pre stretched, aircraft standard hose clamps, hood pins and ragtop boot fasteners all left nothing to chance. This machine would be pacing in public at 130mph.

The race pace cars even had Z28 style 15in rims and tires. These replaced the 14in fare one would normally find on a Camaro SS396, and any 1st

One of the 103 Ermine White '67 Indy 500 Pace Car replicas. However, field studies have shown several more replicas were made. (Courtesy AmericanMuscleCar.com)

This '67 Camaro SS350 Indy Pace Car replica is a numbers-matching car. The factory all vinyl Bright Blue interior lived up to its billing! (Courtesy AmericanMuscleCar.com)

gen Camaro for that matter. The race pace car and back-up mobile shared the pacing chores. One car was shod with Firestones and one with Goodyears, to please the sponsors. 1960 Indy 500 champ Jim Rathmann drove the pace cars, for such pacing duty. With race fans seeing these cool convertibles successfully pace the Indy 500, many wanted one or two. So, the replica pace car total was 3675. These steeds were rationed between the 6400 Chevrolet dealers around in 1969. The orange Z28 style stripes replaced the usual SS stripes, and as such, RPO Z11 pace cars and the Z10 were the

only Camaros outside Z28 to wear so-called 'skunk stripes.'

At a time when 38 per cent of 1969 Camaros came with 396 V8s, such big block pace cars came with a white rear fascia. The Indy 500 door decals were trunk delivered, and it was up to the owner if he wished for them to be fitted.

Not one '69 pace car replica has surfaced with the super rare JL8 four-wheel disk brake option fitted. They were already mighty pricey cars, and that was an option too far. Indeed, although some replicas were snapped up before their tires hit the showroom floor, others lingered for over a year on dealer lots. That color scheme could scare off folks!

The Z11 pace car replica even had a kissin' cousin called the Z10. The RPO Z10 code implied a hardtop, in the same exterior get up as the ragtop Z11. However, there was no orange houndstooth interior. Many of the Z10s came with the 727 code ivory vinyl interior, and half seem to have been ordered with a/c. The Z10s could have numbered as many as 500 hardtops originally, and were sold in the South West and Tennessee. All were Norwood built, and it should be noted that Chevrolet did not

The 1969 Z11 Camaro Indy 500 Pace Car replica had a similarly liveried hardtop cousin called Z10!
(Courtesy AmericanMuscleCar.com)

Sold in the South West and Tennessee, the Z10s were somewhat of a regional special. Many had a white vinyl interior and factory a/c.
(Courtesy AmericanMuscleCar.com)

build cars without a dealer or customer order.

The Z10 never attended the 1969 Indy 500. No Indy 500 door decals were delivered for the Z10. More than that, there is no documentation linking the Z10 hardtop to the 1969 Indianapolis 500. It's all a mystery worthy of Hercule Poirot. Reasons for the Z10's existence could be that the Indy 500 had a contractual pace car requirement for ragtops only. Then too, the Z10 may have been a regional dealer special. A white hardtop, with white interior and a/c, mostly would have provided Southern comfort. However, there is no definitive word on the Z11 to Z10 link. It does show the 1st gen Camaro to be a vehicle of its era – an era with a myriad of optioning, and dealers willing and able to do their own thing. You wouldn't find a Z11 pace car replica or Z10 with a 307 V8. Such cars started with an SS machine, but you could get one with a Glide!

Z28 – The people's racer

The average domestic car buyer wanted a machine that didn't behave like a machine. They wanted maximum automation coupled with minimal servicing requirements. European imports often had major service needs that resembled a complete strip down and rebuild. There was also the saying that the

Opposite top: An automatic SS396 paced the '69 Indy 500. However, many Z10s and Z11s were SS350s, and at an even 300 horse, they weren't that humble! (Courtesy AmericanMuscleCar.com)

Opposite bottom: Why was the Z10 created and what was its true Indy 500 connection? The mystery continues. (Courtesy AmericanMuscleCar.com)

average American buyer felt that the only thing that should be opened was the glovebox.

It also helped if the interior was supremely quiet. There may have been a road under there, but that didn't mean you wanted to feel it. It's little surprise that the Renault Dauphine's game was soon up! However, there was one car that flew completely against convention. Surprisingly it came from Mr Mainstream himself, Louis Chevrolet. The car was the 1967 Camaro Z28 302.

The idea for the 'sock it to 'em' Z28 came from Vince Piggins. There was now a race-ready Camaro available through dealers, and the Camaro's RPO Z28 option code appeared in December 1966. Most people and dealers knew about the 1967 Camaro SS Indy 500 pace car replica, but very few knew of the essentially 1967 ½ Camaro Z28. How many? Try just 602! Was this really mighty Chevrolet, with its usually giant all-points bulletin advertising sweep? However, by the middle of 1968 all the major magazines were reporting, on the by now '68 MY Z28. *Sports Car Graphic*'s Randy Holt Jr noted that when a salesman at a Chevrolet dealer was asked for a brochure containing the Camaro Z28, he asked, "What's a Z-28?"

The Camaro Z28 certainly needed some promotion; at the start it was a mere RPO code. However, before the new version could be promoted Bow Tie style, corporate approval would be necessary. Specifically, that meant the go-ahead from Chevrolet GM Pete Estes, but Estes only drove convertibles, and the Z28 was hardtop only. Well, a ragtop just had to be found. Chevrolet Special Production Division's plan to promote the Camaro Z28 involved a COPO (Central Office Production Order) for one Camaro Z28 convertible. The little Chevrolet elves then placed said ride in the executive garage ... as bait! Fortunately Estes swallowed the Z28 hook, line and sinker. He loved it, and gave approval for its promotion.

So it was that the ads started coming, and dealers and buyers alike began thinking Z28. Try "Z is for

Zap!", "... the mean streak isn't just painted on – it's built in." Plus, expectedly, "It's the closest thing to a 'Vette yet." In the previously mentioned Holt Jr article, it was noted that *Sports Car Graphic* agreed with the advertising. The praise didn't stop there, *Car Life*'s review of the 10 Best Test Cars of 1968 said, "... a car that's gone all the way on everything." Indeed, the consensus was that the Camaro Z28 was the second best handling car from America, after Corvette. There was also praise for the Z28's balanced performance.

It used to be said a sporting car shouldn't break traction at any of its four wheels, and the Camaro Z28 delivered. It could get its power down, handle corners and stop. Fast driving wasn't the Hail Mary pass that it was in some muscle cars. Proving this usability, *Car Life*'s tests of the Camaro SS396 and Z28 showed less was more. For a 30-70mph passing maneuver, it was 5.7 seconds versus 5.4 seconds, in the Z28's favor. The big-engined SS396 got the drop in initial standing start acceleration, but the two were even-steven with 0-90mph, at 12.5 seconds. The Camaro Z28 got to 100mph 1.4 seconds quicker (14.2 seconds). At 133mph, top speed was 7mph higher than that achieved by the Camaro SS396.

The tests revealed that the Z28 really came on strong at high rpm. Braking and handling went all the Z28's way. It did eight stops from 80mph with zero fade. On the other hand, by the seventh stop the SS396 exhibited 30 per cent brake fade. For stopping in a straight line, the smaller engined car was much more controllable. Plus, as long as the road was smooth, the Z28 coupe could carve up corners in a manner that the big block Camaro could not. The 1968 Camaro Z28's $100.10 power front disk brake option, with 11in vented rotors, was a mandatory option. The 9x2in drums were standard Camaro fare, but pads for the front four-piston calipers and rear drum linings were HD items, not stock. Suspension-wise the front 112lb-in coils and 11/16in swaybar, were what you would find on a Camaro 327. However, the rear multileafs were 25 per cent stiffer than a Camaro SS396, at 131lb-in. This accorded with suspension guru Herb Adams' logic of a soft front-end to stay on course, and not get knocked off the cornering line. Stiff rear springing brought the control. Figure in the $184.35 for the Muncie four-speed, because all 1st gen Z28s had a four-speed, but this was separate from the $400.25 (1968) Z28 package. The pack brought the

hi-po jewel that was the 302 V8, a Z28 exclusive. It wasn't even in the Corvette. Then there was the trick suspension, quick ratio steering, and various trim ID and skunk stripe decals. The steering was indeed fast, at just 2.8 turns lock-to-lock. This came from the 17:1 ratio unit. There was also the even faster, 'sneeze at your peril' 15:1 ratio! Unfortunately the $84.30 power steering was the usual over boosted domestic car affair, but essential in parking lots, and it did have more feel than the 'point and pray' Mopar systems. LSD was $42.15, and expected on a Hugger like this.

The Star of the Z28 RPO code, the reason for its racing existence, and deliverer of such good control, was the high-rev 302 cube V8. The 7200rpm redline wasn't just there for decoration, it really could be safely used. It was the old 283 crank, in the current 327 block, with 1967 Corvette 327in³/350 horsepower heads. Add to that a 780 CFM center pivot Holley four-barrel with 1.69in barrels, on an aluminum high riser, and you had much more than the claimed 290 horse at 5800rpm, and,

suspiciously coincidental, 290lb/ft at 4200rpm. Well, GM wasn't racing you know, and the fake rating kept the insurance folks on a low simmer.

An aluminum intake manifold on a sporty car like this was a given. As with all GM aluminum intake manifolds forged at the Winters foundry, the unit carried a Snowflake casting mark. This was a 'W' surrounded by six snowflakes. You would also expect a hi-po V8 to be a solid lifter motor. This was the case with the Z28's 302. Such high rpm capability put bucket tappets out of the question, especially for racing. The ultra big 302 cam had a manic 346 degree duration, and intake plus exhaust valves with 118 degrees of overlap. On an OHV motor that meant little action under 3 grand, but hold on after that! The rocker arms had a 1.50:1 ratio, allowing 0.485in of valve lift. Intake and exhaust valves were supersized, at 2.02in and 1.6in respectively. It goes without saying the 4in bore and 3in stroke motor's 11:1 CR necessitated premium gas.

By 1968 the Camaro Z28 was great value to

So rare that if it was a steak it would be red, this is one of the 602 1967 Camaro Z28s. The original quarter vent icon that started it all. (Courtesy AmericanMuscleCar.com)

the enthusiast, but not cheap at around $4500. By the by, the Z28 was a cool car, but that solid lifter motor implied no factory a/c. Still, if it couldn't get cooler, it could be made hotter with factory-designed parts from an extensive catalog of performance equipment; GM would prefer not to say racing equipment. Participating dealers would gladly install said equipment, that the factory just wouldn't do on the regular assembly line. A more radical cam, not really streetable, and dual four-barrels lifted power from a stock, and genuine, 350 horse to 400 ponies! Then you would need a set of headers, and Bill Thomas Race Cars could oblige for 200 bones. Go to whoa was aided by 1969's JL8 four-wheel disk brake option. This cost a princely $500.30, and 206 Camaro Z28s were so optioned.

Car Life had tried out JL8 on a '68 Camaro Z28 at GM's Mesa Arizona Proving Ground. They were superb, and the magazine correctly predicted that they would be expensive, and a difficult to obtain option concerning 1969 Camaro Z28s. After all, the majority of Chevrolet dealers only sold and knew

about regular Camaros. There was also a general consensus that light feel aside, the Z28's power steering unit just couldn't be beat. This phenomenon was common on domestic cars. Quick changes of direction from side to side, like through a slalom course or evasive maneuver, would usually defeat the power assistance. The power steering pump just couldn't keep up, but not on Z28.

The Z28's Muncie shift linkage was stiff and notchy, and buyers were advised to stay with the stock shifter's rubber boot. The optional Chevrolet-designed console sliding plate shift lever seal could make things tricky. By 1969 the Camaro Z28 got a Hurst shifter for its four-speed, and standard 12-bolt Positraction lsd. The JL8 option involved a different rear axle housing. In 1969 the optional ZL-2 cold air induction hood was at hand. However, earlier Z28s did have provision for cold air induction. This came via cowl venting to the air cleaner tub. Camaro Z28s also possessed a point of distinction over other Camaros, by having 15in rims.

Yes, 15 x 6in Rally rims, with the latest Goodyear Wide Tread E70-15 tires featured steep cord angles, for better handling response. Early '68 MY Camaro Z28s had "302" fender emblems, becoming "Z/28" thereafter. Naturally the original 1967 Z28s still had single rear leafs and quarter vent front windows. This was in common with all '67 MY Camaros. The Camaro Z28 was quickly on the rise, 7199 sales in 1968 and 20,302in 1969.

Who would buy such a madcap machine? Racers, that's who, and racing was what the Camaro Z28 was for: specifically the SCCA's Trans Am road course race series. It's no coincidence the Boss Mustang had a 302 V8, and the Firebird Trans Am a 303, with AMC Javelin on 304 cubes. It was to limbo under the 305ci (5-liter) limit of the Trans Am series. There was also the 2-liter class for Alfas, BMWs and Porsches. The Camaro Z28 quickly proved its worth, beating out the dominant Ford Mustangs in the final two races of the 1967 season. After all, this was road course racing, and the Camaro wasn't called Hugger for nothing!

In the FIA Group 1 to 6 racing era, the Camaro Z28 had to meet a 1000 unit production build requirement in 12 months. This was done, and Camaro Z28 won its class at 1968's 12 Hours of Sebring. A pair of Group 2 Z28s came 3rd and 4th overall. They would have won the event were it not for a pesky pair of Porsche 907 Group 6 prototypes that came 1st and 2nd! So, the Camaro Z28 along with Mark Donohue, Roger Penske and Sunoco,

In 1968, *Sports Car Graphic* said the Z28's 302 was the best street Chevrolet small block V8 it had ever driven. (Courtesy AmericanMuscleCar.com)

The Camaro Z28 challenged and vanquished the existing SCCA Trans Am champ chariot of 1966-67: the Shelby Mustang. (Courtesy AmericanMuscleCar.com)

This '67 Camaro Z28's specification runs to a Muncie M21 four-speed, Deep Water Blue exterior and Style Trim Group with black vinyl interior and simulated woodgrain tiller. Please note the early optional three auxiliary console gauges. (Courtesy AmericanMuscleCar.com)

For history, this Z28's original engine block was replaced under warranty in 1971. By 2000 a full restoration was completed, and, in 2004, this '67 Camaro Z28 came 1st in the Illinois Secretary of State Car Show. (Courtesy AmericanMuscleCar.com)

would become synonymous. You could say the Hugger provided that unfair advantage. However, it was a success that needed work.

Donohue, Penske & Camaro

As part of Ford's Total Performance era, the Shelby Mustang benefited from Henry's involvement with design and homologation parts, but Chevrolet's relationship was more arms length. They did do HD parts, which were available to the public for homologation. However, the interaction between Team Penske and Chevrolet was limited to trading advice and knowledge. There was no actual cash pipeline or interference, and Roger Penske liked it that way. Indeed, Penske did refer to Chevrolet Motor Division as 'The Big House.' There was a Chevrolet engineer acting as liaison man, to assist with information supply from the company. He also got feedback from Team Penske.

Team Penske's Trans Am operation was a relatively small one. Former Shelby Racing team manager Chuck Cantwell was there, but a literal driving force at Team Penske was chief engineer and racer Mark Donohue. Donohue, known as Captain Nice, was in charge of design work, and was always searching for 'The Unfair Advantage.' This happened to be the title of his 1974 book covering his experiences and knowledge in motorsport. As a 1959 engineering graduate of Brown University, car preparation, or 'setting up,' was his specialty. He believed in getting the vehicle's road grip perfected first, with aero work to follow. Roger Penske said Donohue was central in getting the Porsche 917K to work properly, because when they first got that car it was undriveable.

Of course, when it came to unfair advantages, Roger Penske knew a few himself. Famously he qualified the same car twice. Close off the pit area, swap over the racing numbers, and pretend the faster Sunoco Camaro was the slower one! To create a racing Camaro, Penske would order a body-in-white shell through his personally owned dealership. Acid dipping would lighten the shell, and a rollcage was added. The F-body's front subframe was solidly bolted to the central unibody. The front fenders/grille was reinforced, with the entire assembly attaching with four bolts.

Penske used his own front swaybar design, and a system was set up so extra oil could be injected by the driver from his racing cockpit, without having to pop the hood. As for the Goodyear Blue Streak

racing tires, it helped that Roger Penske was the US distributor of those items. The small block V8 was built by the well known Traco Engineering. Even Traco got parts, mostly stock, from Penske's dealership. However, they did utilize a Traco designed custom valve gear. Chevrolet's crankshaft bearings were so durable that they were often used for more than one race. The 12:1 comp ratio motor gave 52/48 per cent front-to-rear weight distribution, and was joined to a M22 Rock Crusher close ratio four-speed. A Corvette aluminum radiator kept the V8 mill chill.

Respecting the rules, the car's fender contour had to be retained. Metal could be neither added nor taken away. Indeed, in keeping with production car racing, many stock items were used and tweaked. So the Chevrolet front coil springs made it through, and so, too, the RPO N44 17:1 fast manual steering, with a small spacer between the steering arm and tie rod to reduce bump steer and roll. Axle hop and binding were tamed using eccentric leaf springs. The spring's forward section was stiffer than the rear portion, for bump compliance and control. Optimal rear Panhard bar location was judged by computer. A normal Chevrolet Positraction lsd was utilized. High quality Koni dampers were employed, with one set capable of lasting one whole season.

The determination and detailed focus of Team Penske, were tremendous. It was apparent from Roger Penske's own words, "The days of the guys who are winning going to parties are over," and "I want my cars sharp". Indeed, the Sunoco Camaro was well prepared mechanically, and presented cosmetically. Roger Penske's determination was shared by Mark Donohue. Donohue ran out a winner with the Team Penske Camaro in 1968. However, this success didn't result in any resting on laurels. In 1969 Mark Donohue said, "Right now, it means more to me to win this Trans Am series than anything I've taken on." [5]

Donohue's determined statement, was made in the face of adversity. By late June 1969 and the round at Bridgehampton, Mark Donohue also known as "the complete race driver," hadn't won a Trans Am race that season. This wasn't going to change at Bridgehampton. Donohue fought from last place on the grid to come home second that day. Even so, Mark Donohue underplayed that feat by saying "We didn't come here to finish second ..." Roger Penske shared the anxiety. The lack of success lay with a typical motor racing combination of problems with

At this 1969 Bridgehampton SCCA Trans Am race Mark Donohue fought from last on the grid to finish 2nd in the Sunoco Camaro. It proved a turning point in Team Penske's race season success.
(Courtesy Car and Driver)

early in the '69 racing season. However, it proved unreliable. One new piece of hardware that did prove a winner, were the British Minilite mag wheels, selected for '69 season. In the winter off season, Donohue and Cantwell tested rim options, and the Minilites came out a winner! Donohue knew that the previous rims used on the racing Camaros, were marginal on durability. Equally trustable, was the Corvette's aluminum radiator.

The largest radiator available for the racing Camaro, had a 2.7in core and carried part number #3016688. An oil cooler was around too, listed as #3157804. An extensive list of Z28 HD chassis hop up parts were optional. Ring and pinion units for the 12-bolt Positraction lsd, were at hand. The custom 4.xx:1 and 5.13:1 sets carried respective part numbers 3961192 and 3961195. These sets were for drag racing, and had a reduced hardness to suit this task. For improved weight distribution, a #3963832 1969 fiberglass hood carried provision for cold air induction.

Smokey Yunick's #13 Camaro

Well, if there was a gentleman that knew his way around a parts book and rulebook, it was Henry Smokey Yunick, proprietor of world famous 'The Best Damn garage in town.' He was also a GM truck dealer, and one of America's foremost engine specialists. Indeed, in his capacity as consultant, Yunick was involved in the creation of The Hot One, the Chevrolet small block V8. As an industry design

and testing consultant, Smokey Yunick worked with Ford, Pontiac and Chevrolet. For in-field research and development, his racing outfit served as an unofficial Chevrolet factory race team. It was a time when racing really did improve the production breed.

Given all this, it was only natural that Yunick would get involved with the Camaro early on. With its cleanly styled body, and availability of those excellent Bow Tie small block and big block V8s, he could see the coupe's potential as a record breaker. Married to this was Smokey Yunick's legendary ability to interpret racing rulebooks. He used to study such tomes with an uncommon rigor. This led to results that, while not technically illegal, did lead to differences of opinion within racing officialdom. Great examples were the #13 Chevelle and similarly numbered, and also very fast, #13 Camaro.

The #13 Camaro looked like a 1967 Camaro, but the modifications were myriad. The coupe had an acid-dipped body, thinner glass, the front end of the body was tilted downwards and the windshield was laid back for improved aerodynamics. Fender flares accommodated bigger wheels and tires, and the front subframe was dropped. The front suspension and floorpan were raised, effectively lowering the Camaro. An added oil line, involving a pressurized hose, permitted the driver to add engine oil from the cockpit. Aside from a mandatory baffled oil pan, this was to prevent oil starvation during high speed cornering, or straight line running, when oil can fail to go or stay where it should.

Yunick's #13 Camaro also featured a racing harness with a military helicopter ratchet mechanism, to aid driver movement. An inertia reel for racing, if you will. Many of the features mentioned would be used on the 1969 Team Penske Sunoco Camaro. This included pushed close drip moldings. Smokey Yunick had raced the early Chevrolet small block V8 in 1955-56, and now it was the Camaro Z28's turn. The venue was the 1967 Mission Bell 250. *Hot Rod* magazine's Jim McFarland witnessed this mid-September event at Riverside Raceway. McFarland didn't buy the informal manner in which things came together.

The #13 Camaro was towed on a flatbed from Yunick's Daytona Beach base, using a beat up '50s pickup. When it reached Riverside, there just happened to be the Goodyear rep, with four racing tires on hand. Indy Car racer Lloyd Ruby was also there. The Camaro was hosed and wiped with motel towels, whereupon Ruby hopped in, and beat

The #13 Camaro lived up to Smokey Yunick's famous lateral thinking concerning racing rulebook interpretation. (Courtesy Eric S Blakely www.edelbrock.com)

Shown in updated '68 form, the #13 Camaro had a tilted down front body, laid back windshield and pushed close drip moldings for that competitive edge. (Courtesy Eric S Blakely www.edelbrock.com)

the pole position time set at the 1966 running of the Mission Bell 250. These things don't happen by accident. Major success for Smokey Yunick's Camaro came in breaking FIA speed records at the Bonneville Salt Flats in October 1967. Three Camaros were prepared for said record breaking: two small block cars, and one big block machine.

The big block entered 'B' production class (305-488in³). For this, a stock bore 540 horsepower motor was built, using eligible optional Chevrolet HD parts. The two Yunick small block coupes concerned 'C' production class (183-305ci), and stock Z28s were fitted with rollbars, American Racing mags and 10.00-15in rayon racing tires. The three Camaros taken to Bonneville had solid lifter motors, Muncie four-speeds, Positraction lsd and stock leaf springs.

The drivers at Bonneville were Mickey Thompson, Curtis Turner, Bunkie Blackburn and Johnny Patterson. The result was over 500 records

The #13 Camaro was a record breaker at the Bonneville Salt Flats in 1967. However, it had to wait for Don Yenko to claim a victory in the SCCA's Trans Am series. (Courtesy Eric S Blakely www.edelbrock.com)

broken in 12 days. The international records broken involved standing starts. At night, the 10-mile unlit course involved very cold conditions. Radiator grilles had to be covered.

The big block Camaro did 174-176mph at 8100rpm for hours. In one 12-hour record attempt, the rear differential even broke. High rpm valve float with the big block motor, resulted in a valve being pushed into a piston, causing the car to expire. One small block Camaro broke a valve, when the car hit some water and over revved.

Smokey Yunick had hoped his #13 Camaro would challenge the dominant Fords in the SCCA Trans Am series. However, this task fell to Team Penske's Sunoco Camaro. The #13 Camaro never actually won a Trans Am series race, while Yunick owned it. As for the legality of modifications done to his race craft, Smokey Yunick always declared, "They never said I couldn't."

Baby Grand Nationals

Smokey Yunick did have his eye on the SCCA's Trans Am series with the Camaro. Increasingly, it seemed like Trans Am racing was where the money was. Pony cars were kings of Detroit, and race fans identified with the cars they owned. There were 102,000 paid admissions for the 12-race series in 1967, as Dan Gurney and Parnelli Jones' Cougars, duked it out with eventual champ Jerry Titus in his

Quaker State Mustang. [7] Well, Smokey Yunick did have an earlier association with stock car racing. In the early days of NASCAR his name and "The Best Damn garage in town" signage were on Herb Thomas' Twin H Power #92 Hudson Hornet. [8]

Stock car racing had been dominant since WWII, and that early '50s Hornet packed a potent inline six. However, with V8s on the rise, NASCAR President Bill France Snr got behind a stock car series that answered what the SCCA had, and complemented the NASCAR pinnacle Grand National series. That answer was the Baby Grand Nationals, in a new series called the Grand Touring Championship in 1968 and 1969.

The new game also attempted to overcome the escalating cost of racing. There were bigger budgets to go with the larger attendances, predicted for the 1968 Trans Am series. In addition, running a Grand National outfit involved a big automaker, and professional race drivers, in a 40-race national series, that required a 35 grand budget per team.

The Baby Grand Nationals spoke to the local racer and mechanic with a modest $5000 budget, and the desire to take part in some events held in their neck of the woods. In using pony cars for NASCAR, the limits were like the Trans Am series. Maximum engine size was 305 cubes, the cars could have no longer than a 112in wheelbase, and the minimum weight was 2950lb. Unlike the pre-1970 Trans Am, it was legal to destroke from 355in[3]. Indeed, in the realm of replacement engines, the Chevrolet mouse motor was cheaper than Ford's Windsor. Apart from helping budget minded participants, the Grand Touring Championship was essential to keep the small tracks alive. It also stimulated interest in local auto racing.

In 1968, there were 19 Grand Touring races, with 35 in the 1969 racing season. In 1969, Buck Baker came second in the championship, with three wins and 1017 points, in his Camaro. Many Baby Grand National coupes were former SCCA Trans Am series cars, adapted to suit. The question did arise, once the Trans Am series imploded after 1970, where did they go? There were this whole bunch of FIA Group 2 pony car racers that used to be part of well-run and financed outfits. They often went overseas, taking part in touring car series in Continental Europe, Britain and Australia.

Camaro Z28 racers overseas

A case in point was the 1968 Camaro Z28 campaigned by Brian Muir in the UK's RAC Saloon Car Championship, the BTCC (British Touring Car Championship). This coupe was formerly a '68 season Team Penske back-up car. Before Muir raced it, it was campaigned on the Continent by German ex-Penske employee Peter Reinhart. It was then purchased by UK building contractor Malcolm Gartlan, and raced with sponsorship from paper product manufacturer Wiggins Teape. In 1970, Brian Muir used this Z28 to win the prestigious RAC Tourist Trophy at Silverstone. He came third outright in the 1970 British Saloon Car Championship, and second in class behind Frank Gardner's Boss Mustang 302.

In the '70s, it was common to see Camaros racing against Ford Capri RS2600s and BMW 3.0 CSLs in West German sedan racing. Similarly, having an American pony car was a competitive thing in UK touring car racing, but you needed the foldin' fun cash. By 1971, the Wiggins Teape Camaro Z28 sported 11³/₄in four-wheel Corvette disk brakes, Muncie M22, Minilites, Firestone racing slicks, staggered shocks and a specially located panhard rod. All the tricks and upgrades gleaned from the peak of SCCA T/A days.

The hard racing was on display at the tight, 1.4-mile, UK Crystal Palace circuit, as contenders battled for the 1971 UK Iberia Airlines Trophy. In the 15-lap, 15-minute race, pole position belonged to Mike Crabtree's RS1600 Ford Escort, and second was Gerry Marshall in a 2.5-liter, fuel-injected Vauxhall

Viva GT. Martin Thomas' 350-powered 1st gen Camaro, with RS front fascia, was third on the grid. For most of the race, Thomas' Camaro was in the lead. It pulled away on the straights, with the Escort gathering it up under brakes. Only one second split the top three for most of the race. By lap ten, the field's Boss Mustang was a distant fourth, and the top three had caught the first of the backmarkers by lap nine.

Unfortunately, constant pressure from the Crabtree Escort forced the Thomas Camaro into driver error. Thomas spun on lap 14, with the Escort taking the checkered flag. Legendary Formula One commentator Murray Walker called the race. However, Camaro success came for Frank Gardner in the 1971 BTCC, when his Chevrolet Camaro placed fourth in the championship. Then there were the ATCC (Australian Touring Car Championship) titles of Bob Jane in 1971 and 1972, at the wheel of his 1st gen, ZL1-powered Camaro. This car enjoyed the modification latitude afforded by Group 2 racing.

It all started when Bob Jane sold his 1967/'68 racing season Trans Am series Ford Mustang, and bought two Camaro ZL1 427s. They were purchased from 1960 Indianapolis winner Jim Rathmann, who had a Chevrolet dealership in Florida. General Motors informed Jane that two ZL1 coupes were located in Melbourne, Florida. One was a Hugger Orange #33 VIN 610732 coupe, with the other a Le Mans Blue #52 VIN 620934. The blue car was an automatic intended for drag racing, but Bob Jane bought 'em both! The COPO (Central Office Production Order) Camaro's ZL1 427 V8 motor was meant for drag racing, and, alluding to its all aluminum nature, was developed for Can Am (Canadian American) racing.

The lightweight ZL1 was a natural for road course racing, and Bob Jane proved it with a purpose-built racer using Harrop brakes and a Holinger modified Muncie M22 four-speed. The result was over 600bhp and 600lb/ft. After all, with cold air induction, it was the most powerful production engine Chevrolet had offered to Joe Q Public. Even the standard COPO Camaro 427 heeded the ZL1's abundant power, with front disks, HD radiator/suspension, and 12-bolt Positraction lsd with 4.10 gears being mandatory options. The problem for Jane was the ZL1's propensity for devouring gearboxes, "The problem with the 427 was it used to eat gearboxes. It was so powerful that there was no gearbox built in that era that would stand the torque."

Racing at Sandown, Bob Jane scored his first win in the Camaro, but lost 2nd and 3rd gears in the process: "This thing went half the race in top gear, which is totally amazing, but that's what torque can do for you." In the seven-round series that was the 1971 ATCC, Jane won three races, but had two seconds and one third. He beat out Canadian rival Allan Moffat, who was campaigning his 1969 ex-Trans Am series Mustang. The Camaro was too good, so the Confederation of Australian Motorsport (CAMS) banned the ZL1 427 V8! This forced Bob Jane to switch to a four-barrel 350 V8 for the 1972 racing season.

The combination of Jane and Camaro still won the championship, with four victories, two seconds and one third. He had defeated Moffat's Mustang yet again, 76 points to 53. The Bob Jane Camaro ran again in 1973, this time under the Z28 tag. It won the round at Calder Park, but was disqualified due to a homologation infraction. Bob Jane still had an edge on Allan Moffat, who was now using a local Ford Falcon GTHO Phase III, but CAMS said there weren't 25 similar Z28s in Australia, so no deal.

Jane had worried about the Camaro being competitive sans ZL1, but as it turned out the Hugger was such a road course natural, it didn't matter, "I was quite surprised that the chassis was so good that the power of the 350 was enough," he said. Unable to race the Camaro in the ATCC, it was eventually taken up by drag racer Mike Tyder as a $1/4$-mile machine. In 1998 Bob Jane bought back the car, and it was restored to its 1971 ATCC glory state.

Bob Jane won the Australian Touring Car Championship (ATCC) in 1971 and 1972 using this 1969 COPO Camaro ZL1 427. He was forced to switch to a 350 four-bbl V8 in 1972 due to the ZL1 being banned.
(Courtesy Sicnag)

CHAPTER
Three

Big Blocks, Speed Shops & ¹/₄ mile

The big blocks are coming!

Observing the VIN of a 1st gen Camaro, 1 signifies Chevrolet Division, 2 indicates the Camaro vehicle line, 4 means a V8 engine, 37 the coupe bodystyle and 7, 8 or 9 the model year of the car. After this, the letter L says the coupe was built at LA's Van Nuys factory. It was appropriate to look in 'The Valley,' since Southern California was the mecca for muscle cars, custom cars, imports and anything representing self-expression on four wheels. With an added interest in performance (ironic given California would soon become smog control central) cars packing big block V8 power, the best of the best, were the hot ticket.

Chevrolet weren't so well placed for ultimate power, earlier in the 1960s. GM's anti-racing policy had seriously curtailed Chevrolet and Pontiac Divisions. Both were placed at a disadvantage during Ford's Total Performance era with the Cobra 427. So entered the 396in³ big block V8, in the 1965 Corvette. To many, this one-year-only 425bhp engine for the two-seater seemed better value, compared to the pricey and less powerful Fuelie 327. Then came the 1966 L72 427 V8, and the Plastic Fantastic's Fuelie was history! Now you just had to have a big block.

For Camaro, a big block option became a very necessary thing. A month or so after the 1967 Mustang 390 V8 came the Camaro SS396. The L35 and higher output L78 396s were enough for most, and more than the Mustang's meek 390, but you can never have enough of a good thing, right? Factory options aside, which was the first big block Camaro? *Hot Rod* magazine felt they had the skinny on that phat rat motor, with its converted Camaro SS350 V8. It was June 1966, and this Camaro SS350 had arrived at Petersen Publishing for prototyping, prior to the Camaro's 1966 fall launch.

It was normal in those times for a new Detroit design to go around the aftermarket industry, with companies looking at the new jalopy. They would try and work out what products could be designed and offered to the public post haste. All in all, 16 companies studied this new Chevrolet, with *Hot Rod*'s Jim McFarland in charge of the coupe for the automotive show and tell. A major upgrade applied in this timeframe was a 396 big block conversion by West Coast Chevrolet guru, Bill Thomas Racing Cars of Anaheim, California. Bill Thomas would become linked with Nickey Chevrolet, and knew the factory had big block fitment in mind for Camaro. There was also the new Super Stock class at the Winternationals to consider.

The *Hot Rod* magazine car was to be featured in a series of 1967 upgrade articles. The coupe was the first of its kind in many ways: as a Camaro in California, road-tested in print media, with a street driven big block, Edelbrock intake, four-speed Hurst shifter that got into the 11s in a NHRA event. Jim McFarland took this newbie to Lions dragway, and in third gear at 6200rpm, its 396 was blown to the four winds. It seemed that this 396 had done 500 tire-testing miles earlier for NASCAR, at Riverside raceway. No problem, Bill Thomas put in another 396, and McFarland took the Camaro to Irwindale, where the car encountered Bill 'Grumpy' Jenkins. Jenkins looked over the Camaro with some concern.

The Camaro went to Pomona and drew Grumpy Jenkins during first-round eliminations. Jim McFarland speculated that there must have been something at Irwindale that spooked Jenkins, because in a Chrondek crisis at Famoso, Bill Jenkins made an error. "With one yellow light still showing on the Tree, Jenkins red-lighted." The *Hot Rod* magazine (HRM) crew was there with Don Evans as driver, McFarland as mechanic and John Thawley as helper in SS/C class like Jenkins. Evans did a 11.84-second pass at 119.86mph on his second run in A/MP class. It seemed Grumpy knew something that HRM did not.

The journal retired the car immediately from competition. Those involved just didn't think it would be so competitive out of the box. It turned out that Bill Thomas had sneaked in a huge 490ci V8, not the 'little' 396! Indeed, it used to be an old racer's trick. Whenever anyone asked if modifications had been done, you just said nah, it's stock! After such revelations, Thomas refitted the coupe's original 350 small block. *Hot Rod*'s Jim McFarland kept this Camaro, and it would be used as a test bed for prototyping during the fuel crisis/smog control era. Now the aftermarket was using this Camaro to work out what performance and economy parts could be offered in those challenging post-1974 times.

Dana Camaros

In the '60s it was all about the street & strip. To win on either, you had to toss out that 350 cube grocery getter and install a 427 V8. That's where the speed shops came in, because the factory didn't normally put 427s into Camaros. The earliest outfit

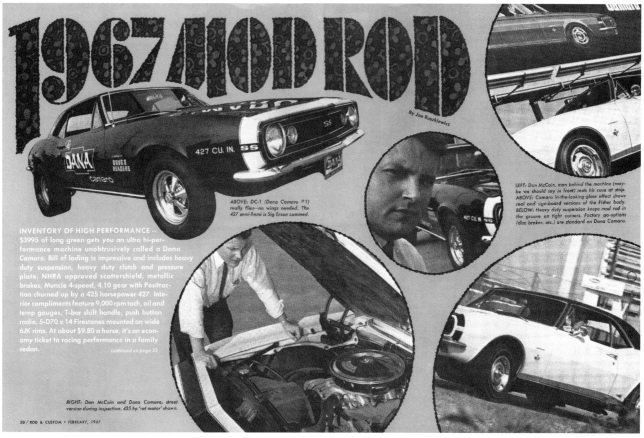

continued on page 52

This is believed to be the first Dana Camaro built, and Dana's Don McCain did local drag racing to promote Dana Chevrolet. (Courtesy *Rod & Custom*)

to accomplish this task with a coupe available for purchase by racers was Dana Chevrolet.

Dana Chevrolet, and the man behind it, Peyton Cramer, had a clear mission statement. It was stated by John Ethridge, in the July 1967 issue of *Motor Trend*, that "in his new undertaking, [Cramer] intends to do with the Camaro pretty much what Shelby did with the Mustang. Even the $3995 base price is te same as that of the Shelby GT350."

All of the above came as little surprise, given Dana's genesis. Peyton Cramer and Don McCain were former Shelby American employees. Cramer was Shelby's general manager, and had a hand in the creation of the Shelby Mustang GT350. McCain was a drag racing specialist. It transpires that Carroll Shelby himself had examined the possibility of Shelby American offering the Camaro as well as the Mustang. It made commercial sense to cater to both sides of the street. This didn't happen, but it's believed the first Dana Camaro may have been created while Cramer and McCain were at Shelby American's Phoenix shop. Indeed, the caper may

have involved the two gentlemen installing the 1966 Corvette L72 427 into that first coupe, with M21 four-speed and Hurst shifter.

This first Dana Camaro was delivered in November 1966 to Brown & Hoeye Chevrolet of Mesa, Arizona, as a gold painted coupe with small block V8. Peyton Cramer and business partner Paul Dombroski, were turned down by FoMoCo concerning a Ford dealership. So, they bought bankrupt So Cal South Gate dealer Dana Chevrolet. The goal was to make Dana the first Chevrolet dealer in the region to focus on high performance. Don McCain handled sales, and drag-raced the converted Camaro to publicize Dana Chevrolet's 427 conversions. Well-known SCCA racer Dick Guldstrand held a managerial position at Dana.

In a pattern replicated at other speed shops, early conversions began with a Camaro SS350 coupe. This was for body rigidity, and to start with essential hardware: HD suspension, 17-quart rather than 13-quart cooling system and 14x6in rims with D70-14 Firestone Wide Ovals. To this, and with an early

Wearing its correct shade of GM code 55 Azure Turquoise, this 1969 Dana Camaro 427 has that street sleeper look Dana was famous for. (Courtesy RKMotorsCharlotte.com)

1967 Dana package costing $1078, was added: 425 horse 427, Muncie four-speed, 3.55:1 12-bolt Positraction, metallic brake linings, headers, dual exhaust system, HD clutch and pressure plate with NHRA approved scatter shield, chrome plate dress up valve covers/air cleaner, extra instrumentation (8500rpm electronic tachometer, oil pressure and coolant gauges).

There was a delete option credit worked out for the unwanted 350 motor that the Camaro came with. This was $475, the parts counter price for a 350 small block sans starter and alternator, both of which 350 items were retained on the converted Dana Camaro 427s. The new motor was a '66 L72 Corvette 427 making 425bhp gross. This four-bbl solid lifter edition made max power at 5600rpm and 460lb/ft at 4 grand, on an 11:1 comp ratio. The hotter Corvette triple deuce 427 reached 435 horse, but the vacuum method of bringing in the outer carbs was temperamental, and the 425 horse 427 was more tractable.[9]

The 435bhp L71 427 V8 was a $150 option at Dana. Either way, the semi-hemi 'porcupine' head

427 was more motor than the Camaro SS350 was car. In the July 1967 issue of *Motor Trend*, John Ethridge found out by just how much. Concerning the L72 427, "Too much and the rear end wants to come around." At least unlike in the smog era, there was some power to keep an eye on. The test subject's 3.73 rear axle meant 130mph was reached with ease. A 3.07:1 final drive ratio equaled a possible 158mph at the 6200rpm redline. Given the L72's muscle, you had better believe it!

Standing start acceleration in the Dana Camaro, and cars of its ilk, was a challenging affair. The trick was getting all that power down using existing chassis and tire technology. Traction Master torque arms were present, but didn't really compensate for Dana's hi-po camshaft kit. John Ethridge found the upsized F70-14 Goodyears useless in containing 1st gear wheelspin. Start in 2nd or 3rd if you like, it made no difference. The 1/4 mile still took 14.2 seconds at 105mph. Similarly, *Car Life* in April 1967 reported a 14.2 second pass at 102mph.

Ethridge said that with the biggest tires that would fit, 9.00/9.50-14 Goodyear slicks, matters

Former Shelby American general manager Peyton Cramer was in charge of Dana Chevrolet. He wanted to make Dana the Shelby of Chevrolet. (Courtesy RKMotorsCharlotte.com)

Early Danas had L72 427 V8 punch, no power steering, and utilized the Camaro 350 V8 alternator and starter motor. Even with a 3.55 rear end, flooring it in 4th brought wheelspin! (Courtesy RKMotorsCharlotte.com)

Most Dana Camaros were 1967 and '68 models. This 1969 edition has Dana tag brackets. Like the Z28, but unlike other 1st gen models, this Dana Camaro rides on Goodyear Polyglas 15 inchers. (Courtesy RKMotorsCharlotte.com)

improved to 13.3 seconds at 107mph. The Camaro's body had to be raised to clear said tires. Uncorking the headers reduced the ¹/₄ mile time to a limbo low 12.75 seconds at over 110mph. Such uncorking crested the legal limit for drive by noise levels. The Dana Camaro that went around the magazines, had the optional power front disk brake option, plus

metallic linings for the rear drums. However, *Car Life* still encountered brake fade from the second stop. There was also the contemporary problem of rear brake lock up.

There was a common plea from road testers for more balanced performance, than the Dana Camaro offered. In addition, the Muncie shift linkage for the four-speed required man handling, but this car was for a certain purpose. In its role as a $^1/_4$ mile winner, that could also be street driven, the Dana Camaro made more sense. As John Ethridge said for *Motor Trend*, "To be perfectly frank, the Dana Camaro is not everyone's motorcar, and it was never intended to be … But to the enthusiast who can afford it, it offers a combination of the highest order of performance and utility value that is hard to match."

With the A-body Barracuda big block not offering the option of power disk brakes, even in mild versions, the Camaro's greater versatility was a boon. When it came to its true purpose, the Dana Camaro delivered. The buyer of car number one did intend to race it. This caused some legal problems that Dana Chevrolet helped with. Given Gary Dodd's intention to race, he couldn't get car insurance, and without insurance the bank wouldn't approve a car loan. Dana pulled a few sleights of hand, to get Dodd over the 1320ft line.

Prior to the insurer discovering the intention to race, Dana convinced the bank to approve the loan. State regulators were then maneuvered around. Dodd allegedly received his coupe with no transmission oil, and the incorrect camshaft for the 427 V8. In return for these snafus, Dana took over the loan and Gary Dodd got Dana Camaro number one, plus its ownership pink slip. It was also claimed the Camaro was still in the alleged state of disrepair, to keep matters on the level, as it were.

Dodd certainly raced hard, and to that end his Camaro eventually used a 1957 Olds differential and Connell Chevrolet-sourced ZL1 427, with a tunnel ram intake. The coupe was originally gold, and changed to black prior to Dodd's ownership. The original 12-bolt Positraction broke under the strain of the earlier L72 427. With the '68s coming, this Camaro was visually updated to a blue exterior, and Dana's dual aperture fiberglass hood was fitted. This number one Gary Dodd car did heads-up West Coast Pro Stock racing, and its competition career ran into the early '70s. At this point, the fuel crisis and recession were making finding funding for drag racing difficult. By the end of its career, local newspapers referred to the coupe as "Old Dana Camaro." So many were obviously wise to its historical pedigree.

In general, Dana Camaro 427s didn't carry much exterior decoration. Rocket SS rims and Fenton SS center caps were popular. West Coast solid pipe guru Doug Thorley supplied headers.[10] Showing the uncompromising nature of such Camaro 427s,

the pipework fitted had certain tube sections uncollapsed, with zero provision for accessories like power steering. Dana's Don McCain did local drag racing in Dana's cars, to promote the dealership's speed shop work. As per other shops, you could order a Camaro from any Chevrolet dealer, and have it sent to Dana for whatever extent of upgrade you wished: have a L72 or aluminum-head L88 427 crate motor with 12.5:1 comp.

Most Danas were '67 or '68 Camaros, with the rare L88 427-powered Dana Camaro 88 being extra special. Sadly, times and Southern California change. Compared to other speed shops that tried to placate regulators, or offer emissions compliant models, which mostly could only pass at the 49-state level, Dana Chevrolet challenged authority head on.

It all culminated in an EPA (Environmental Protection Authority) raid on, and take down of, Dana Chevrolet in 1974. Vehicles were seized and sent to the LA County Sheriff's impound lot, where they were auctioned off. Dana took on the law, and the law won. In this new age, speed equipment became strictly for 'off road use.' This meant you could use it on a track or strip, but not on public roads.

Just a few years earlier, Dana Camaros had been a fixture of SoCal street racing, but the days of racing for pinkslips were history. Increasingly, federal agencies were using high-handed actions, at the behest of special interest groups to threaten personal liberty. By the mid '80s, Lee Iacocca and Carroll Shelby were associated with front-drive, turbocharged, four-banger Chrysler Corp cars. For traditional enthusiasts, that wasn't an option. It only served to increase the value of Dana Camaros, and those made by rival speed shops.

Baldwin Motion

Sometimes the cars with the biggest impact and media coverage are built in the smallest numbers. This was the case with the high performance Baldwin Motion Chevrolets made from 1967 to 1974. Only around 500 cars were created, and not all were even sold in America. It's also the case that lightning certainly struck when the paths of Joel Rosen, Ed Simonin and Martyn L. Schorr crossed in the late '60s. Rosen ran Motion Performance Inc, a company that made racing cars to order, and sold performance items and body modification parts through its shop and catalog. The Baldwin Auto Co was where Ed Simonin came in, it involved family-run Chevrolet dealership Baldwin Chevrolet

Showing how late the '69 Camaro ran into the '70 MY, this Baldwin Motion Camaro LS7 454 was purchased from Baldwin Auto Company on June 29, 1970 as an SS396.(Courtesy David Griffiths www.legendarymotorcar.com)

of Baldwin Long Island, New York. Then there was Marty Schorr, contemporary editor of *Cars Magazine*, who did public relations and catalog promotion for the speed shop. Schorr also had a hand in model development concerning the Baldwin Motion combine.

Well, it wasn't exactly the coming together of Charlie's Angels, but Baldwin Motion certainly created auto magic. The surprising thing was that Baldwin Chevrolet had no prior association with selling hi-po Chevrolets. The firm just did regular, standard issue models. Motion Performance had built race cars, and Joel Rosen had participated in drag racing, hillclimbs and rallies, but had no prior GM links. However, at this time there was indeed a market for Chevrolets that went beyond the already very impressive performance of stock models. So, one could order a Camaro, Chevelle, or Corvette and eventually Vega, from Baldwin Chevrolet. It would then go to Motion Performance, where, money and mind permitting, you could have anything you wanted!

The finished result was an expensive, turnkey performance car that could be financed through the usual GMAC (General Motors Acceptance Corporation). All without leaving the Baldwin Chevrolet dealership. What you got was usually a Camaro with a big block. Early on it was the discontinued 1966 425-horse Corvette 427 V8, with Holley four-barrel, solid lifter cam and cast-iron tube headers. Apparently, the single quad flowed more air than the triple deuce. Baldwin Motion's take on the big block Camaro was designed by Joel Rosen, and was logically referred to as an SS427 early on.

Compared to Dana, Baldwin Motion didn't hide its light under a bushel. Its work was known to include colorful hoodscoops, chrome plated side exhausts and orange painted engine blocks. Baldwin Motion badging, custom fiberglass body parts, plus Stinger hoods, all appealed to more street driven use, than pure competition vehicles. Mechanical upgrades were myriad. If you desired triple deuce carburetion on an aluminum high riser intake, Phase III ignition by

An ultimate of ultimates underhood: LS-7 454 V8 (casting code no. 3963512), plus Winters Foundry aluminum heads and dual plane aluminum intake manifold. The traditional Baldwin Motion orange painted block is also present. (Courtesy David Griffiths www.legendarymotorcar.com)

Motion, Sun Super Tachometers and auxiliary gauge sets, it could be done. Super Bite suspension parts, Bill Thomas traction bars, Cure Ride shocks and depending on purpose, M&H street slicks.

A big block Camaro with slicks and 4.88 HD axle wouldn't be much use in the snowbelt. That's what VWs were for! One thing Baldwin Motion cars lacked was a factory warranty. As stated on the invoice, "This is a race car – No warranty on powertrain." That isn't to say the cars lacked a warranty of the kind that counted. As Joel Rosen said, "We think so much of our Phase III Supercars that we guarantee they will turn at least 120mph in 11.5 seconds or better with a [Motion Performance - Approved] driver on an AHRA or NHRA – sanctioned dragstrip."

The Baldwin Motion cars had the go to match their show, thanks to Joel Rosen. Underlining the functional nature of speed shop big block Camaros, and their very real chance of usage in stock classes of drag racing, a Schiefer conversion pack

aluminum flywheel, and Super Revlok diaphragm style pressure plate were often fitted to stick shift examples. Metal was sprayed on the forged aluminum flywheel, which weighed just 10lb. It was a strong unit that avoided inertia during speed shifting.

A diaphragm clutch was handy in road cars. They made the often-found BW Super T10 reasonably light and easy to use on the street, in terms of clutch action. However, in full scale redline fever, the clutch would get hung up between shifts. To aid high rpm clutch disengagement, there was Super Revlok. One of the few concessions to practical use was an aftermarket Hone transmission overdrive, which made highway driving semi-bearable with a super short rear axle ratio.

Outlandish though the Baldwin Motion cars were, it all proved a successful business. A few exports even went as far afield as Kuwait, Mexico and Norway. In the end, these were some of the few places that it could legally supply.

This four-speed benefits from a Schiefer conversion pack aluminum flywheel. The powerful 454 V8, with Baldwin Motion Phase III cam & CD ignition, put the traction bars to good use!
(Courtesy David Griffiths www.legendarymotorcar.com)

Baldwin Motion majored in evocative print ads, in a way that other speed shops didn't. As a showstopper, getting a big block V8 in a little subcompact Vega was truly something else. GM was going to put a small block in the related H body Chevrolet Monza, once its rotary engine program had failed ... but a big block?!

Somehow, Joel Rosen snaked the LS7 454 V8 into the Vega. The 454 was a replacement for the 427, to overcome the pending 1971-72 industry-wide compression ratio drop that GM was leading, and dictating, to cut emissions. You could call the Baldwin Motion Super Vega overkill, but *Car Craft* magazine simply called it King Kong. Its 1974 article was titled "King Kong lives on in Long Island," a reference to the 1933 movie *King Kong*, which was partly set in New York. The EPA didn't much care for the automotive King Kong, being most unappreciative of Mr Rosen's engineering epic. Indeed, the EPA got the Department of Justice to send a cease and desist order to Baldwin Motion.

This decree from the Gods of Mount Washington DC forbade Motion Performance from building street racers, or tampering with factory smog controls. Then, too, there would be a $10,000 fine for every smog device removed or disabled. To avoid a Dana style raiding party, Baldwin Motion paid a $500 fine and complied with the EPA. It continued for a time, with its invoices marked "For Export" or "For Off Road Use Only," but with the fuel crisis, subsequent recession and apocalyptic smog law coming for 1975, Baldwin Motion's business was no longer viable. Indeed, even the Baldwin Chevrolet dealership closed in 1974.

Given that less than 10,000 speed shop cars of all makes were produced annually, out of a 10 million unit American market, a low volume manufacturer exemption could have been permitted by the EPA. The pollution from such expensive specialty cars were but a drop in the ocean. However, the Feds were only interested in blanket laws. In a similar manner, the 55mph national speed

The color is code 76 Daytona Yellow, and the price for this 1969 Baldwin Motion Phase III Camaro 454 was $6193. With 4.88 rear gears, a very extreme $1/4$ mile machine.
(Courtesy David Griffiths www.legendarymotorcar.com)

limit was intended to save gas, to help the nation's trade balance in the wake of the fuel crisis. In reality, a car with overdrive traveling at 70mph was more economical than one driven at 55mph. At lower speeds, a car would be straining in overdrive on a slight gradient. However, the powers that be were more interested in listening to environmental groups and 'experts,' than to reason.

As a postscript to the Baldwin Motion story, Joel Rosen came out of retirement in 2005. A 1969 Baldwin Motion Camaro was on display at the 2005 SEMA show. There was a plan to build 12 1969 Baldwin Motion Camaros, but sadly it never came to pass. The plan was probably a victim of the 2007 global financial crisis. In 2012 such new Baldwin Motion Camaro coupe and convertible prototypes, were auctioned off for 450 grand a piece.

Nickey Chevrolet

Most domestic car dealers either didn't know about the high performance parts an automaker offered, or didn't wish to carry them. The hi-po sports specialty area wasn't where the money was. No, the serious money and volume sales were in the loaded up family cars. Or so they thought. However, Nickey Chevrolet of Chicago, Illinois was an exception. From the late 1950s, this Chevrolet dealer offered high performance parts. By the '60s things got heavy duty, with speed shop work on a number of Chevrolet models. With the arrival of the Camaro, the performance market was reaching its zenith. 1967, the first year of the Nickey Camaro, was the last year a practically smog-control- free car could be bought. So, there was the desire and ability to drive on the street what were essentially race cars with license plates.

To turn dreams into reality, Nickey Chevrolet teamed up with Bill Thomas Race Cars. Nickey Chevrolet came up with the development money, and Bill Thomas' speed shop would build the cars. The former would sell the finished machines in the mid west and on the East Coast, and the latter dealt

This LS6 454 Stage III conversion of a 1973 Camaro 350 represented the penultimate year for Nickey Camaros. (Courtesy Sam Cameron sanfranciscosportscars.com)

with the West Coast. After all, Bill Thomas Race Cars was located in Anaheim, California. Thomas had been working out modifications for the Camaro, before said pony was even available to the public. Indeed, a Nickey Camaro 427 was around prior to the factory Camaro SS396.

As per other early 427 swap exponent Dana Chevrolet, Nickey Camaros started with a Camaro SS350. This was the top Camaro of the time, and came with essential hardware, namely: HD suspension, front swaybar, HD radiator, drums with metallic linings, four-speed Muncie, Positraction lsd and red stripe Firestone Wide Ovals. The Nickey Camaro conversion work was all done prior to customer delivery. A turnkey car if you will. A basic early Nickey Camaro 427 listed for just $3711. However, headers, HD clutch, pressure plate, scatter shield, auxiliary dash instruments etc. were all extra. It was a new kind of Detroit optioning.

Even though most Detroit management didn't see profit in performance cars, Nickey Chevrolet did. It noticed sales increases, due to the 'Win on Sunday, sell on Monday' phenomenon. So, it sponsored Corvettes and Chevrolet-powered sportscars. This

included the Colson & Wood gas dragster, and match racer Dick Harrell. Harrell, from Carlsbad NM, was an AHRA stock car champ. Given the Nickey Camaro could do stock classes in AHRA, it was handy to have Harrell as a Nickey performance advisor. Then there was Nickey Chevrolet parts manager, Ken White. The dealer had 27 people working in the parts department. Project manager for the Nickey Camaro at Bill Thomas' operation was Pierce Marshall. Creating a Nickey Camaro involved stock Chevrolet high performance parts, help from the aftermarket, and planning. Yes, the factory boys had designed the Camaro so a big block would fit. However, prior to the SS396, the details rested with the speed shops and racers. Dick Harrell found that if you removed the hood, battery, radiator and 350 motor, the 427 dropped right in!

On the positive side, the big block lined up with the small block V8's engine mounts. There was no cutting, bending, or welding required either. When speed shop Randall American dropped a 401 V8 into the AMC Pacer, it had to roll and weld the front crossmember for clearance and strength. With Camaro, there were indeed a few clearance issues. Bill Thomas' headers, as used by many speed shops on Camaros, required $1/16$in to be ground off the number five left-side header tube, to clear the steering box. Yes, tighter than Jack Benny!

Axle wind up and brake tramp were long standing muscle car bugbears. This was especially so for single leaf '67 Camaros, but Nickey had solutions. For one, Chevy II traction bars were swapped from left to right. The Chevy II traction bar shock absorber bolt was cut off, and replaced with a $7/16$in bolt in a new location. Now the shock absorber was mounted ahead of the traction bar bracket. The Nickey traction bar replaced the Camaro's stock spring plate, stopping just behind the spring hanger, and clamped to the leaf spring, instead of the car body.

It was hard to see the Nickey Camaro 427's raison d'etre as a response to the Shelby Mustang GT500 428. The Ford was very tame in comparison. Shelby or no, it came with 355bhp, and you could have a/c and automatic transmission, if you liked. The specification of a Nickey Camaro really

Nickey Chevrolet's Stage III LS6 454 is shown. The name of parts manager Don Swiatek was on the Nickey work order for this coupe. Swiatek would go on to work at the revived operation Nickey Chicago. (Courtesy Sam Cameron sanfranciscosportscars.com)

depended on the requirements of the customer. However, even in its mildest econo form, the 427 from Chevrolet – with one four-barrel, hydraulic

Aside from the stove hot 454, Nickey Chevrolet, famous for its 'backwards K,' added Rocket rims, traction bars, Lear Jet AM/FM 8 track stereo, if you could hear it, and lsd.
(Courtesy Sam Cameron sanfranciscosportscars.com)

lifters, 10.25 'you could almost use regular' comp ratio and humble cast-iron intake – made 385bhp. As per other speed shops, Nickey, or Bill Thomas to be precise, started with the L72 427, and then as Thomas said "We just make it run a little better."

As a bare minimum, that implied blueprinting a special Bill Thomas camshaft kit, 12.5:1 pistons of extruded aluminum nature, and Thomas' custom headers, naturally. On the intake side it could be a Nickey intake manifold, with dual Carter AFB four-bbl carbs. For a combination safe from detonation up to 8 grand, Dick Harrell put HD points in the formerly single-point 427 distributor, utilized 396 V8 weights and six-cylinder Chevrolet springs. For clearance with advanced carb setups, a custom dual aperture Nickey fiberglass hood was employed. For exhaust work post headers, Ced's Muffler of Chicago was used for custom work. Indeed, the left-side header pipe going onto the muffler was modified so the Camaro's oil filter could stay in the stock position.

Nickey claimed going from the 350 to the 427 V8 represented a mere 90lb front end weight gain, but it was more like 200lb. Weight distribution was 59/41 per cent front-to-rear, and an a/c system spacer was placed under the front coils to maintain ride height, with the heavy big block V8. A factory a/c radiator was used to keep the 427 cool. This HD radiator had an extra row of cooling tubes. With gearboxes it was wide ratio Muncie four-speed with 3.00 (1st), 2.20 (2nd) 1.47 (3rd) 1.00 (4th), or for $10 more a close ratio Muncie four-speed 2.54 (1st) 1.80 (2nd) 1.44 (3rd) 1.00 (4th) and the THM 400 automatic. Positraction lsd 12-bolt with 3.31, 3.70, 4.10 or 4.56 rear axle were available. No ratio charge if the car was in stock, and only the cost of labor if you wanted a different ratio.

As for prices in 1967, Bill Thomas' headers were $139.95, his big cam kit (310 degrees duration, 84 degrees overlap, 0.565in lift) was $164.55, dual quads on an aluminum intake were $150.95, and 1in front swaybar $29.95. The Nickey/Thomas Traction Kit was $39.95. Interestingly, Bill Thomas could work in an independent rear suspension, based on the C2 Corvette's IRS, but no one asked for it. Similarly the metallic brake linings were half the price of power front disks, and drag racers didn't much care for disk brakes. Drum brakes offered less wind resistance and were lighter. In any case, brakes just slow you down!

Fully equipped to turnkey level, the Nickey Camaro 427 was a six-grand car in 1967, enough

to get you into a Jag XKE. Similar price, but different purposes, and not the same buyer group. Out of the box in mild tune with 3.73 gears, wide ratio Muncie four-speed, and some civility, it was a 13.9-second pass at 108mph. This was the kind of street moxie absent from domestic cars between the mid '70s and late '90s. However, when tuned to drag racer specifications, with 4.88 gears and those Carter AFB dual quads rejetted to drink heartily, it was an 11.35 at 127mph. This result was recorded by *Car and Driver,* and stated in its September 1967 issue.

Even in mild state, *Car and Driver* found the Nickey Camaro idled at 1800rpm, and needed over 2 grand on the tach all day to keep the sparkplugs from oiling up. Then there was the 6-9mpg gas mileage range, which took one's breath and cash away … The four wheel drums were adequate, in a very qualified way. If you mostly did strip work, and rarely tackled mountain road driving, they did okay. Still, for a few years Nickey and its famous 'backwards K' script made sense on the street and strip. In the '60s this was a crossover vehicle!

Come the 1974 model year, and it was a very different final Nickey Camaro for a changed world. Rampant insurance premiums, Muskie's smog bill and a fuel crisis were all affecting Nickey Chevrolet, and *everyone* else. So, it was time for one last throw of the dice, and in 1973 Nickey Chevrolet became Keystone Chevrolet. In January 1974, the production of modified cars from this dealership, stopped completely. The last Nickey Camaro was a 1974 model year car. The starting point was a new Type LT coupe, which was then converted in the 'backwards K' tradition. The coupe was delivered to the Nickey Chevrolet dealership in November 1973, and finished in December that same year.

This final Nickey Camaro had a softer, more road car compliant specification. Objectively, it was more practical and pleasurable for most enthusiasts. It was finally answering that 1967 journalistic request for more balanced performance. By this stage you couldn't order a complete L88 427 from GM. However, you could get a short motor, and to this was added sturdy cast-iron heads. The 12.5:1 comp, and Holley 4053 780 CFM carb on a LS6 intake, all still spelled performance. A Positraction lsd was still to hand for this impact bumper Camaro Type LT, but the 3.23 econoaxle meant one could now complete Thanksgiving trips to see Aunt Patti without going deaf!

For the time being Nickey Chevrolet was also still going, but as Nickey Chicago. In January 1974,

On June 23 1974 this Nickey Camaro set an $^1/_8$ mile stock class World Record of 8.12 seconds!
(Courtesy Sam Cameron sanfranciscosportscars.com)

The first owner got a best of 10.52 at 129mph, a points championship win, with first prize being the
four-speed fitted. (Courtesy Sam Cameron sanfranciscosportscars.com)

In an interesting life, this Nickey Camaro was with a collector in Japan from 1990 to 2010, before returning to America. It has been repainted once in the original Midnight Green.
(Courtesy Sam Cameron sanfranciscosportscars.com)

former Nickey Chevrolet owners Jack and Ed Stephani got hold of the fabled dealership's former parts manager, Don Swiatek, and Vice President Al Seelig. Working as Nickey Chicago, the reunited crew continued to sell hi-po parts, offer tuning services and turnkey modified cars. Sadly, even this new incarnation closed down in 1977. Compared to 1967, the auto world of 1977 had very different concerns. However, there was one guy from those early times that was still going, and modifying Camaros as well.

Yenko Camaros
Don Yenko's 1st gen Camaros were like those from other speed shops, but his background, how he reached these coupes, and what he did afterwards, set him apart. Don Yenko's family had an automotive background. His father had started a Durant dealership, an endeavor that led to a Chevrolet showroom in the 1930s, and later another. Don Yenko was a business graduate of Penn State University, and was a pilot in the US Air Force prior to coming to the family's Chevrolet dealership in Canonsburg, Pennsylvania.

Yenko's racing background was more like that of Mark Donohue, than Dick Harrell. He had been doing road course racing in Corvettes until … "I got tired of looking at the rear bumper of Mark Donohue's Mustang." Compared to Donohue's Shelby GT350, Corvettes were too heavy, so Don Yenko looked for something else. He used his Chevrolet dealer connections to do a new Chevrolet for racing. The coupe was based on the Corvair Corsa. Don Yenko wrote an article on this racer's genesis, which appeared in the June 1966 issue of *Sports Car* magazine. In this account, Yenko stated he had designed aerodynamic body addenda using cut up pizza boxes!

Don Yenko's goal was qualifying the Corvair for the SCCA's D production car class. To meet the requirement of 100 cars by January 1 1966, Yenko utilized the COPO system plus dealer parts to create 100 Yenko Stingers in under two weeks! The Corvair-based Stinger was the first car Yenko offered to the public. It could be purchased in a number of stages, depending on how much performance a buyer wanted. The Stinger sold successfully into 1967. A network of Chevrolet dealers was organized to sell the Stinger, with one of them being Nickey Chevrolet of Chicago.

With the Corvair commercially winding down, and Yenko looking to A-production sedan racing and the SCCA Trans Am series, a decision was made to switch resources to the new Camaro Z28. Embodying the knowledge gained from Stinger, Don Yenko created the Yenko Camaro Stormer. However, he only managed to sell two cars. With GM's anti-racing policy preventing over 400 cubes outside intermediates, Yenko redirected his special Camaro towards drag racing. In doing so, and for competitiveness, the assistance of Dick Harrell and Bill Thomas were sought.

Harrell had been with Nickey Chevrolet, and high performance guru Bill Thomas had helped Nickey, too. Advice from both parties was instrumental in creating a 450-horse Camaro 427 conversion, capable of getting 11s at the strip with tuning. It was the familiar combination of L72 427, courtesy of Corvette, HD suspension and 4:10 rear axle. To this was added Yenko's own fiberglass hood design, which resembled the Corvette's Stinger hood, as per the two-seater's 1967 incarnation. A M21 four-speed came with the L78-powered SS396s that Yenko ordered as base vehicles for conversion. As a further factory upgrade, in 1968-69 there were aluminum heads for the SS396/375 horse motor that saved 100lb. This was the L89 396 V8.

The 1967 Yenko Camaro sold well, and the 1968 edition also used the SS396 with 375bhp L78 as a starting point, plus close ratio Muncie four-speed. To this combo was added a COPO 9737 pack, involving 140mph speedo, larger $1^1/_8$ in front swaybar, along with a special Yenko trim tag. For profitability, the '68s were converted using a L72 block swap. All remaining L78 items like heads, carb, intake manifold etc were then added back. Visual and functional points of distinction were the Yenko twin snorkel fiberglass hood, Poncho 14x6in steel rims with Yenko caps, and Yenko emblems on front grille and front fender. The front fenders also carried a '427' script, as did the tail panel.

Going a step further, an 'sYc' (Super Yenko Camaro) serial number tag now resided in the driver's door jamb. There were Stewart Warner pedestal mounted tach and auxiliary gauges. They were more in the racer's sight line than the factory console gauges. Early Yenko Camaros utilized an aftermarket rear spoiler, but later cars adopted factory front and rear spoilers. So far so good, with around 64 Yenko Camaros made. For '69 MY, Don

Yenko talked to Chevrolet about the COPO program being utilized to create factory Camaro 427s.

A COPO Camaro 427 was the base car for the '69 Yenko Camaro. This made use of factory power front disk brakes, spoilers, ZL2 cowl induction hood, and 4:10 axle with Positraction lsd containing heat-treated gears. For '69 MY, 9560- and 9561-coded engines were offered under COPO. The former was the all-aluminum ZL1 427, the latter the solid lifter L72 427. Yenko ordered 201 L72s, and other speed shops used COPO too, once they were wise to the program.

For the Yenko Camaro, upgraded hardware ran to an oversize front swaybar like on the '68s, an HD four-core radiator, and M21 four-speed or THM 400 automatic. Yenkos, like Baldwin Motion Camaros, weren't street sleepers. It was fashionable to flaunt by the late '60s, early '70s and into the early '80s. To this end, Yenko 427 badges, side and hood striping, plus 'sYc' insignia on head restraints, all served notice to kids on the street that you had a white hot ride. 1969 turned out to be a Yenko Camaro zenith,

Don Yenko's Canonsburg PA Chevrolet dealership successfully sold 1st gen Camaros with 427 swaps. This '68 Sequoia Green Yenko Camaro 427 has M21 four-speed and 3.73 Positraction lsd.
(Courtesy Mark Pieloch AmericanMuscleCarMuseum.com)

with 201 coupes. 171 were four-speeds, and the remainder had the THM 400. All involved a base car with code 711 standard black interior.

The dream kind of stalled at this point. Interest in pony cars was past its peak, the formal COPO Camaro 427 program was at an end, insurance companies were getting real nasty, and what about those smog laws? Air pollution was getting more strictly controlled by the year. The economy wasn't what it should have been, either. Acknowledging all of the above, Don Yenko tried a couple of smaller emergency performance fighters: the Yenko Deuce, and the Yenko Stinger II. The Deuce was a small block-powered Chevrolet Nova, and the second coming of the Stinger involved a turbocharged Vega. The Deuce was aimed at circumventing the latest insurance company supercar loading of 25 per cent. Observing horsepower, power to weight ratio and displacement, a sporty car had a limit to meet.

With tightening pollution laws, many in the industry were turning to turbo power. Make a small engine behave like a big one, on demand. The theory was that during the smog car certification test cycle the motor would be running non-boosted, and would therefore be polluting less. In spite of Yenko's determined efforts, the Deuce didn't last long in the marketplace. In addition, the Stinger II couldn't satisfy the EPA long term. However, there was a third option: Yenko's Super Z 400.

GM was leading and determining the industry's method of meeting emissions law. For now it was the compression ratio drop, and GM cars got in there a year early, 1971. So, for the early '70s, the route to maintaining performance involved larger displacements and free flow breathing. Don Yenko's Yenko Sportscars Inc employed Chevrolet's 400 mill, for the usually 350-powered 2nd gen Z28. The thing was, the 400 wasn't a high performance motor. It was a 250 horse (gross) two-barrel, low speed, family type engine, but now it was getting spicy!

Normally the 400's 0.138in shorter conrods, nodular cast-iron crankshaft, low flow heads and heavy 8.5:1 low comp pistons didn't get pulses racing, but it could be modified. Yenko applied

This Rally Green Yenko Camaro 396 with M21 four-speed and black vinyl interior is one of the 66 1968 Yenko Camaros made. (Courtesy Mark Pieloch AmericanMuscleCarMuseum.com)

the Z28's aluminum intake manifold, an 800 CFM Holley four-barrel carb and a hot, if still hydraulic, cam. The changes pushed output to 290 horses. With an all-in weight of 3200lb, the Yenko Super Z 400 didn't incur the insurance company supercar loading. However, it was plenty lively, and bucketloads of tire smoke were attainable, if that was your want.

With such a low comp, the Super Z could even run on regular, but the changing times meant very little demand for speedshop supercars. It was getting hard to find customers for normal Z28s, Trans Am SD 455s, 'Cuda 340s, AMX 401s – you name it. A 400-powered Z28 was a good idea in such low comp times, but Chevrolet didn't swallow the bait with a factory facsimile. Don Yenko used the performance hiatus to do Corvette racing, and the continued sale of Chevrolet high performance parts through his dealership catalog. That said, even now the dream of a Yenko Camaro wasn't over. A surprise and welcome comeback was made by the 1981 Yenko Camaro Turbo Z.

The Camaro Z28 had gone for a nap during

1975 and 1976 model years, but increasing sales of its Trans Am sibling prompted a return for '77 MY. By now the Z28 was a standalone model, not an option package. What's more, the Z28's former special, Corvette-shared, L82 four-bolt main 350 had left the building at the end of '74 MY. Upon its '77 MY return, the Z28 was motorvated by the relatively 'cooking,' plebian but effective, two-bolt, main LM1 350 four-bbl V8. By this stage, the respected Canonsburg, PA operation of Don Yenko was an official performance partner of GM. The new Turbo Z had GM's blessing, and carried a partial Chevrolet warranty. Such was its faith in Yenko's work.

The Yenko Camaro Turbo Z represented an amalgam of two very popular elements on the contemporary North American auto scene. That is, the Camaro Z28 and the turbocharger. Both elements were saviors in a high performance auto era, laid low by legislation, insurance companies and two fuel crises. Don Yenko personally addressed such challenging times. "Ever increasing numbers of emissions controls have sapped their share of horsepower from once potent engines. To recover

these accumulated horsepower losses without increasing pollution presents a real challenge. After months of testing and development, we have done it."

Indeed, making power while passing smog law has become the conundrum of the modern age, akin to alchemy. Chevrolet itself had created a 1979 Turbo Z28 prototype that worked, but couldn't meet the tighter emissions regs of 1980. In addition, formalized corporate policy was against any new machine trumping the Corvette, a sportscar that had been ailing since 1974. Don Yenko solved the emissions riddle, and GM corporate policy was of no concern to him. So the Yenko Camaro Turbo Z was free.

The starting point for the Turbo Z was the automatic-only 1981 Z28 350 automatic. Yes, you could get a four-speed Z28in Chevrolet's normal range, but that tied one to a mere LG4 305. In any case, automatic cars could more easily pass smog law. With legal calibrations, stick shift cars had poor drivability, and were difficult to drive steady enough under the EPA's 50,000 mile smog certification test. So, Yenko worked with Turbo International to come

Only ten Olympic Gold '69 Yenko Super Camaros were built, and this 450bhp 427-powered coupe is one of them! (Courtesy Mark Pieloch AmericanMuscleCarMuseum.com)

The Turbo Z's Turbo International system was of 'draw through' design, using seven pounds of maximum boost. There was no turbo bypass valve which helped eliminate turbo lag. Note the retention of the factory a/c compressor, at lower right. (Courtesy RKMotorsCharlotte.com)

The Yenko Camaro Turbo Z was slushbox only because of its Z28 350 basis. All the usual luxury Z28 options, such as a/c, cruise and tilt steering, came along for the ride. (Courtesy RKMotorsCharlotte.com)

In trying economic times only 19 Yenko Camaro Turbo Zs were made and sold. However, with the Turbo Z, Don Yenko had created a modern supercar. (Courtesy RKMotorsCharlotte.com)

This DKM 30 grand custom dream car had hi-po V8s, courtesy of Traco Engineering. It was a turbocharged 457bhp at 6800rpm, 350 small block, with Chevrolet no. 5754 solid lifter cam. This bolide was export only, the Middle East providing DKM with clients. That said, there was a 'mild' 350 horse version that was legal in DKM's home state of Arizona. This green motor had an 850 CFM Holley four-bbl, 11:1 TRW pistons and Edelbrock Victor intake manifold.

COPO Camaros

Right from the start, big power was available in Camaros. With the Corvette leading the way, and theoretically it being the only model exempt from GM's racing ban and power-to-weight limitations, there were great V8s on the parts shelf. The Camaro was quickly available with the 396, launched in 1965 model year. In 1966 came the L72 427, and from the spring of 1967, the hallowed L88 427. This L88 motor featured aluminum heads, and Chevrolet was very secretive on the subject of power outputs. In the words of Karl Ludvigsen from his book *Corvette, America's Star Spangled Sports Car, The Complete History*, "There was no hedging on the output of this engine; Chevy didn't say anything about it at all." [11]

The consensus was around 560bhp gross on 103 octane juice for the L88 427. Production numbers of the motor were 20in 1967, 80in 1968 and 116in 1969. Then, too, the L88 motor was available over the parts counter for decades as a short motor. Hundreds were made up, with appropriate parts completing the picture, even though fully assembled L88 427s from GM were no longer around. However, there was no 427 of any kind available to Camaro, as a regular production option (RPO). You could just get a crate motor and drop it in, but then there was COPO (Central Office Production Order).

Unknown to most, it was possible to order a factory fresh 1st gen Camaro 427 using the COPO system. COPO was a back door, small parts order setup initiated by Chevrolet performance guru Vince Piggins, who was also behind the Z28's availability. This was all a boon for racers and speed shops that wanted ¹/₄ mile worthy Camaros, factory made. Or at least a starting point. A Camaro 427 was a kind of unofficial option package, starting via a L78 SS396, with mandatory options within. The Camaro's front power disks were a given, so too F41 suspension, M21 four-speed with G80 4:10 Positraction rear axle and 'BE' 12-bolt differential. It was Chevrolet's toughest axle, but there was more.

The holy grail of COPO Camaros was any of the 69 sold '69 MY cars, with the ZL1 427 V8. Yes, this 427 had aluminum heads and block. Indeed, it was the first Chevrolet production motor with an alloy block, and came with press-in iron cylinder liners and specialized racing internals. This very special 427 even went through a quality audit at the Tonawanda engine plant in which it was assembled, and so it should have been. This was because the ZL1 427 with option code #9560 cost a whopping $4160.15! This was three grand over the L88 427, and much more than a base Camaro Sport Coupe, which was a mere $2727.

In terms of genesis, the all-alloy ZL1 427 had been developed for Can Am racing. The decision to fit the Can Am Chaparral 427 to Camaro has been attributed to Vince Piggins. For the Camaro, the intended goal was drag racing. All-alloy allowed less weight, which aided weight transfer and traction in stock classes of the sport. Indeed, there was a 50-unit build minimum for NHRA Super Stock. Fifty cars were ordered by Illinois Chevrolet dealer Fred Gibb, via COPO. The remaining 19 low-volume special order ZL1 Camaros were taken by other dealers.

Bringing the ZL1 into the COPO Camaro's engine compartment has also been attributed to Dick Harrell and a desire for drag racing, ordered through Fred Gibb Chevrolet. Each ZL1 was hand assembled in a surgically clean room. It took 16 hours per engine, with the ZL1 427 coming under the watch of Corvette engineer extraordinaire Zora Arkus Duntov. Completed ZL1 427s were either fitted to Corvettes, Camaros or sold over the parts counter.

The ZL1 saved 160lb over the L88 427, and 200lb compared to the L72 427. As a big block, the ZL1 weighed the same as a small block 327 V8! Fitted to the Camaro, the ZL1 provided front-to-rear weight distribution equal to a Z28, at 56/44 per cent. Overall a Camaro ZL1 427 weighed around the same as a Z28 302. This was all combined with horsepower and torque equal to an L88, which was to say stupendous. As part of continual engineering refinements, exhaust ports were now larger and round, not square. Plus, there was a more Hemi-like open combustion chamber, under the sparkplug.

The camshaft of the ZL1 had a duration of 356 degrees, and a standard Z28 style exhaust system. Due to engine compartment space constraints, the stock square port 396 exhaust manifold was fitted, and this apparatus for exhaling was less than ideal. On the Chevrolet parts list was a Chevelle/Camaro/Corvette chambered pipe option. This series of resonating chambers could reduce your ET (elapsed time) by several tenths. For intake, it was the familiar aluminum job seen on L88s, and the '69 Camaro ZL1 427 came with the ZL2 cowl induction hood, seen on Z28.

There was an aluminum case M22 Muncie four-speed, which saved 70lb. This box with close ratios and HD synchros involved lower gear helix angle and thicker cog teeth. This was all a $311 option. Standard tires were E70-15 Polyglas GTs, the biggest one could have sans fender clashing. Roger Huntington reported on a '69 Camaro ZL1 427 for *Cars* magazine. In the August 1969 issue, it was stated a car prepared with the help of Midwest performance specialist Berger Chevrolet did a 13.16-second pass at 110.21mph. This was with one 850 CFM Holley four-bbl on a L88 intake. Huntington also mentioned the coupe was civil enough to be street driven, but the idle turned rough in hot weather, plus gas mileage was around 6mpg.

This 1969 COPO Camaro ZL1 was ordered with M21 four-speed and G80 4:10 Positraction lsd, in code 57 Fathom Green. (Courtesy David Griffiths www.legendarymotorcar.com)

The respected L88 427 Chevrolet V8 had aluminum heads and a reputed 560bhp (gross). It was available over the counter in short motor form for decades. (GM Archives)

low 10s and many Super Stock records broken. However, in the final analysis, drag racers mainly stuck to the much cheaper L88 427. The L88 was more of a known quantity in terms of thermal properties and reliable horsepower production. The ZL1's lightweight nature was best suited to the Can Am road course format for which it was developed.

Going with the usual story, COPO Camaro ZL1 427s are worth a fortune today. However, a performance prophet is seldom respected in its era. As per other slow selling homologation specials of the day, the Camaro ZL1 gathered dust in showrooms. Costing as much as 8 grand for a well-specified car, 30 of the '69 Camaro ZL1 427s were returned to Chevrolet unsold. Indeed, the final cars were offloaded in the early '70s, by which time Super Stock racing was far from Chevrolet's mind. Twelve of the coupes even had their engines removed and sold. It was commonplace to sell powertrains after racing purposes were met. Some

If you were expecting faster, it was easily done. This was a stock car that could be driven to the local shopping mall with reasonable decorum. Going faster, and overcoming stock limitations with exhaust, tires and suspension etc was up to racers and their teams. This indeed came to pass, with

Rated at no more than the L88 427's bogus 430 horse gross figure, the $4160.15 ZL1 427 V8 was the ultimate Camaro option. (Courtesy David Griffiths www.legendarymotorcar.com)

racers switched back to L88s, and the ZL1s went into Corvettes or various project cars.

Drag racing

All the elements came together with the first COPO Camaro ZL1 427 made, which was a base six-cylinder coupe, to which the COPO 9560 option code was applied. With its racer purpose there was no need for a deluxe interior, a/c etc. It was a combination of Vince Piggins, La Harpe, Illinois Chevrolet dealer Fred Gibb and Dick Harrell. This first car went to Harrell's Performance Center in Kansas City, Missouri, for preparation. Originally, this Camaro ZL1 427 had a THM 400 automatic, before switching to a Clutchflite transmission, which joined other dedicated racing hardware. With AHRA, there was no need for inner fender panels, nor front brakes, and the no. 1 Camaro ZL1 had fiberglass fenders and hood, a scatter shield, rollcage, single seat interior, Dana 60 rear end, ladder bar suspension and initially a single quad.

Harrell's Camaro made its debut at the February 1969 AHRA Winternationals in Phoenix. In testing at Kansas City International Raceway Park, Dick Harrell managed an 11.64-second pass at 122.15mph, using M&H 8.00/8.50in tires. At the same venue, with one Holley 850 four-bbl, matters improved to 10.41 seconds at 128.10mph, and with dual Holley 660s on a Weiand tunnel ram intake, a 10.29-second ¹/₄ mile. Fred Gibb employee Herb Fox even reached the Winternational's semi finals, and had a qualifying win over Mr Four-Speed himself, Ronnie Sox.

More results for this seminal Camaro ZL1 came

in AHRA and NHRA, using dual Holley 4500 quads. Racing under revised AHRA Super Stock rules in 1971, this Gibb-Harrell Camaro ZL1 427 had Gibb driver Jim Hayter achieve an AHRA record of 9.63 seconds at 143mph. The coupe won the AHRA Championships in Super Stock and NHRA Pro Stock. This historically significant COPO Camaro ZL1 underwent a five-year restoration in 1988, at the hands of Olds engineer Bill Porterfield, in its original Candy Apple Red with gold lace. Authentically, the giant hoodscoop is in clear plexiglass, and the engine compartment houses a Winters Foundry sourced ME code, all-aluminum ZL1 427.

After his association with Nickey Chevrolet, Dick Harrell campaigned the Yenko Camaro, which led to Yenko Chevelle and Nova 427s. It was significant in this era how race cars, Camaros in particular, made use of stock hardware. They also retained their production car look, even in the world of funny cars. An early example was the Pisano brothers' 1967 Camaro funny car. This 2400lb class racer kept the center Camaro steel, GM Fisher unibody. To this base were attached fiberglass nose and tail sections, produced by Fiberglass Trends.

There was a ducktail spoiler and expected Simpson drag chute. The chassis came from leading builder Don Long. The front saw a dropped axle, coils and radius arms, with the rear involving a four link and Monroe coil overs by Doug Kruse. On the inside were aluminum interior panels, and a fuel burning 427 with GM 6-71 blower, connected to a B&M shifted THM 400. The motor featured a Howard camshaft, favored by the Pisano brothers, and the THM 400 autobox was much used by Chevrolet funny car racers back in the day.

The car was raced by Frankie Pisano with older brother Joe, a Bonneville Salt Flats ace. At the Long Beach Drag Strip, their Camaro commenced with low 8s at over 170mph. The coupe quickly gained notoriety. *Car Craft* magazine editors named the Pisano brothers' racer, as among the "10 Best Rods" of 1967, adding in October of the same year: "An entry in the wild 2400-pound class that was an immediate winner." While it's true that this '67 Camaro funny car was successful in SoCal racing, it was a little too heavy for the highest level of match race funny car competition.

A Camaro funny car that *was* an unqualified winner, was the 1969 machine of Kelly 'The Professor' Chadwick. The drag scene wasn't overly represented by '69 Camaros, as such. However, this particular car was one of the best. Chadwick gained

Only 69 1969 Camaro ZL1 427s were built. A stock car could do low 13s, but that was just the beginning! (Courtesy David Griffiths www.legendarymotorcar.com)

his handle from many years of teaching high school. Previously he had run a steel bodied '67 Camaro funny car, and would go on to a 1971 Camaro funny car. The '69 machine was created by foremost builder Don Hardy, who also served as chief mechanic. Hardy took the unorthodox approach of going with a Torqueflite, rather than a THM 400. He had been a former student of Chadwick!

The Don Hardy build featured an innovative chromoly chassis, and popular Hilborn fuel-injection. Sponsor Jardine provided the headers. Once again, Chevrolet racers stayed faithful to Chevrolet hardware. Compared to the exotic Ford Boss, SOHC Cammer and Mopar Hemi crowd, the Camaro was of the people. The story here was a Chevrolet 427, like you could buy over the counter, bored out to 438 cubes. The factory steel crank was kept, rectangular port heads were prepared, and a flat tappet cam, rather than a roller, was utilized. Nitro methane was the power adder, but largely the Chadwick Camaro went for reliability and consistency.

While traditional funny cars just used rear stoppers and a chute, the Chadwick Camaro

This Camaro ZL1 was originally ordered from, and sold by, Seltzer Chevrolet of Yukon, Oklahoma. In Fathom Green, it's one of only nine four-speed ZL1 coupes built. (Courtesy David Griffiths www.legendarymotorcar.com)

harnessed the brakes of sponsor Hurst-Airheart. Originally rolling on Halibrand mag wheels, the results were quick in coming. Kelly Chadwick won the lucrative Coca Cola Cavalcade of Stars in 1969 and 1970. In 1970 the Chadwick Camaro also won the *CARS* magazine meet at Cecil County Raceway. By the close of 1970 racing season, the car did a 6.90-second pass at 212mph. During 1970-72, Ray Sullins was the coupe's mechanic. In modern times the '69 Chadwick Camaro was restored by Holzman

The '69 Camaro ZL1's genesis involved drag racer Dick Harrell, Chevrolet dealer Fred Gibb, and Chevrolet division's performance guru Vince Piggins. (Courtesy www.mecum.com)

It started with a solitary four-barrel, but eventual Offenhauser heads and dual quads saw Dick Harrell leave his mark, and rocker cover badge! (Courtesy www.mecum.com)

Race Cars of Wichita, with exterior paint by Lavern Kelly.

There was another Camaro funny car racer that didn't win a lot nationally, but did win a lot of friends. Jungle Jim Liberman was one of the best known drag racers of the 1970s. Famous for his "Far Out!" exclamation in funny car commercials, he was a Chevrolet man in the cars he owned and raced. His personal transport was a Corvette, which he was driving when he first met legendary back-up girl, Jungle Pam Hardy.

Somewhat a party animal, Jungle Jim's 1000ft burnouts and decision to never lift were well known. Race meet fans went bananas when he turned up at the last minute and performed such displays. There was much accompanying chanting of "Jungle Jim, Jungle Jim!" Revell kits immortalized Jungle Jim, Jungle Pam and their Vega with a scale model. However, for all this, Jungle Jim Liberman only achieved a single national victory, and did so in a 2nd gen Camaro funny car.

As with all his racecraft, Jungle Jim was interested in having his Camaro perfectly prepared, and running flawlessly. It certainly did that day in 1975, when he won at Old Bridge Township Raceway, during that year's NHRA Summernationals. This Camaro was certainly a rarer sight than the hot pants Jungle Pam liked to wear. Only ten mini Camaro funny car bodies were built, and Jungle Jim Liberman had one of them.

Fred Gibb's employees, Herb Fox and Jim Hayter, enjoyed competition success in this coupe. The Gibb-Harrell Camaro ZL1 427 was an AHRA Championship winner in Super Stock and NHRA Pro Stock. (Courtesy www.mecum.com)

Below: For the 1970 Super Stock season the AHRA chose Dick Harrell and Bill Hielscher as two of six Grand American Professionals. Both their cars were AHRA-denoted as '70 Camaros, even though only Hielscher's coupe was a 2nd gen model. (Courtesy www.mecum.com)

The Kelly Chadwick '69 Camaro Funny Car was built by Don Hardy. Chadwick used it to win the 1969 and 1970 Coca Cola Cavalcade of Stars. (Courtesy *Hot Rod*)

Chevrolet 1969

Car and Track's report on the 1969 Chevrolet Impala provided an idea of Chevrolet's pre-eminence in the American auto industry. Host Bud Lindemann, with good humor, said that every time they tested a new Impala, they wondered about the No 1 sales position. Was it the styling, engineering or performance? Whatever the reason, Lindemann noted that Chevrolet had more dyed-in-the-wool fans than any other auto producer. He added, "Many of which would probably buy anything that comes off the assembly line, as long as the name Chevrolet is stamped on it."

Bud Lindemann also acknowledged that Chevrolet had an uncanny ability to come up with new ideas and innovations, that oftentimes became standards in the industry. He went on to say that while, in the past, Impala had never failed to impress, with this '69 edition Ford and Chrysler may have a shot in the sales race. The test confirmed Chevrolet's reputation for quality craftsmanship and construction. It also noted traditional good feel Bow Tie power steering. As for performance, an HD suspension and 427in place of the 396 two-bbl, would have been a whole different ball game. Then again, not everyone wanted speed, and as Lindemann concluded, "From the Corvette to the Caprice, Chevy tries to be all things to all people. Maybe that's why they're number one."

Outside the main business of full-size family cars, not everything was going Chevrolet's way. The new C3 Corvette of 1968 had quality and handling shortfalls, noted by the critics. Major magazines felt the two-seater was too big and heavy, and wasn't put together as well as it should have been. There were also some new design teething problems that had delayed the C3's original planned '67 MY release. Critical comments didn't stop the public from buying the new Corvette. Sales were always rising, and put pressure on quality. It was said that Corvette quality suffered because the two-seater was put on regular Chevrolet quality control standards, not the previous special Corvette level. This was hard to understand, since Chevrolet always had a good reputation for careful assembly, fit and finish.

Also at variance with traditional Chevrolet life was the Vega. This small, economy car was Chevrolet's subcompact entry, intended to tackle imports in a growing market segment. The Vega was initiated by a design committee, headed by GM

The new subcompact Vega picked up accolades, but its genesis and subsequent quality snafus were unbecoming for a Chevrolet. However, its mini 2nd gen Camaro styling was judged appealing. (Courtesy GM Archives)

President Ed Cole. It was then handed to Chevrolet division as a fait accompli, hence the lack of a 'C' name as per other wearers of the sacred bow tie. The proud Chevrolet designers and engineers were not pleased with this car being foisted on them. They didn't really want anything to do with it. However, the Vega quickly amassed critical and commercial success.

The Chevrolet Vega was Motor Trend's 1971 Car Of The Year, and Car and Driver's Best Economy Sedan. Thanks to a well located four-link live axle, import loving Road & Track called Vega, "The best-handling car ever sold in America." Vega was innovative, it had a linerless aluminum block, plus a very tall cast-iron head. Chevrolet fast tracked the design cycle, and even assembly line processes were geared for speed. At the Lordstown Ohio plant, a new Vega could roll off of the assembly line every 36 seconds. However, quality and reliability were lacking. Fenders were so thin you could practically see through them, and that aluminum block inline-four was none too dependable. Sadly, cheap parts and a militant UAW workforce conspired to make the attractive Vega a disposable car.

The Super Hugger arrives

Fortunately, Chevrolet had a new model that was a critical, commercial and largely quality success. It was the 2nd generation Camaro called 'Super Hugger,' and most certainly lived up to its name! Unlike with the 1st gen F-body, GM's designers and engineers had greater time, budget and latitude to reach the new car's lofty ambitions. The goal was a world class grand tourer. A GT that really lived up to its appellation. A combination of refinement, comfort and acceleration, heretofore never seen at the price. In the 1970 March issue of *Road & Track*,

engineering editor Ron Wakefield talked about the interchange between American and European design. Aside from floor-shifted, four-speed sticks and disk brakes, the new GM F-body possessed exotic, Italian-influenced styling from yesteryear.

The new Camaro was judged to be Ferrari-like, whereas the dual aperture Firebird grille made PMD's F-body sibling seem like a Maserati from a few seasons back. It all contrasted with the high impact styling of rival ponies, the Mustang and Barracuda. These established players majored in the expected unbridled horsepower, and stiff suspension for performance editions. However, GM's 2nd gen F-body was different. The stated intention of GM designers was a true European GT car. So, refinement and comfort would have to be designed in, not tacked on with an option package.

At first glance, the basic specification of the 1st and 2nd gen F bodies was similar. A partial unibody with front subframe, SLA/coil independent suspension at the front, and a leaf sprung live axle out back. However, all elements had been

The 2nd gen Camaro emerged in the psychedelic era, but its refined design allowed it to last into the '80s. The stock J52 front disk brakes are shown but not discussed. (Courtesy GM Archives)

completely redesigned for what was virtually an all-new car. The unibody and front subframe were now stronger, for refinement, rigidity and safety. The double shell roof structure was better for roll-over accidents. The roof cavity could also accommodate insulation material.

There was much thought given toward active and passive safety. The feared federal roll-over testing explained the stouter roof, so too the absence of a factory-available ragtop during the 2nd gen coupe's run. There were standard door impact beams built into the door cavity. GM also took the unprecedented step of making front disk brakes standard. The 2nd gen F-body Camaro and Firebird were the first pony cars to feature this. It took a while before rivals did the same, and industry voices through the early '70s often criticized domestic cars for having disks optional. So, on every base Camaro it was a GM Delco-Moraine, non-power, but vented, floating caliper disk/drum setup. Front disks were 11in, with rear drums 9.5x2in. Swept area was 332 sq in.

For refinement there were fewer inner panel holes, and even low-line Camaros carried improved soundproofing, but with no increase in material weight. In 1969, some low-powered Camaros still rode on single rear leaf springs, but it was now multileaf springs and staggered shocks for all. Suspension springing was also softer. Front spring rates on six-cylinder models were 100lb-in, on V8s it was 110lb-in. At the rear, the base model spring rate was lowered from 1969's 100lb-in to 90lb-in. Like 1969, the standard front swaybar was 0.6875in, but now, for the first time on any Camaro, you could get a rear swaybar. This optional rear bar was sized 0.625in.

Previous pony car practice was a big ol' front baseball bat-sized swaybar and stiff springs all around. However, the Super Hugger took the European route. You could contain body-roll with front and rear swaybars. Therefore, spring rates could be softer for an improved ride. This also implied that the 2nd gen Camaro was less likely to be bumped off-course on imperfectly surfaced turns. Super Hugger handling was aided by front and rear tracks, increased by a respective 1.68in and 0.5in also. There was greater wheel travel, front and rear. It was most noticeable at the back, with a driveshaft permitted to rise 0.75in more. There had been an F-body policy change, with Camaros and Firebirds no longer 4+1 seaters. As a pure 2+2 with rear buckets of a kind, the driveshaft tunnel could be higher, making for an improved ride.

The F-body would lead to purchases of more expensive intermediate and fullsize cars. Which was GM's plan. (Courtesy GM Archives)

It was now easier to enter the rear compartment, because the 2nd gen F-body's doors were 5.5in longer. In addition, there were no rear $1/4$ windows, like in 1st gen days. With revised seating, there was greater front and rear legroom, and more headroom. For the driver the steering wheel was now further away. Indeed, the whole steering mechanism had been moved forward. With the longer steering column, it was now possible to have two shock absorbing couplings, compared to the previous one. The increased length, also made the steering less affected by side deflections. This spelled fewer steering corrections.

The steering itself came courtesy of a recirculating ball system. This was better able to cope with road shock absorption than rack and pinion setups. Optional power steering was integral with the steering gear, and was variable ratio in nature. The steering got faster the more you turned.

It was 15.5:1 on center, and 11.8:1 on full lock. Showing divisional differences, the Camaro had quicker steering than the Firebird. It was 27.3:1 versus 30.8:1, meaning 4.8 turns lock-to-lock, rather than 5.4. The top dog Z28 even offered a 21.4:1 fast manual ratio. However, many would prefer the Camaro's power steering. At just 2.3 turns lock-to-lock, it was video game quick.

Chevrolet set up its version of the F-body for more understeer than Firebird. Pontiac favored oversteer, but the Chevrolet clan felt understeer was safer for the average driver. In either case the new F-body handled in a genuinely new way, and for once that TV ad wasn't exaggerating. The commercial for the '70 $^1/_2$ machine showed a red coupe, sporting faux wires and RS nosecone. It was carving up twisty roads. The driver voiceover spoke of glued to the road handling, "You expect it from Corvette, but this Camaro's really a pleasant surprise." There was mention of chassis refinements, and the standard front disk brakes.

GM engineers regarded the 2nd gen F-body, as more of a driver's car than the 1st gen iteration. It was softer, but with more control and a rebound/jounce ratio of 3:1 compared to the 1st gen's 2:1. Reflecting European practice, the shocks were revalved to go down stiff, and come up relatively softer. As part of an improved ride, this all helped resist bottoming out, a problem of the era that affected the 1st gen F-body more so. Continued from 1st gen days, were the use of staggered shocks. For all Camaros it was the right shock ahead of the live axle, with the left behind. The goal was to tame axle and brake tramp, which was important given the new Camaro's abundant firepower.

Matters started humbly with the familiar 250 cube inline six, with 155bhp at 4200rpm. The opening V8 was the 307, making 200bhp at 4600rpm. Then arrived three 350 V8s. First was the L65 350 with 250bhp at 4800rpm, followed by the L48 350 packing an even 300 ponies. At the 350's apex was the Z28's LT1 making 360 horses gross. The L48 and LT1 both had 380lb/ft torque, but their respective horsepower outputs occurred at 4800rpm and 6 grand. If you wanted the serious torque of a big block, then there was the well-known 396 V8. The L34 made 350bhp, with the L78 396 on 375 horses. For the two 396s the maximum outputs came in at a respective 5200rpm and 5600rpm. The difference with the 2nd gen Camaro was that the 396 was now a 402 V8.

The latest version of the 396, was still called

Separates the men from the toys.

Remember when you were a kid and you put a lot of trick stuff on your bike to make it look like something it wasn't?
A lot of so-called "sporty cars" still operate that way.
But not this one.
The new Camaro Z28 is as good looking underneath as it is on top.
With a 360-horse Turbo-Fire 350 V8. And with a Hurst shifter that comes along for the ride when you order the 4-speed.

Then there's the suspension that lets you feel the road without feeling the bumps. And the quick ratio steering. And the special wheels with the F60 x 15 tires. And on, and on, and on.
But don't just take our word for it. Pick one up at your Chevy dealer's Sports Department and take it for a road test.
You'll see we're not kidding around.

Putting you first, keeps us first.

CHEVROLET

The Z28 continued with the 2nd gen Camaro, but was now available with optional THM 400 automatic transmission. (Courtesy GM Archives)

the 396. In Camaro life the model was still the SS396, and even more was planned. Early magazine articles spoke of the LS6 454 arriving with 450bhp at 5800rpm and 500lb/ft at 3600rpm, using an 11.25:1 comp ratio and single four-barrel. The 454, as already seen in Chevelle, and to be used in Corvette, did appear on specification sheets and sales brochures for the Camaro, but didn't reach production. However, the 396 was plenty powerful, and gearbox choices were myriad.

With entry level powerplants, there was no chance of a four-speed. It was a three-speed manual, or for the automatics the legendary Powerglide and the three-speed THM 350. The L65 350 V8 was the first motor eligible for a four-speed, and the L48 was the first level available with the new 11in clutch. Try a M20 wide ratio Muncie four-speed, close ratio M21 or heavy-duty close ratio M22. The M22 was a $232.35 option, and 1185 1970 $^1/_2$ Camaros were so fitted. With Muncie four-speeds, the low duty unit had a cast-iron case, coded R. The heavy-duty M22 had an aluminum case with code P.

Hidemi Aoki with the Dave 'Big' Deal Camaro ZZZZZ-28. Artist and designer Dave Deal took the 1970 ½ Z28 as his inspiration. (Courtesy www.nepoeht.com)

Style-wise, you could recognise a '70 ¹/₂ Camaro thanks to the chrome 'C' header panel, and 'Camaro by Chevrolet' trunk lid script. Inside it was the one-year-only low back Strato buckets, with their adjustable head restraints. A big stand-out, and optional on any Camaros including SS and Z28, was the RPO Z22 appearance package. This involved bumperless central Endura nose section, flanked by round parking lights on the catwalks, and bumperettes on either side. The licence plate went under the right side bumperette, and that wasn't all for the $168 option. RPO Z22 included $19 C24

Hide-A-Way windshield wipers, a custom black painted grille and RS insignia.

RS callouts would be replaced with SS or Z28 equivalents if the Rally Sport pack was applied to those two performers. It's said the 2nd gen RS look was inspired by the big grille fascia of the Series 1 Jaguar XJ6. However, in the Camaro's case, RS made the coupe look mighty beaky. But don't worry, that rubberized Endura nose could take a licking and keep on ticking! Pontiac liked to prove this courtesy of demonstration hammer blows to the GTO's front. Aside from dent resistant rubber facings, state of the art discussions also revolved around tires. There were no radials for the latest Camaro, all choices were familiar bias belted types.

Six-cylinder 2nd gens rode on 14x6in rims with E78-14s, V8s got F78-14s covering 14x7in wheels. Top of the totem pole, higher than even the SS396, were the Z28's Goodyear Polyglas GT F60-15s, on 15x7in rims of stamped steel nature. Dimensions saw length, width and height at a respective 188in, 74.4in and 50.4in, all on a 108in wheelbase. It's what used to be called a small compact domestic car. Front and rear tracks were a very Super Hugger respective 61.3in and 60in. Weights for the pre-fuel crisis era were par for the course. A base six-cylinder Camaro was 3060lb, a small block V8 edition weighed 3180lb, and big block Camaros came in swinging with 3450lb – even with an all cast-iron big block, a very restrained figure. Then again, the Camaro was a very restrained coupe next to rivals.

Chrysler Corp had a new E-body Barracuda, with Challenger offsider, for 1970. These cars possessed extrovert styling, stock drums and the option of a Hemi 426 V8. It was the kind of pony a 1968 buyer would have flipped over, but in 1970, and especially thereafter, folks were starting to count their pennies. The Hemi E-bodies were seldom purchased because they were very expensive. With rising insurance premiums and general costs, a Hemi was just too much. Similarly, FoMoCo's '71 Mustang talked the old line of bigger and flashier is better, but with diminishing commercial returns. Ford's elephant in the garage was the Maverick.

Even little AMC debuted its 'Humpster' Javelin for '71 MY. This new coupe got sales traction, and even had a 2+2 AMX. However, by 1971 you had to question the wisdom of Hemi-powered ragtops with four-wheel drums. The game had changed, and GM was hip to it, with a Camaro putting the heat on Henry's pony in the sales race. The 70 $^1/_2$ Camaro

Dave Deal's Leeroy Carzero character liked to cruise Rev Street, Midtown USA at 6000rpm in his Camaro ZZZZZ-28! (Courtesy Marc Cranswick)

amassed 12,578 sales for inline sixes, 112,323 with V8s, for a grand total of 124,901.

Concerning model 123-12487, information was given to Van Nuys, California and Norwood, Ohio assembly plants in February 1970. A dealership introduction transpired on February 26 1970. The opening chassis sequence commenced with 500001, with the 7th VIN digit indicating L for Van Nuys assembly, or N for a Norwood build. It was a significant start for what would be the best selling Camaro generation to date.

For decoration, Chevrolet used 'Magic Mirror' Acrylic lacquer. Ford and Chrysler employed enamel finishes. Rubbing paint thinner in an inconspicuous location is a quick way to test the presence of lacquer; some paint should rub off. There was an absence of a two-tone paint option with the 2nd gen Camaro, but you could have a vinyl roof. Said vinyl came in white, black, dark blue, dark green and dark gold. Soft Ray Tinted Glass was $37.95 and coded A01.

A question of demographics

The writing was on the wall for GM's competitors that the 2nd gen F-body's refined manner was the way to the future. *Consumer Reports* observed sporty cars in a July 1971 group test of domestic and imported makes. The consumer magazine chose to test a base Firebird six-cylinder, but could have easily sampled the similar Camaro, and it noted this. Either way, its conclusion was the same: "If a specialty car is what you want, you could do a lot worse than a Firebird (or the basically similar Chevrolet Camaro). We found the Firebird far more satisfactory, overall, than the Mustang."

In refinement, as a practical car, the new F-body made the genre-starting Mustang appear like a one trick pony. Poor ride, a lack of moveable dash vents, and poor outward visibility all led one away from Henry towards Louis Chevrolet. Pontiac's Bunkie Knudsen had moved to FoMoCo after work on the 2nd gen F-body was completed. At Ford, Knudsen's managerial role saw a 'more is more' approach to Mustang, which did not sit well with Lee Iacocca. The early '70s Mustang sales slide confirmed Big Lee's concerns.

The 2nd gen F-body avoided the one dimensional pony car approach of rivals, but why? Why go to the trouble of creating a decent coupe, for a pony car segment that was contracting in size? Pony cars peaked at 11.9 per cent market share in 1967, by 1969 that figure was 9 per cent and falling. Small cars were on the rise, hence the feverish development of the Vega. In addition, pony car buyers were not very loyal. The Mustang had the highest repeat ownership at 26 per cent, with Firebird on a mere 9 per cent. Hot intermediates like Chevelle SS396 and GTO fared much better. That said, pony car buyers did routinely stay with the same brand, for example going from Camaro to Chevelle.

GM Customer Research staff knew all this, and more. They knew the contemporary youth market was disproportionately large, going into the 1970s. From this they recognized an opportunity to sell pony car owners, their second and third cars,

Carzero's antics woke retired hermit Jed Cluffer. Cluffer alighted with his 12 gauge shotgun to shoot the offending ZZZZZ-28 varmint.
(Courtesy Marc Cranswick)

within the same brand. Pony cars were often the first new car for a young buyer. That very humble starting point for a 1970 $^{1}/_{2}$ six-cylinder, secretary special Camaro was $2749. So, Customer Research estimated a good pool of buyers for well-equipped, value-added, mid-size and full-size family cars by 1980. Get them young, as it were.

It was that existing older buyer group, which bought full-size cars, that would shrink through the '70s and '80s. When reviewing the new Cadillac Allante on TV's *MotorWeek* in 1987, host John Davis said Cadillac had been burying its customers, by the cemetery's worth. Of course, the new 2nd gen Camaro had Corvette-style tail-lamps, which gave it more youth appeal. One thing the new Camaro didn't have was the 1st gen's JL8 four-wheel disk brake option, although J52 front disks were standard. However, for the most part, buyers were still into that 'go angle,' and Camaro could oblige.

Good sports – Camaro SS350 & SS396

In its wide-ranging fleet ambit, common with volume selling brands, Chevrolet offered Camaro in taxi/police packages, with the 250 cube inline six. The latter involved local patrol work, not high speed pursuit. Indeed, super fast cop cars mainly went to the South to deal with moonshine runners. In the case of the straight talking six, economy of purchase and operation were key. There was the flexibility of specifying a Powerglide or THM 350, beyond the stock, all synchro three-speed manual box. Still, rental fleet specials with spill combating poverty interiors, weren't going to enchant the private buyer. Much more desirable was the SS package, which, as per usual Chevrolet parlance, stood for Super Sport.

The V8-only SS package (RPO Z27) got you power-assisted front disk brakes, the sensible 300 horse L48 350 and Firestone's F70-14 Wide Ovals on purposeful 14x7in W-I-D-E rims. In this case, the path led to the 1970 $^{1}/_{2}$ Camaro SS350, with the SS pack adding $290. The F41 sports suspension package, which included 1.0in front swaybar and formerly optional rear swaybar, was outside the SS pack, and cost $31. A Positraction lsd was also separate, and optionable. However, then there was the Big Kahuna, the Camaro SS396. The L78 big block SS implied F41 and Positraction rear end, as mandatory options. As usual, 396-powered Camaros had a black painted rear fascia panel.

You could have factory a/c with either SS version, and it was the 402 cube powered SS396 that was the revelation of the 2nd gen Camaro's debit line-up. Previously, 1st gen Camaro SS396s had proved a handful in acceleration, braking and cornering. However, the new SS396s showed the chassis benefits brought by the 2nd gen redesign. The greater wheel travel, softer suspension settings, dual swaybars, wider upper and lower control arm bushings, new rear multileaf bushings and larger front balljoints, meant the new Camaro SS396 could corner flat, avoid axle tramp and cope better with imperfect back roads.

The very quick, $105 variable ratio power steering was a must. *Road & Track* judged this power steering to be Mercedes-like. This was a time when Mercedes' power steering was considered the gold standard in high effort, good feel power-assisted tillers. *Road Test* sampled a four-speed Camaro SS396, and its August '70 issue said the new 2nd gen big block Camaro coped with challenging Big Sur country, and California Highway One, with aplomb. Yes, you could now use that big block's power, which made the latest Camaro SS396 a fine GT car. *Road Test*'s four-speed example had the 350 horse L34 396, and turned in a 15.3-second $^1/_4$ mile at 92.7mph. It also got 10-11mpg in town, and 13.9mpg on the highway.

The test car had the factory $380 a/c option, and sensible 3.31 rear gears, a stock SS396 fitment. The 10.25:1 CR helped create the 415lb/ft, but also seemed to make the coupe octane sensitive. Indeed, it pinked on lesser grades of hi test, and was judged a thirsty car overall. Even in those pre-fuel crisis days, magazines were weary of the 2nd gen's size and operating costs. *Road & Track*'s SS350 automatic managed a 16.6 second $^1/_4$ mile at 86mph, 0-60mph in 8.8 seconds and 115mph. *R&T*'s May 1970 issue said this car, also with 10.25:1 CR, garnered 14.4mpg overall. In a common contemporary assessment of domestic designs, *R&T*'s import leanings saw them judge the new Camaro as too large and heavy for its passenger and cargo capacity.

It expressed concern over poor gas mileage, and future times when gas might not be so cheap. With inflation, gas, insurance and a $4500 purchase price, the average buyer could find things tough. However, for the time being the 2nd gen was a shoe that fit, and *Road & Track* disclosed and supplied praise. It drove this Camaro SS350 a week prior to the 2nd gen's launch. The public went nuts over the styling. However, the magazine noticed that current 1st gen Camaro owners seemed to ignore the coupe. *R&T* speculated it might have been because the new car

Fortunately, Cluffer missed and Leeroy exclaimed, "Outasite, man, that was really a far out buckshot solo." (Courtesy Marc Cranswick)

looked so different. Existing owners may have felt abandoned by Chevrolet, or they might not have realized it was a Camaro at all!

The journal felt the 2nd gen had greatly improved upon the Camaro's ride and handling compromise, and that F41 was no teeth-rattler. It also judged it a superb American GT machine, and said, "... it's the best American car we've ever driven, and more importantly it's one of the most satisfying cars for all-around use we've ever driven." Indeed, the following year *R&T* declared the Camaro SS396 to be "The best car built in America in 1971". [12] In contrast to *Road Test*'s experience, *Road & Track* judged its 1970 $^1/_2$ Camaro SS350 to have poor brakes for mountain driving. Front power disks notwithstanding, its coupe exhibited discernible brake fade in standardized testing.

R&T also said it chose the excellent GM THM 350 automatic because the four-speed was stiff in action. It's true there was a general consensus that the standard four-speed Hurst shift linkage was awkwardly stiff. There were a number of safety and anti-theft measures built in that made the four-speed stick a tricky choice, and not just in Chevrolets. In some cars you had to fully depress the clutch to shift gears. Starting procedure involved fully depressing the clutch pedal, too! You also had to shift into reverse to remove the key from the ignition. Such foibles were affecting domestics, industry wide.

The auxiliary $84 instrument option brought welcome, but not complete readouts. Leftwards saw fuel gauge and ammeter, with the right side supplying a temperature gauge and clock. An oil pressure gauge would have been more useful than a clock, but this was also an industry-wide omission. The optional factory a/c carried no reservations. It had many outlets, was powerful, and recommended by all who tested it. The intuitive HVAC control panel lay to the lower left of the steering column. A little out of the way, Pontiac placed its panel high in the dash, inline with the instruments.

In any case, such HVAC controls were well illuminated at night, and easier to fathom than equivalents on imports. One similarity with the diminutive captive import Opel GT was the trunk – it was virtually the same size! That 6.5ft^3 trunk volume was the price of the 2nd gen's handsome proportions. Like the little Opel, the Camaro also borrowed the tail-light treatment from Corvette; no bad thing. Still, unlike the Opel or Corvette, the Camaro did offer a separate luggage compartment, and in every way was a more practical ride. Indeed, even the Camaro Z28 was learning to compromise.

The Zee with zip – Camaro Z28

Somewhat of a prelude to the new Camaro Z28, at least in terms of engine, was the 1969 *Car and Driver* Blue Maxi Camaro, dubbed the Z29, due to spiritually taking the Z28 concept to the next level. The hardtop coupe's creation was linked to the Penske racing organization, Mark Donohue and deputy Sam Eckerd to be precise. When it came to making the ultimate Camaro road racer, Team Penske would know. The coupe had expected hardware, Camaro's four-wheel disk option, Konis, American Racing 200S rims, Goodyear Polyglas GT F60-15s, Positraction and permanently open cold air induction hood. However, there were a couple of surprises.

The *C/D* Blue Maxi had factory a/c, at a time when many speedy domestics either weren't optioned so, or could not be optioned so. Stahl headers were connected to a 1970 LT1 350, the kind of small block you would expect in a Corvette. SCCA rule changes for the 1970 season of the Trans Am series permitted larger engines to be destroked. This had always been an impediment for the big inch crowd. Pontiac and Mopar didn't have a small block V8 that could snake under the 305in^3 limbo pole. The Blue Maxi motor was a converted 1969, 350-horse Corvette 350in^3 V8. This solid lifter job had a Z28 cam, Z28 intake, 800 CFM four-bbl Holley, forged 11:1 pistons, four-bolt mains and 370 horses. It all implied speed and comfort, with *C/D*'s 13.7-second pass at 103.69mph backing up the promise.

The series production 1970 $^1/_2$ Camaro Z28 was also 350 V8-powered, with a slight detune. All one had to do was tick the $572.95 Z28 option box and let the good times roll. They rolled quickly thanks to 360bhp at 5600rpm and 370lb/ft at 4 grand. The Z28 package brought several hardware items: Holley 780 CFM four-bbl carb, new high rise aluminum

This 1970 ½ Camaro Z28 four-speed was ordered through the COPO program. With its chassis upgrades, the new Z28 was truly worthy of its 'Super Hugger' sobriquet.
(Courtesy David Griffiths www.legendarymotorcar.com)

The solid lifter LT1 350 was Corvette-sourced and rated at 360 horses. The comp ratio was 11:1, and a single Holley four-barrel provided the premium juice. (Courtesy David Griffiths www.legendarymotorcar.com)

intake manifold, cast aluminum rocker covers with internal galleries, Z28 302 heads and valves, '69 optional camshaft, HD radiator, F41 suspension and 4.1 turns lock-to-lock manual steering.

The internals of the LT1 350 weren't cheap, with four-bolt mains, forged steel crankshaft and TRW impact extruded pistons making the 6500rpm redline a safe one. There was a new 11in clutch for four-speed fiends, and the 12-bolt 1970 only Positraction lsd was a $44.25 separate option. *Car and Driver* was of the opinion the Positraction made things worse, not better. The Z28, and all Camaros, adhered to the Chevrolet credo that understeer was best for most drivers. So, the optional lsd would only exacerbate this trait. The Z28 had staggered shocks, as did all 2nd gen Camaros. However, the THM 400 automatic was a $221.80 option.

Just for the Z28 package, the automatic had a 2400rpm torque converter stall speed. This was tailored to the 350's high output, low torque nature. The automatic rear gear choice was between a stock 3.73, or optional 4.10:1. The latter was commonly

agreed to be necessary to get the poky-motored Z28 off the line with some alacrity. Indeed, the torque converter's torque amplification nature helped

With the four-speed stick many Z28 buyers went close ratio, 2.52:1 not 2.20:1. However, in practical terms, a taller 1st helped acceleration times. (Courtesy David Griffiths www.legendarymotorcar.com)

maximize the LT1's torque delivery. As for the four-speed, 1185 1970 ½ Camaro Z28s were specified with the $232.35 close ratio HD M22 unit. With Z28, many buyers went close ratio with a short 2.52 low, when the 2.20:1 1st actually aided ¼ mile times. It was useful being able to wind out the LT1 350, and this V8 could certainly make the Z28 dance at high rpm.

More than a grand tourer, the 3550lb Camaro Z28 four-speed was also more sports car than muscle car. Many felt it was more sports car than the contemporary Corvette! This was one coupe that could get all its power onto the road. Helping such matters were the Z28's 15x7in hoops, wrapped in Polyglas GT F60-15s. It was Goodyear's state of the art tire for domestic sporty cars of the day, and tried to combine the best of the bias belted and radial tire properties. The 2nd gen Z28's rims resembled alloys, but were in fact stamped steel units, with welded steel centers. They were stronger and less corrosion-prone than cast alloy wheels. The rims had a dull gray finish, bright lugnuts, center caps and trim rings. Blue bowtie emblems adorned said center caps.

For all that the Z28 had, there were a few surprising omissions, such as an absence of cold air induction, as with the 1st gen's ZL2 hood. It was odd seeing an air cleaner tub taking in warm underhood air on a performance car. The former four-wheel disk brake option was also gone, so too the front spoiler. With Trans Am racing rule changes, these last two items were no longer homologation necessary.

However, you did get a high-performance oil pump, and baffled oil pan. This all made comparisons with the in-house, quasi rival Firebird Trans Am 400 Ram Air IV somewhat interesting. The Trans Am was nearly one half second quicker in the ¼ mile, and 10mph slower in top speed, compared to a Z28 also fitted with four-speed and 3.73 rear gears.

The Trans Am was around 200lb heavier, and about $200 more expensive. The Pontiac had cold air induction, and could have a/c. The Camaro Z28 could have neither, but did have a baffled oil pan, which the Trans Am didn't receive until the 1977-79 W72 400s. Both Z28 and Trans Am had the same footwear, rim sizes, plus an amazing handling reputation. However, with no special oil pan, engine damage was a Poncho possibility in hard cornering. *Car and Driver* offered some comparisons between its automatic Z28 with 4.10 gears, and a Hemi Challenger and Boss Mustang that it had recently tried. The Z28 stopped in 228ft from 80mph, the Challenger and Boss took over 290ft.

The Hemi Challenger edged the Z28 in the ¼ mile, just, 14.1 playing 14.2 seconds, with FoMoCo in the high 14s. At 11mpg, overall the Camaro Z28 was slightly more economical than the Dodge. It was also a tad pricier than either Mopar or Ford. However, such comparisons meant little, because the Boss 302 was gone at the end of '70 MY. The Hemi departed at the close of 1971. For a comparable high output, low torque superb handler, the Z28's closest competitor was the Plymouth 'Cuda 340.

GM President Ed Cole planned a comp ratio drop to meet tightening federal emissions regs. This made the 1970 ½ Camaro Z28 a highwater mark for 2nd gen performance.
(Courtesy David Griffiths www.legendarymotorcar.com)

Like the 'Cuda, the Z28 would also circulate between 1970 and 1974. In spite of the age-old Ford versus Chevrolet rivalry, character made the Z28 and 'Cuda closer spiritual kin.

So what could a Camaro Z28 do? According to *Car and Driver*, 0-60mph in 5.8 seconds, trap speed of 100.3mph, with top end being 118mph. *Motorcade*'s four-speed Z28, with more sensible 3.73 gears, did a 14.5 second ¼ mile at 98.2mph and 10.6mpg. In May 1970, *Motorcade*'s Dave Epperson dismissed the original Z28 as being too Chevy II close, and technically unimaginative. The new Z28 went several steps further though: "I'd like to shake the hand of the guys who worked up this car." Britain's oldest car magazine, *Autocar*, also had praise for the 1970 ½ Camaro Z28. It tried a three-year-old Canadian import in 1973, finding no rust, great used condition, and the coupe tough enough to be manhandled in recording performance figures.

Autocar dropped the clutch at 4 grand, getting 0-60mph in 6.3 seconds, 0-100mph in 16.5 seconds and a 13.6 second ¼ mile. The car was slightly modified with headers and a custom intake manifold. It had tried a 1970 ½ Camaro SS350 automatic earlier, achieving 0-60mph in 8.5 seconds, 0-100mph in 22 seconds and a 16.3 second ¼ mile. The 4-second flat 50-70mph passing time of the SS350 was identical to the figure the journal would record for a new 1984 C4 TBI Crossfire Corvette, tested in Belgium.

Autocar judged the Z28's four-speed to be heavy, but precise. The disk/drum brakes were a tad light, but hauled the Camaro Z28 down from 120mph straight and true, with no fade. Handling was neutral, but the ride was firm and a little under-damped. Roll was minimal and confidence-inspiring. Problems concerned the Polyglas GTs, judged a little squirrelly and lacking in wet road grip. One day soon, the Z28 would get radials. One thing Chevrolet promised on the 2nd gen's debut was an adjustable seatback. However, one had to wait until the 3rd gen Camaro, for that nickel and dime trick. Another problem encountered by *Autocar*, and common to many cars of the era, was an inability to work the foot-operated park brake, when wearing the separate lap and shoulder belts.

Once again, inertia reel belts would come to the rescue, but 120mph would arrive sooner. Zero to 120mph was recorded in 26.6 seconds, but the gas tank would empty shortly thereafter! The Z28 recorded 10mpg in town, 12mpg cruising at 70mph, and that was with larger UK measured gallons. However, the Camaro Z28 had proved itself a true

In 1971, the new Camaro made *Road & Track's* Top 10 list; the only domestic car to do so. The journal proclaimed Camaro SS396 to be the best car made in America. (Courtesy GM Archives)

enthusiast's car, and with 24,800 miles on the odometer, a durable one. There were some detailed Z28 recognition points. Compared to regular Camaros the Zee had a floor hinged gas pedal. Other Camaros had a firewall hinged pedal with bracket. Camaro Z28s had an 8000rpm tach, others ceased and desisted at 7 grand. All Z28s had F41 suspension, implying brackets welded to the rear frame rails, for that second swaybar.

The big 'Jim Hall' three-piece COPO 9796 rear spoiler became available from April 20 1970, with 8733 coupes fitted. Camaro Z28 and Camaro SS had special hood insulation as standard equipment. The optional THM 400 automatic featured electric kickdown; there was no cable, and all '70 ½ Camaros had low back Strato buckets and adjustable head restraints. The Chevrolet brochure declared "Camaro 1970. A most unusual car from the place you'd expect: Chevrolet's Sports Department." Objective testing and subjective experience lent credence to its assertion.

Chevrolet. Building a better way to see the U.S.A.

Camaro for 1972: Nineteen years of Corvette taught us a lot about sports cars.

We've been building the Vette for nearly two decades now and it's still the only two-seat production sports car made in America.

In those 19 years, we've learned about braking, steering, suspensions, aerodynamics, engines and a lot more from Corvette. And the sum total of all this

learning has turned up in our Camaro.

In fact, August *Road & Track* magazine called the Camaro 350 SS one of the 10 best cars in the world. No qualifications.

Camaro's front disc brakes, road-hugging suspension and wide-base wheels and tires make it

handle amazingly like Corvette. And for '72, there's a new manual steering gear ratio for quicker handling, cleaner burning engines, and even handy map pockets in the door panels.

A lot of people think our Camaro is the closest thing to a Vette yet.

See your Chevy dealer and take a ride in a '72 Camaro.

It's the one with four seats. We want it to be the best car you ever owned.

Chevrolet

Camaro Sport Coupe winding through Southern California hills.

Apart from energy-absorbing A pillars, a rear steel bulkhead beefed up the partial unibody. So, no rear folding seats for the 2nd gen F-body! (Courtesy GM Archives)

1971-1972

The TV show *Car and Track* delivered a comprehensive test of the 1971 Camaro RS two-bbl 350 automatic on Grattan Raceway in Michigan. Host Bud Lindemann's report touched on many points affecting Camaro and the auto industry in general. For openers it was "In the pony car race the Camaro left the gate late. They've been trying to catch the Mustang ever since. This year they did, and both cars are neck and neck in sales. Now we wonder if the race is worthwhile, since the sporty car market seems to be on the downhill treadmill." Indeed, *Car and Driver*'s May 1971 issue on the '71 Camaro Z28 noted that, whereas the Mustang used to outsell the Camaro three to two, they were now even steven at the time of writing.

The statistic's bore out Lindemann's assessment of a market segment in decline. Pony sector sales fell from 1967's 11.9 per cent to 7.2 per cent market share in 1970. *Motor Trend* offered some illuminating sales stats in its October 1971 issue. Mustang had fallen from a 1966 sales peak of

540,802 units to 165,414 in 1970. Camaro had declined from an early 229,335 peak to 143,664 in 1970 annual sales. Firebird had recovered somewhat to 58,757 in 1970, with AMC Javelin/ AMX and Plymouth Barracuda languishing on a respective 31,090 and 30,267 unit sales. Whether it was model year sales, or calendar year sales, the writing was on the dealership wall.

Ford had spent big on the re-jigged 1971 Mustang. It continued with a three body-style range, but really, Henry was pumping against a slow puncture. There was no '71 Boss Mustang 302, despite one being planned.

While Mustang was overheating, Camaro seemed to be coming on song. *Car and Track*'s '71 Camaro RS coped well with Grattan Raceway. Indeed, Bud Lindemann described the coupe as a good handler. It had an acceptable highway ride, but acquitted itself even more admirably on track. The Camaro RS snaked through the pylon course with ease. The cones were closed up, and the tester still managed an easy 35mph slalom. Rebound was smooth, no jacking up, and recovery was called excellent.

The Camaro was rated agile and predictable. Lindemann noted that if you got into trouble on the road, there was a pretty good chance of maintaining control. He said "The term Hugger was aptly applied." Unfortunately, the stopwatch showed the expected decline, since *C&T* tried an equivalent '70 $^{1}/_{2}$ Camaro. Contemporary smog controls weren't meant to affect full throttle performance, but did. The test subject was deemed no neck snapper, with 0-30mph in 2.7 seconds, 0-50mph in 6.1 seconds, and 0-60mph in 8.9 seconds. Lindemann acknowledged the presence of Chevrolet's tried and true two-barrel 350 V8. He passed along the engineer's assertion, that there could be a more than 15-horsepower variation, between two motors made on the same day.

With the Camaro RS 350 two-bbl on 245 horse, 15 ponies may not have been crucial. If the go was restrained, the whoa was satisfactory. The coupe shut down from 30mph in 40ft, 50mph in 97ft and 70mph in 196ft. The front disks dissipated heat well. There was only slight correction needed for straight stops. Nose dive was slight also. *C&T*'s criticisms concerned the ever diminutive trunk: "Even the trunk remains too small to carry anything that goes in a trunk." The revised '71 Strato buckets were also of limited value. They had integrated high back head restraints, which were developments of Vega units. Indeed, that subcompact at one time even bestowed its steering wheel to the Corvette. Sports fans were expecting such hardware to arrive at, not come from Vega.

The latest buckets had a mere two position, four degree adjustment range. Was this really the promised Camaro reclining seats? They had deeper, full foam construction, and a new manufacturing process, but weren't suited to spirited driving. Initially they seemed comfier, to rope in showroom prospects no doubt. However, *C&T* wanted a firmer base, and more backrest bolstering. In the end, *Car and Track* judged Camaro and its ilk, a very good thing. They kept the driver in control, at a time when many

The Camaro Z28 continued into 1972, with the package retailing at $766. Stripes, emblems and handling pack were included. (Courtesy Steelside Classics)

domestics didn't. Lindemann said that in an era of softer suspension, sporty type cars provided security through firmer springs, shocks and heftier swaybars, "… because of it they're safer, and they're fun. I hope we don't lose them to a thing called progress."

The progress Bud Lindemann was referring to were shifting buyer patterns, against a background of greater government regulation of emissions. Traveling to the result of the Muskie Smog Bill, GM President Ed Cole set his corporation, and the industry on a path of reduced compression ratios for no lead gas. This implied an 8.5:1 CR across the board, bar Camaro Z28 which for '71 MY had 9:1 compression. The great Z28's LT1 V8 was now down to 330bhp at 5600rpm and 360lb/ft arrived at 4 grand. However, Z28s still needed premium gas. Perhaps even worse was the inclusion of a CEC (Combined Emission Control) valve, to keep the EPA at bay.

In the vein of GM's transmission controlled spark, CEC cut vacuum advance in 1st and 2nd. It also held the throttle part open in deceleration in 3rd and 4th, and in 3rd on automatic cars as well. Car and Driver found the four-speed Z28 now did 0-60mph in 6.7 seconds, a 15.1-second pass at 94.5mph and 130mph with a 3.73 rear axle. It still had enough moxie to hit the redline in 4th. At $786.75, the Camaro Z28 package was still worth it. The Camaro SS396 was also still available, but now possessed just 300 ponies. These were all gross ratings, but the industry was changing over to net horsepower for '72 MY. GM cars were getting ready for the emissions apocalypse early. However, some domestics and imports retained their 1970 specs in 1971.

Notable Camaro performance changes for 1971 included the absence of the 12-bolt Positraction lsd. It was now a ten-bolt 8.5in unit. The new D80 spoiler pack, included a new front spoiler, made of ABS plastic. The big Jim Hall rear spoiler brought up the rear, replacing the short 1970 1/2 unit. The latest Z28 cam had the same lift and duration as per 1970. Hurst-shifted four-speeds and 2400rpm stall speed torque converters also made it through. For improvements, the Z28 had stronger engine mounts and a larger fuel filter. The Camaro Z28 HD U joints were kept, but the variable ratio power steering was now slower.

On the detail front, side markers now flashed in synch with turn signals. The Camaro 'C' on the header panel changed from chrome to red, and the dashboard had more international symbols. '71 MY

also saw new wheel covers, larger back-up lights, and two new optional vinyl roof colors. 1971 also witnessed the end of Van Nuys' F-body production, as all the eggs were placed in the Norwood, Ohio basket. For '72 MY there was a coarser grille mesh, and the mid-year introduction of a three-point seatbelt incorporating a shoulder harness. A smog pump made tighter emissions easier for the Z28 to meet, in terms of drivability, for which GM had a reputation as- the best in the industry. However, this was an area that was rapidly going south, in terms of increased stumbling and lean carburetion surge.

Tightening emissions meant the 307 and 396 V8s were about to go absent from California in 1972. So, the new starting point for the Golden State would be the first optional 49-state V8, the L65 two-barrel 350. This 8.5:1 CR motor ran on regular and made 165bhp at 4 grand, with a useful 280lb/ft at 2400rpm. According to Motor Trend's October 1971 issue, a L65 Camaro 350 with THM did 0-60mph in 10.2 seconds, an 18.5 second 1/4 mile at 79mph, and could stop from 60mph in a nifty 123.4ft. Not bad for the day, and E78-14s as footwear. Weight for the power steering equipped coupe was 3336lb. However, excitement dictated one should tick the Z28 option box.

With 255 net horsepower at 5600rpm, and 280lb/ft at 4 grand, the 9:1 CR-engined Camaro Z28 could now run on 94 octane regular (RON). It was 15 net ponies stronger than the Camaro SS396, and its stats were respectable for the era. Road & Track's example managed 0-60mph in 7.5 seconds, a 15.5 second 1/4 mile at 90mph and 60mph to zero in 159ft. Its braking performance was no better than plainer Camaros, but its performance spelled 12.3mpg overall, with an associated 209-mile cruising range. The coupe carried a 4.10 rear axle on the automatic Z28 tested. Much of the Z28 hardware from earlier times was still present. That said, like rival high output handler the 'Cuda 340, these were performance cars gradually succumbing to federal smog law.

For 1972, the Z28's 16:1 straight ratio power steering was revalved for more feel. Specifically, the torsion bar actuator was now stiffer. The rear spoiler and fast manual steering were now optional, rather than standard. Hood and deck striping were now a delete option. Observing the sales figures, 6562 SS (Z27) coupes were ordered. In VIN 5th digit terms it was 'K' for the SS350 and 'U' for the SS396. Z28s were denoted by 'L', and sold 2575 units. The Z22 RS appearance pack accounted for 11,364 takers in 1972, and cost $118. Sports appearance was getting more traction, as insurance and other costs bit hard. Commercially, Camaro descended from 114,630in 1971 to just 68,651 coupes sold in 1972, and the UAW was a big reason for that.

There's little doubt Camaro would have dusted off Mustang in the sales race, three bodystyles or no. However, UAW strike action proved to be the ultimate fly in the ointment. In late September 1970, a 67-day strike hampered the '71 Camaro's introduction, but there was more to come courtesy of the UAW. In an interview, Jeff Teague, son of AMC's long-serving styling boss Dick Teague, recounted how UAW strike action in 1970 had largely been the reason that the AMX/3 missed series production. More than that, Jeff Teague, also a noted stylist, said such strike action nearly bankrupted AMC. He said the UAW were using little AMC to send a message to the Big Three. Give in to our demands, or else …

'Else' turned out to be the 174-day strike at the sole GM F-body Norwood, Ohio plant. The strike started on April 7 1972, and resulted in 1100 part made '72 MY cars that were either scrapped or sent to vocational schools. It was too expensive to modify them to comply with 1973 bumper and smog law. The strike action cost an estimated $125 million to dealerships in lost sales revenue, associated with an estimated 40,000 F bodies that weren't made.

The Norwood, Ohio industrial action prompted management to examine whether the GM F-body should continue, and the figures showed why. Chevrolet's total for 1972 production was 2,151,076, compared to under 70,000 Camaros sold, resulting in voices saying 'was it worth it?' The pony car segment was in decline, including arch rival Mustang. Rising insurance premiums, general inflation and a public cooling for sporty cars were in the mix. It seemed like the 1968-70 peak of buyers ponying up to buy expensive fast cars, with tailored power teams and suspension setups for road course and strip, had gone. If anything, Joe Q Public was taking an increasing shine to intermediate-sized personal coupes, of a luxurious nature. Fortunately for Chevrolet that included the Monte Carlo.

This is one of the 2575 Camaro Z28s built in 1972. The 174 day UAW strike at Norwood nearly brought about the F-body's demise. (Courtesy Steelside Classics)

By 1972 the solid lifter Z28 350 LT1 motor was rated at 255bhp net. Optioning the 12 buck 4.10 rear axle, implied mid 15s. (Courtesy Steelside Classics)

This '72 Camaro Z28 was specified with a wide ratio Muncie M20 four-speed. The Hurst shifter was gone at the end of '71 MY, making it easier to slot that stick around the gate. (Courtesy Steelside Classics)

Good fortune, too, that owner loyalty groups and some sporty car die-hards in GM management were on the F-body's side. They could see that enthusiasts couldn't live on Corvette alone. Then, too, how could Henry's pony be allowed to gallop free without a response from the Bow Tie boys? So it was that the GM F-body lived to fight another day. This faith placed in Camaro and Firebird would yield financial dividends as the '70s wore on. Even so, 1972

Genuine Z28s had rear swaybar brackets welded to the rear frame rails. Mods to this coupe include a 383 stroker motor, with spark assistance from a MSD ignition box. (Courtesy Steelside Classics)

The big Jim Hall three-piece COPO 9796 Trans Am series rear spoiler, and ABS plastic front spoiler, were part of the D80 package. (Courtesy Steelside Classics)

would prove to be the end of the Z27 SS package, and big block V8s in Camaros for that matter. No big engines anymore for Mustang or Mopar. Only Pontiac and AMC would be in the 400-cube plus pony corral.

Camaro's speedo was now a 130mph job, not the previous 150mph unit. However, not everything was slowing down at Chevrolet. In keeping with the rest of the auto industry, the turbocharger was seen as a savior from tightening smog law, and an increasing need for better gas mileage. To this end, Chevrolet Engineering worked on a Turbo Camaro in 1972. The ingredients were the familiar 250in³ six, but with export spec 7:1 CR truck pistons, Schwitzer Model no. LDA 319 turbo, Vega air cleaner, Rochester Monojet carb, Holley electric pump with boost pressure sensing hose, stock mechanical fuel pump and stock AIR smog pump.

The system was a blow-through affair. Max boost was set at 10psi, with a bolt-on bar fitting on the side of the sump for the turbo's oil return line. Only the inlet side of the Z28's dual muffler system was

utilized. This non-RS '72 coupe had a gold exterior, white accents and similarly painted Z28 rims, plus a small 'Turbo Camaro' script. The results were a 16.18-second pass at 86mph, with THM 350 and lower emissions than a stock six, according to *Hot Rod*'s June 4 1972 issue. It was slightly swifter than an automatic '70 ¹/₂ Camaro SS350, and with the promise of superior gas mileage. The Turbo Camaro seemed to have everything but an intercooler. Such was the way of turbo packages before the '80s.

An important stat was the 50-70mph passing time. A normal automatic '72 Camaro six-cylinder took 12.87 seconds, but the blown Camaro cut that figure to just 5.12 seconds! The non-turbo Camaro six took a leisurely 20.28 seconds for the ¹/₄ mile, with a 67mph trap speed, close to a VW Beetle. The Turbo Camaro was a safer car, and cleaner concerning smog testing. Chevrolet had also planned a 400in³ small block Camaro Z28, for mid '72 MY release, following in the tire tracks of Don Yenko's example. Sadly, neither the Turbo Camaro nor the Z28 400 V8 eventuated. Indeed, given

Nova. A few smaller cars cost less. That's what they're worth.

Nova costs little more than a little car. But you get so much more with it.
To wit: some actual room. Coupe seats five. Sedan, six. In comfort.
Body by Fisher with inner fenders and flush-and-dry rocker panels that help prevent rust.
A travel-size trunk with a cargo-guard steel barrier. Springs selected by computer to give Nova the right ride for the way you equip it.

Five regular-fuel engines to save you money—including standard Four, Six or V8.
A range of transmissions in manuals, automatics and the low-cost Torque-Drive that never makes you clutch.
Don't saddle yourself with a small car. It isn't worth it. Not with Nova around.

Putting you first, keeps us first.

CHEVROLET

Assembly of the Chevrolet Nova was moved from Norwood to protect said compact from the UAW. (Courtesy GM Archives)

surrounding events, it was lucky the Camaro even made it into 1973.

1973-1974

The '73 Camaro didn't look much different, but there were many detail changes in a rationalized range. Standard motor was the 110bhp net 250in^3 inline six, with the remainder being variations on the small block V8. There was the 130-horse 307 V8, unless you lived in California, then came three 350s. The two-barrel 350 made 165bhp, the L48 350 was on 190 horse, with the Z28's L82 hydraulic lifter 350 producing 245 ponies. Hydraulic lifters meant factory a/c could be a first-time Z28 option. However, some late '72 MY Camaro Z28s have come to light with factory a/c also. With the SS396 history, it became commercially imperative to offer the top performer

Opposite: A sales total of 68,651in 1972. However, if it wasn't for the Norwood strike, Camaro would have blown off Mustang's doors in the sales race! (Courtesy GM Archives)

with a/c. After all, Pontiac's chief Trans Am, the SD 455, did so.

1973 saw the option of fast glass return, for the first time since '69 MY. This necessitated the optional console for the power buttons. Being a coupe, the GM bean counters saved $$$ by having two console buttons, avoiding the usual three with two on the driver's door and one for the passenger door! The arrival of a space saver spare was a necessary evil for anyone wishing to use the trunk for anything larger than a copy of *Readers' Digest*. Smog law dictated EGR (exhaust gas recirculation) for all Camaros. However, you also snagged a coolant recovery system into the bargain. That said, what you couldn't see was perhaps the biggest treat.

The Chevrolet designers cleverly got the Camaro up to speed, with 1973's front 5mph bumper law. The rear required just a 2.5mph bar. So, there was a slightly heavier bumper that you didn't really notice. The RS nosecone also made it through intact. There were now reinforcing bars from the front fenders to a core support, and from the support to the urethane nose section. It all added a scant 0.4in to vehicular length, and avoided the unbalanced look that affected many '73 MY cars, like Corvette. Of course, insurance companies offered rebates for owners of cars with stronger bumpers. However, you could bet that within a few years, all owners would have higher premiums ... plus the impact bumpers!

Of greater annoyance was the new seatbelt warning buzzer and light. Chevrolet did its best to make the raucous device palatable. Now the incendiary notice only sounded in forward gear, and cancelled with the park brake invoked on stick shift Camaros. Stick shift implied three-speed normal or HD three-speed Muncie plant-made boxes, and a choice of Saginaw type four-speed and aluminum-cased Muncie four-speed. If you bought a Z28 four-speed with factory air, figure on the wide ratio M20 box, not the M21 close ratio four-speed. The 1973 Z28 total was 11,574 split, 6107 stick and 5467 automatic. For the most

Opposite: This Camaro Z28 shows you could still get the Endura nosecone in 1973. Chevrolet did some beefing up to meet the new 5mph bumper law, adding 0.4in to length. (Courtesy Richard Budman www.FlemingsUltimateGarage.com)

Chevrolet. Building a better way to see the U.S.A.

part, it was Z28 business as usual, but there were some softenings and economisms necessary to make said racer more accessible.

For one, the formerly aluminum Z28 intake manifold was replaced with a cast-iron job. Then, too, a GM Rochester Quadrajet superseded the Holley four-barrel that the Z28 used to employ. With smog law resulting in leaner running and hotter motors, the cooling system was upgraded from 15 to 17 quarts. The Z28's suspension was also softened some. Front swaybar was reduced to 0.938in, complementing 300lb-in front springs. The rear bar was the usual 0.6875 unit, with multileaf spring rate at 99lb-in. Indeed the only difference between Z28 and F41 suspension was different rear shock valving. Axle ratios were now curtailed, and more highway amenable. A stock 3.42 rear axle was for automatics, with the familiar 3.73 rear gears for the four-speed. The rear Z28 emblem was now a foil decal, and the U14 auxiliary instrumentation pack, was now optional.

The Z28 pack was combinable with Type LT, and this implied some Z28 insignia omission, as Type LT took its place. The Type LT ensemble was a plush luxo deal, and made the Camaro Type LT an equivalent to Firebird's Esprit. To make way for this new luxury variant, the Z87 Custom Interior option was dropped at the end of 1972. No one really knows for sure what 'LT' stands for. It's suspected that the nomenclature signifies Luxury Touring. Chevrolet billed the new version thusly, "Type LT. For those who want a little more Camaro." To this end, standard equipment included the 350 two-bbl V8, 7in wide Rally rims, variable ratio power steering, hidden wipers, blackout rocker sills and moldings, dual exterior sport mirrors, U14 instrumentation pack, extra body and underhood insulation, deluxe seat trim, plus bright beaded woodgrain trim concerning both instrument panel and door cards.

There were Type LT badges placed on the steering boss, rear fascia, C-pillar and front catwalk

For 1973, the "Zee" rode with 245 net horses, but the 350 V8 was now an hydraulic lifter job. This made factory a/c a first time official Z28 option.
(Courtesy Richard Budman www.FlemingsUltimateGarage.com)

location. In spite of the obvious luxury raison d'etre, the Type LT came with a standard four-speed. The coupe was also much desired by all kinds of potential owners, including young ones. Indeed, some youth buyers even preferred Type LT to the Z28 package! Chevrolet had read the market early, and well, concerning the American driver's usual desire for plush and hush, but in a smaller vehicle. To this end, Type LT utilized Amberlite insulation blanket within doors, rear $^1/_4$ panels, roof cavity and C-pillars, behind the rear seat, under the rear package tray, and under interior carpeting.

What was it all like together? *Car and Driver*'s September 1973 issue let you know. The journal sampled a '73 Camaro Z28 four-speed replete with RS and Type LT packs. Zero to sixty happened in 6.7 seconds, no slower than *C/D*'s '71 Camaro Z28 four-speed. The $^1/_4$ mile was close, too, a 15.2 second pass at 94.6mph. The Z28 shut down from 70mph in a respectable 192ft. Gas mileage was in the 10 to 13.5mpg range, on regular. One could cruise at 70mph, with 76 decibels recorded, or 85dBA with the pedal to the metal!

As occurred with rivals in the '70s, like the plush AMC Concord in AMX form, you kind of wondered how the sport and comfort packs coexisted? The 1973 Camaro Z28 had an open element air cleaner, for what Chevrolet called "power on demand" sound. Still, buyers did increasingly want a mix of show, go and nice surroundings. There were no strippers at Chevrolet. The madcap 4.10 rear end was gone, but automatic Camaros adopted the Grand Haven ratchet effect console shifter. It was an equivalent to Pontiac's user friendly slap shifter. There was also a perforated headliner from mid '73 MY.

The marketplace rewarded the '73 Camaro with 96,751 sales, only 3614 of which possessed the humble 250in³ six. 1973 had been a very good year for the auto industry in terms of sales, and pony cars were looking up. Indeed, in the intermediate class, Chevelle hadn't done so well against the new '72 Torino. In 1973, Chevelle was taking a third position, behind both Torino and Olds Cutlass. The blame was attributed to styling. Perhaps they were right; after all, Camaro looked the same in 1972-73. So, tricks looked pleasant for Camaro heading into 1974. In spite, or perhaps because of the fuel crisis, the Camaro was sitting pretty in Chevrolet's range.

At a time when industry sales were flagging, and dust was gathering on the roofs of full-size dealer stock, the Camaro and Z28 sold more. 1973 had seen pent-up demand for Camaro and Mustang

The 2nd gen's high driveshaft tunnel made for an improved ride, but limited the Camaro to 2+2 status. Two things backseat drivers wouldn't know about the '73 Z28: a stiffer torsion bar actuator improved steering feel and rear axle ratio effect. The 3.73 rear end was for non-a/c cars, with the 3.42 rear axle for a/c cars. (Courtesy Richard Budman www.FlemingsUltimateGarage.com)

satisfied in the wake of strike action. However, in 1974 Camaro was overcoming circumstances on pure merit. The grand total moved onto 151,008 units, 22,210 of which were with the L22 250in³ six. It seemed that in a fuel crisis storm, buyers called at the inline six Camaro port. The RS package was gone, its famous Endura grille a victim of the '74 MY restyle, which incorporated 5mph aluminum impact bumpers at both ends.

The restyle brought a new fiberglass nose, new rear $^1/_4$ panels and a new trunk lid. The bumpers sat on flat leaf springs. There was a revised front grille, and wraparound tail-lights. On the lower level Sport Coupe, baby moon hubcaps were replaced with aluminum caps. It was a very successful reworking of a popular shape, that used the F-body's length to good effect. Like the Firebird for '74, the impact bumpered F-body was a good-looking lesson to many barge bar domestics and diving board equipped imports. Practical improvements saw an indicator light for front brake pad and ball-joint wear. Three point belts with an inertia reel shoulder portion were welcome. So too, the absence of federally mandated Interlock by mid-1974.

The Interlock mini logic sequence computer had proved an unreliable nuisance. In contrast, the Chevrolet 350 V8 small block continued to help all. The base 307 was history, making the 145bhp 350 two-bbl the first V8 choice. In California, it was a four-barrel 350 with single exhaust and manual

In 1973 only you could have Type LT, Z28 and RS packs ... on the one car ... holy options Batman! 11,574 Camaro Z28s were sold in 1973. (Courtesy Richard Budman www.FlemingsUltimateGarage.com)

brakes; a spec also shared with high altitude areas. Also for California was the LM1 350 V8, making 160bhp at 3800rpm and 250lb/ft at 2400rpm. On a 49-state basis, the L48 350 was rated at 185bhp, with a useful 270lb/ft at 2600rpm from an 8.5:1 CR.

The Z28's L82 350 still made 245bhp on a 9:1 CR, and from mid '74 MY featured GM's HEI (High Energy Ignition) transistorized, no points system. HEI would prove key for all Camaros soon. All '74 Camaro V8s came with power steering as standard equipment, but the new four-color D88 striping decal pack option was a Camaro Z28 exclusive. 1974 Z28s had their fifth VIN digit denoted 'T,' and still retained the special engine internals used by previous Z28s. The export Camaro Z28 of 1973-74 was a little different still. If you missed the Camaro SS396, all you had to do was move. You see, Z28s exported to Europe and Britain used the 402in³ big block.

Simplifying export matters, the Camaro Z28 and Monte Carlo were sharing the 402 V8/THM 400 power team by 1973. In 1974 Britain, there was

the Camaro Z28 listed at £3420 sterling, with the Type LT version costing £120 more. All Chevrolets listed for 1974 UK sale were automatics, with the Corvette only listed with the LS4 454 big block. Pontiac Firebird Formula and Trans Am, were only stated as having 455 V8s. The Firebird Formula was identically UK priced, to the Camaro Z28 Type LT. At this time, the final Jaguar XKE V12s, went out the door for £3365 sterling. However, you couldn't get a/c on a RHD Jaguar XKE, and that wasn't cool.

This 1974 big block 402in³ powered automatic export Camaro Z28 was featured on the ITV network, Thames Television UK auto show *Drive In*. It was part of a segment looking at the sale of American cars in the UK, and the commercial future of selling V8-powered automatic cars in the wake of the fuel crisis. TV presenter Tony Barstable noted that the latest US cars could run on the UK's 3-star leaded gas. Plus, the UK spec Camaro Z28 came with air-conditioning as standard equipment.

On *Drive In*, the test driver did a tire-squealing, brake-torqued take-off in the Zee. In ever-changing

In the wake of the Norwood plant strike, GM had considered axing the F-body in favor of better-selling lines like Impala. (Courtesy GM Archives)

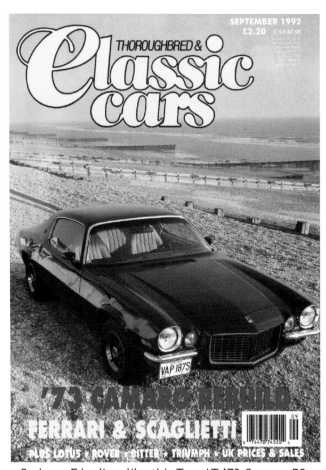

2nd gen F bodies, like this Type LT '73 Camaro RS, were probably the most popular American cars sold in the UK. (Courtesy IPC Magazines)

buyer trends, a higher percentage of Camaro buyers selected C60 $397 factory a/c. The total was 79,237 Camaros with a/c in 1974. 124,010 selected the J50 power brakes and radial tires appeared as an option, but only in FR78-14 form. The Camaro Z28 still sported Goodyear Polyglas GT F60-15s as standard equipment. 1974 saw the first time the Camaro could be optioned with an AM/FM stereo radio, and the Borg Warner Super T10 took over from the Muncie in January 1974, concerning high-performance Camaros and Firebirds.

Pony cars – the industry's viewpoint

When the 2nd gen Camaro made its debut, a *Car and Driver* choice poll saw it gain twice as many votes as the Mustang. A very likeable coupe, but there must have been more reasons for the Camaro's

and pony car genre's survival. Even as late as the start of 1974 model year, all pony players were still around. 1970 had seen rising interest in the intermediate class, hence Ford giving the Torino so much attention. 1971 belonged to the subcompacts, as buyers increasingly sought a cheaper way. However, pony cars still hung in there. In March/April 1972, the segment's sales even picked up after what had seemed an interminable decline. Why?

Jim Brokaw offered some explanations in the November 1972 issue of *Motor Trend*. Skyrocketing Corvette insurance premiums, a Datsun 240Z waiting list, a small family's need for the pony's +2 seating, pony car loyalists, sporty car fanciers in general and even returning Vietnam veterans with combat pay burning a hole in their pockets. In detail, yes, but more generally, pony cars were increasingly the kind of car buyers wanted, as they downsized from family intermediates. A reasonably sized, easy to handle sporty car, with good driving manners.

The Camaro was a long-time associate of the Corvette's image. In 1973-74 the Z28 and plastic fantastic shared a L82 350 V8 to good effect. (Courtesy Gabriel)

They were cheaper to buy and insure than a full-size luxo sled, or even a mid-size.

With the right engine and appropriate optioning, a pony coupe could very well sock it to ya! Even in the early to mid '70s, it was still possible to tailor order a pony car to personal tastes. They could bring the right combination of sport, luxury and economy. This accommodating nature became even more attractive with the fuel crisis. Indeed, in April 1974, *Motor Trend*'s John Fuchs said ponies had the power to save buyers from the "Energy Circus" of artificial shortages, OPEC grandstanding and oil industry refinery capacity snafus concerning unleaded gas. With their reasonable nature, pony cars could adapt to buyer needs.

There was another reason for the spike in sales: the rising interest in sporty personal cars. These coupes were luxury mid-size 'Chariots of the Gods.' They had style, and whatever desirable power options were still to be had. This hedonistic class

represented the lion's share of the cars that TV show *Car and Track* tested in 1974. They were of major interest to viewers, and out of all the ponies, the Camaro Type LT seemed a mid-size personal car alternative. All the good stuff, but at a slightly lower price, and in a smaller size. *C&T* host Bud Lindemann introduced the 1974 Camaro Type LT thusly: "This LT version is designed to appeal to those who lean towards the European GT road

Now with aluminized 5mph bumpers front and rear, the '74 Camaro Z28 held onto the 245 horse L82 350 for one final year. (Courtesy Ryan Baliski)

machines." The mezaluna, Type LT-based, rear fascia tail script seemed in keeping with this Continental dream.

The Camaro Type LT tested had the 145bhp 350 two-bbl and THM 350. Indeed, the test driver used the slap shifter gate to go up and down gears on Grattan Raceway. He pushed the coupe hard round the track, as with all test subjects, smoking the outside wheel at will due to the non-lsd rear end.

The figures were 0-30mph in 3.9 seconds, 0-50mph in 7.5 seconds, with 0-70mph in 12.4 seconds. All this, plus a 16.7-second ET at 82mph, were very respectable for the time and class. Even the Feds couldn't keep a good small block down.

Braking performance saw 30mph to zero in 35.5ft, from 50mph in 101ft with hot brakes, the 70mph stop took 201ft, and the coupe couldn't be kept straight. The comment was made that

This 1974 Camaro Z28 has the Type LT pack, which implied some interior and exterior Z28 callout omissions and LT substitutions. The 1974 Camaro gained a dash indicator light for front brake pad and ball joint wear.
(Courtesy Ryan Baliski)

the Camaro Type LT was much like the Mercury Cougar XR7 also tested – comfortable and very soft. Through the pylon course the Type LT suspension made for performance that was very loose, with excessive body lean and a front end that wanted to wash out. Recovery through the slalom was only fair. The *C&T* test driver said: "The Z28 it ain't."

Fuel economy, a pressing concern in the aftermath of the fuel crisis, was fair for the class, but all of a sudden many were desiring more. At 60mph on the highway it was 17.4mpg, falling to 14.7mpg at 70mph, with 15 to the gallon overall. Bud Lindemann liked a car that handled, so even though the '74 Camaro Type LT had many good points, like lively acceleration and comfort, he was disappointed, "Chevrolet seems to be famous for building cars with a little something for everyone. We found however, that this LT model may exclude the performance driver."

With the 55mph national gas saving speed limit trying to save America's balance of trade from

OPEC, how many performance seeking drivers were there? Judged by the other 1974 domestics that *Car and Track* sampled that year, the Camaro Type LT seemed to be the kind of personal car buyers now wanted. It also seemed to be a better exponent of the art than rivals. Bud Lindemann was taken aback by Lincoln-Mercury's personal car interpretation, the '74 Cougar XR7. After some derisory comments concerning FoMoCo's propensity for badge engineering, he said: "Whatever happened to the posh, jazzy little pony car? Well, it obviously fell into the Ford calorie tank and fattened up, like so many entries from the Ford stable."

The interior was likened to Cleopatra's chamber, and acceleration with the top 460 four-barrel V8 was found wanting. An 18.2-second $^1/_4$ mile was combined with brake swerve and dive into the asphalt, not to mention smokin' binders. Ford had gone separate chassis with its mid-sizers for '72 MY, and that made for a lean producing, sluggish performance through the pylons, in spite of the

In 1973-74 the Camaro Z28 was L82 350-powered. However, the export Z28 shared its 402 V8/THM 400 power team with the Chevrolet Monte Carlo. (Courtesy Ryan Baliski)

optional HD suspension being fitted. As Lindemann said, he would have hated to try the one marked standard. Then there was the Olds Cutlass, a top rear-drive seller for years, and well into the '80s. The Olds' take on the personal car brought an excellent ride/handling compromise with its HD suspension, but woeful braking. Even with standard front disks the Cutlass Salon's brakes faded into oblivion. They involved enough swerve to place you side-on after a 70mph stop.

A Cutlass Salon with the Olds Rocket 350 four-bbl V8 and 2.73 snooze axle, spelled a 19-second ¹/₄ mile. A couple of years hence, this motor with fuel-injection would power the Caddy Seville. Base-engined Cutlass or top optioned Cougar, the result from Car and Track was 12mpg overall. Both cars were very luxurious, and carried a whale of a price tag. You would probably have to sell seven Datsuns to equal the mark-up on one of these babies, so dealers were happy.

As a sign of the Eldorado that was the intermediate personal car boom, for 1974 Ford had moved Cougar from compact to mid-size and Mustang to subcompact. Camaro's position as a happy medium was also shown by Car and Track's test of the hot selling new '74 AMC Matador Coupe X 401. Whereas the Cougar and Cutlass were separate chassis jobs, the Matador retained the Rambler tradition of the unibody. In between was Camaro's partial unibody. So it was that the Matador Coupe was judged as trapping all the bumps, rattles and noises associated with pure unibodies.

American Motors' budget shortfalls versus the Big Three were revealed by the HD suspension handling with too much lean and a lack of body control compared to the Cutlass. Rear brake lock up, tail slewing and brake fade from 70mph also put the car sideways after an emergency stop. The coupe's big 401 cube four-barrel V8 just edged out the Camaro LT in acceleration, with an ET of 16.57 seconds at 89mph. However, the trade off was a thirsty 11.3mpg overall. The styling was judged an attractive and functional result of AMC's success with Mark Donohue and the 'Flying Brick' in

Hydraulic lifters and a smaller front swaybar crept in by 1973, but wheels and tires were still the same as in 1970. The specialized engine internals also made it through, plus the all-important baffled oil pan.
(Courtesy Ryan Baliski)

NASCAR. That said, Bud Lindemann questioned the emphasis placed on styling versus gas mileage in the wake of the fuel crisis.

The reason behind Detroit's priorities was that such designs were completed and released before the Yom Kippur Arab Israeli conflict, and subsequent economic reprisals from OPEC. This left the Camaro Type LT and other ponies as the new default personal cars, as buyers downsized. If you wanted that ideal package with more sport, then the '74 Camaro Z28 was your bag. And remember, you could include Type LT too! *Motor Trend* met up with said Z28 and three other ponies in 1974. The magazine's April 1974 report of 'The Fearsome Foursome' carried the header line: "Camaro Z-28 13.3mpg Javelin 15.2mpg Challenger 15.5mpg Firebird 19.2mpg".

The emphasis on gas mileage was a sign of the times. It was a varied mix of sport compacts, with Camaro Z28 a top performance dog, Javelin and Challenger employing thrifty 304 and 318

V8s respectively, and Firebird Esprit with a luxury oriented, low-speed 400in³ two-bbl unit. However, they represented the final refined state of the pony car that the public first met a decade earlier. Even now, the Camaro Z28 still packed heat. Quick, comfy, fine handling and mid 15s at over 90mph. As John Fuchs wrote, "Not too shabby for a '74 car." At $513.45, the Z28 option was cheaper than ever, and Fuchs added, "It's a lot of money, but the Z is still a lot of car."

Given the era, *Motor Trend*'s assessment of ye olde Camaro Z28 wasn't too surprising. The firm ride could be hard to live with, and '70s inflation was a friend of no one. Fuchs even suggested the Camaro Type LT with automatic, a/c and fast glass to be a better deal. At 195.4in long, 74.4in wide and 49.2in tall, the Z28 seemed to fit buyers better than ever. After all, 1974 was the Zee's best selling year, to that point.

Surprisingly, *Motor Trend* praised the commodious nature of the Camaro's back seat. It

The 1974 Camaro Z28 set a sales record with 13,802 sold that year alone. However, only 6978 of those buyers sprung for the new four-color, D88 $77 exterior striping option. (Courtesy Ryan Baliski)

also expressed a willingness to try the Javelin with the 258in³ I6, to save even more gas. Indeed, AMC Javelin had come first in the test, with the Camaro Z28 in second place. Unlike the Javelin, Camaro's nameplate would live beyond 1974. However, the times dictated weighty concerns for the auto industry.

Troubles for Detroit

As was normal for top executives and management, GM's styling supremo Bill Mitchell had some special cars over the years. These included a ZL1-powered 1970 ¹/₂ Camaro. Mitchell likened stroking the gas pedal to laying a whip across a mare's ass. However, times were changing. In 1971, the first year of the compression ratio drop, one Chevrolet engineer said "All our engines will respond to more spark (advanced ignition timing) and more fuel because we've got them leaned out so far for emissions." In October 1971, *Motor Trend* said when testing a '72 Camaro with 350 two-bbl V8, that the slushbox coupe did an 18.4-second ¹/₄ mile. It achieved its

best time on the first run, and got slower thereafter due to overheating.

That performance and drivability were being sacrificed on the high altar of environmental concern came as no surprise. That said, political representatives did get a shock when the public said enough was enough over 1974's Interlock: "… congressmen are coming under increasing pressure to pull out of the industry and stop meddling altogether."[13] Many drivers were irate over the technical problems caused by the mandatory Interlock device on 1974 vehicles, which obliged drivers to buckle up prior to starting their car. Apart from many seatbelts of the time being awkward to use, the mini logic sequence Interlock computer was often unreliable. This was an era when cars themselves were becoming increasingly problematic, due to federal controls.

The upshot was: excessive government interference equals no votes. So, in the House of Representatives an amendment carried, 339 to 49, to stop Interlock and the move to make a

Sports fans said goodbye to the Camaro Z28 at the end of '74 MY. The sporty Z28 would return in 1977, however. (Courtesy Ryan Baliski)

passive restraint system (airbag) mandatory for 1977 model year. The amendment, or climbdown, came from congressman Louis Wyman, who felt Interlock and airbags should merely be options. The casual manner in which politicians proposed mandatory introduction of industry wide hardware, was incredible. These devices had never been available on volume-produced automobiles, and yet congressmen wished to make them compulsory in short order.

Special interest groups had the ear of politicians. Information was supplied by 'experts' who made their case seem imperative and feasible for regulators to implement. In 1974, CARB (California Air Research Board) tried to retrofit smog controls on 1966-70 cars. There were immediate protests, and it prompted this response from seasoned automotive journalist Roger Huntington: "Why don't we just hang on until the old cars are junked? Is air quality really going to be helped enough to be worth the hassle?" [14]

Naturally, the possibility of service stations

overcharging to retrofit smog controls was real. There would be the cost of inspections and other factors. There were just too many new laws and too much interference, without enough preparatory study. For example, the NHTSA pushing for mandatory airbags as the passive restraint system of choice. At the time, many in the auto world felt better seatbelts were the answer. However, the politicians couldn't be stopped. There was even a proposed bill to get NASA involved, at taxpayer expense, to come up with cleaner, quieter and more economical engines.

A small example of the upshot of all this was the introduction of dual resonators on the 1974 Corvette; Zora Arkus Duntov and team tried to hush up their two-seater to meet tighter Golden State drive-by noise regulations. September 8 1974 was the date confirmed for Evel Knievel to jump Snake River Canyon in his Skycycle X-2. It seemed with all the proposed bills and experimentation, soon the whole nation would be composed of daredevils trying something risky at the behest of the Feds.

Meanwhile all the legislative changes were taking place during difficult economic times. Due largely to the fuel crisis-initiated recession, auto sales were down 24 per cent during the first half of 1974. 1973 had been a bumper sales year.

Apart from the fuel crisis, cost push inflation was exacerbated by the stricter government safety and smog laws. It was increasing the cost of car ownership to the point that a compact car in 1974 cost the same as a full-size sedan in 1970. Overall cost was pushing buyers towards smaller vehicles. Of course, imports were generally smaller and more economical. So, an indirect consequence of government action was the domestic automakers being placed at a competitive disadvantage. Apart from an eroded manufacturing base, national security was possibly compromised in subsequent years.

In April 1973, the EPA checked how ready the domestics were for 1975 smog law. GM was 93 per cent there, Ford lagged on 55 per cent, with AMC and International Harvester on 26 per cent. Chrysler Corp registered a big fat zero! It was no secret that, since 1968, much of Chrysler's cash had been taken up trying to meet federal smog and safety dictates. It hadn't come up with a commercially needed subcompact of its own. This was partly because it had given development money to the Plymouth Cricket captive import (Hillman Avenger). Also, Chrysler Corp thought small cars were a fad. Lastly, it started work on its own subcompact, but abandoned it. Lack of money was key.

Chrysler had enough problems at home, and overseas, without legislative burdens bestowed from Washington DC. The upshot was a 1979 Lee Iacocca makeover, involving closure of 13 plants, much unemployment and a $1.2 billion taxpayer funded bailout. By the late '70s, American Motors was also feeling the squeeze. The new age of functionalism predicted by its former chairman, George Romney, seemed to have only helped VW and the Japanese. AMC was caught between the Big Three and the imports. Instead of begging from the taxpayer, it merged with Renault in 1979. The largely government-owned French automaker wanted to make it big in America.

To prop up its entry partner, in the wake of the second fuel crisis-induced recession and falling Jeep sales, Renault took a 46 per cent stake in AMC in 1980. AMC owned AM General, a defense industry contractor majoring in the supply of tactical military vehicles. Soon AM General would supply the famous Humvee, but before this icon reached production, AMC sold AM General. It had to, following pressure from the government. Uncle Sam didn't like its defense contractor being owned by an automaker controlled by a foreign government. Plus, AMC needed the cash.

By the early '80s, domestic automaker survival was tough going. Their share of a shrinking market had declined to 72.2 per cent by 1982. Between 1970 and 1982, Japanese car companies had increased their stake from 3.7 per cent to 22.6 per cent.[15] Although not the sole reason for the decline in domestic market share, federal regulation had contributed to the weakened positions of Chrysler and AMC, with a negative impact on employment. At this time, Japanese cars sold in America were fully imported. So, greater sales of such imports led to fewer American jobs in US plants. The rougher conditions for making and selling cars Stateside, had even pushed AMC towards being foreign-owned, compromising its position as a defense contractor.

As the two biggest automakers in the world, GM and Ford could weather the 1970s storm. However, even their positions had been weakened. Consequences were set in motion, which have flowed on since 1975. Through the '80s there was a desire to move production to Mexico and utilize backdoor imports from low-cost producing nations. Remember the Pontiac Le Mans from South Korea?

By the 1990s, a great reliance on truck and SUV sales, combined with the aforementioned '80s gambit, maintained the bottom line. Since the '90s, there has been a move to relocate production to China. Indeed, under GM boss Mary Barra, there are more GM factories in China than America. It calls into question the value of the post-Global Financial Crisis GM taxpayer bailout, which was supposed to protect American jobs. The consequences of legislation and regulation, and the future scenarios they create, can be hard to foresee. However, ultimately one thing is certain: the public will pay.

CHAPTER
Five

On The Right Track – 2nd Gen Racing

Road course racing

The Camaro had been a 24-carat winner with Team Penske, but those guys had moved to American Motors for the 1970 season. There had been many rule changes for the 1970 SCCA Trans Am season. Cars couldn't use dual quads, and it was now possible to destroke a big motor under the 305in³ limit. It was getting the racers down to earth, so 1970 was like starting over. Certainly there was an all new GM F-body, joining an all new Chrysler E-body; the latter represented by the Barracuda and Challenger siblings. One thing that didn't change was the arm's-length relationship between the GM cars raced by private teams, and the factory.

So, this time Team Penske gave way to Team Chaparral when it came to campaigning the Camaro in Trans Am racing. It was the Texan outfit with the white cars, courtesy of Jim Hall and Ed Leslie. The Chaparral team was associated with Can Am racing, so the T/A series was a real change of pace: it was a more restrictive discipline. However, behind the scenes, the Titus/Godsall Firebird was getting Poncho engineer support, and the Chevrolet clan was helping, too.

The relationship and connection to the road cars was hinted at in Don Fuller's account of how the big 2nd gen Camaro rear spoiler came about, in the September 1975 issue of *Road Test*. It seems that one day prior to the 1970 Trans Am championship commencement, the Camaro and Firebird people encountered each other at GM's Black Lake proving grounds in Milford, Michigan. It was an area for handling evaluation. The Firebird folk were testing aero aids on the 2nd gen Firebird. Chevrolet's Jim Hall was amazed at the Firebird spoiler's king-size nature. At the time, the Chevrolet people had a '69 Penske Camaro at the proving grounds. They were still working with the old coupe and its small spoiler.

It transpired that the Pontiac styling department wanted the new rear spoiler's edges rounded off, which did look nice on production cars. Jim Hall found out that the Pontiac engineers wanted straight edges, both horizontally and vertically. At this time, all early spoiler production was allocated to Pontiac. This made it hard for Chevrolet to get spoilers early on.

It all explained the final form of that big Jim Hall Camaro rear spoiler, and why it took so long to homologate the item. In the end, it all seemed to have greater bearing on the 2nd gen Camaro's looks, than on its racetrack success. The front

The 1970 SCCA Trans Am season saw many rule changes, an all-new Camaro, and Jim Hall's Chaparral team handling matters. Unfortunately, major Camaro success wasn't forthcoming.
(Courtesy www.historictransam.com)

Frank Gardner's SCA sponsored 1970 ½ Camaro was powered by a ZL1 427 V8 in Group 2 sedan racing. It got him the 1973 British Saloon Car Championship. (Courtesy Castrol)

runners in the 1970 Trans Am series were Parnelli Jones in the Boss Mustang and Mark Donohue in the Javelin. The former won out in the end.

Jim Hall managed three fourth places at Lime Rock, Bridgehampton and Road America. Ed Leslie got pole position at Mid Ohio, and Vic Elford won at Watkins Glen! In the final analysis, Jim Hall and Team Chaparral probably found the move from Can Am racing too big. Even the Titus/Godsall Firebird Trans Am didn't do that well in 1970. Nor did the Mopar entries.

In racing, a proven package that works is essential. The GM and Mopar clans were starting from scratch in 1970, and that put them behind the eight ball. In any case, the Trans Am series imploded thereafter. The costs were too great for the manufacturers to get involved, arm's length or otherwise. Public attendances seemed to mirror pony car sales, with both cooling off some.

To find high level road course success with the 2nd gen Camaro, you had to try overseas. In

Britain, it was racer Frank Gardner using the Adrian Chambers SCA Freight-sponsored Camaro. The year was 1973, in the British Saloon Car Championship, with top contenders adhering to FIA Group 2 regulations. These permitted a fair amount of latitude and low homologation number. Gardner's Camaro was a 1970 ½ model with RS visage, with a ZL1 427 V8 under the hood, backed by a Holinger-modified Muncie gearbox. The power team came from the 1st gen Camaro winner, campaigned by Bob Jane in 1971's ATCC (Australian Touring Car Championship).

When the Australian authorities banned Jane's Camaro from using the ZL1, the 600 plus horsepower V8 and beefy gearbo x were sold to Gardner. In Britain, the SCA Camaro competed against Ford Capri RS2600s and the BMW CSL coupe of Brian Muir. Plus, there was defending champ Bill McGovern in his Hillman Imp. Muir had campaigned an ex-Penske '68 Camaro Z28 in 1970 and 1971, but now had the Batmobile. At the 1973 Silverstone meet, Muir's CSL beat out Gardner's Camaro to win. However, it was Gardner in his Camaro that got 6 wins and 66 points, to claim the championship.

The 1973 BSCC was a Chevrolet versus Ford battle of sorts. Second through fourth in the championship were taken by rear-drive European Ford Escorts. Under Group 2 regs, such Escorts and McGovern's Imp were pocket rockets. On tighter tracks, the smaller cars could pressure the brakes of the heavier, faster machines. Frank Gardner had come from open wheelers, and spoke on what it took to catch a tiger by its tail; or should that be a panther?! "The big cars, you'd hang on to them and hope that you didn't get them over the limit, because with any big car you get out of shape there's no chance rectifying the error. You'd be a passenger. It was a challenge to find some sort of balance." [16]

Up and coming Formula One star James Hunt certainly found balance in a Camaro. Driving the Hesketh Racing March 731/1, he came 6th in the 1973 French Grand Prix. However, he won that year's Avon Motor Tour of Britain in a Camaro Z28 RS. Sponsored by Avon Tyres, the tour took place from Bath to Bath. It was a new event for FIA Group 1 cars. There were factory-prepared and privateer cars, plus big names: Graham Hill, rally ace Roger Clark and Frank Gardner all participated. Cars included Alfa GTVs and Datsun Bluebirds, in a diverse field of production cars. The first event was held at Snetterton at night. It was the first nocturnal race in Britain in eight years.

In this 1973 Silverstone outing, Gardner's Camaro was in a three-way fight with the Ford Capri RS2600 and Brian Muir's BMW CSL. (Courtesy Ford UK)

Tony Lanfranchi's BMW 3.0Si leading James Hunt's Camaro Z28 at Oulton Park. However, Hunt was the overall winner of the 1973 Avon Motor Tour of Britain. (Courtesy *Motor Sport*)

James Hunt's Camaro Z28 lining up with Gordon Spice's Ford Capri at Snetterton for the start of the 1973 Avon Motor Tour of Britain. (Courtesy *Motor Sport*)

Lining up at Snetterton were the top contenders of Hunt in his #6 Camaro, and sedan car star Gordon Spice in the #3 Ford Capri. Hunt's drive in the A.J Rivers Racing Camaro was a last minute move – Richard Lloyd was injured, so James Hunt stepped into the coupe. The A.J. Rivers Racing Camaro wasn't known for its race reliability. However, this time was different, with the machine holding up. Hunt blasted into the lead, drove sensibly on the rally stages, and won overall. This was in spite of a broken gas pedal at Oulton Park, and other problems. Indeed, Tony Lanfranchi's BMW 3.0Si was leading Hunt and won, but was disqualified for being over the time limit on a road course section. Gordon Spice came second overall in the Capri, and rookie journalist Robert Fearnall successfully served as James Hunt's co-driver in the July 1973 event. [17]

From 1979 to 1983, a Camaro was also raced by Kevin Bartlett in the ATCC (Australian Touring Car Championship). Bartlett was an F5000 expert, whose career in that once popular discipline was coming to an end by the late '70s. Australian media mogul Kerry Packer suggested Bartlett should do touring car racing. Packer owned TV commercial network Channel 9, and would sponsor Kevin Bartlett's coupe. Kerry Packer also suggested Bartlett choose a slightly unusual car, rather than the local default Ford Australia or GM Australia (Holden) selections. This was so Packer wouldn't have to pay the Ford and GM subsidiaries any money!

That offbeat choice was the Chevrolet Camaro, a car not officially sold in Australia. Kevin Bartlett took the Camaro route, partly because it had

been homologated under FIA Group 1 rules, with some decent hardware. Secondly, being an F5000 specialist, he knew plenty about the Chevrolet small block, and the where and what to get concerning hotting up the 350 V8. He also had connections with Chevrolet Racing Division, and the skinny on chassis stress figures. The latter turned out to be promising for Australian racing. So, a new '79 Camaro was purchased from Unser Chevrolet of New Mexico.

The slight problem was that the Camaro was a Group 1 racer, and Australia worked under unique Group C rules, so adaptation was necessary. Stock weight was 1630kg, with Group C limited to 1442kg, meaning the Camaro had to visit Weight Watchers! Kevlar was used for the front and rear spoilers and fender flares. The standard coupe's

steel leaf springs were also swapped for fiberglass equivalents, weighing just 4.5kg. These originated from speedway racing, where Bartlett learnt less load capacity was required. In the end, the Channel 9 Camaro, nicknamed Ol' Blue, was only 15kg overweight.

Local racing authority CAMS did the Camaro a favor by insisting the coupe be backdated to 1974-77 styling. This substituted aluminum rather than steel bumpers, bringing a handy weight saving. That said, CAMS prevented Bartlett from using four-wheel disk brakes. This was probably because they had been homologated for the 1st gen Camaro, and only offered as a production option on that generation. This forced Bartlett to baby the brakes to survive races. Team Highball had a similar problem with its Group 1 AMC Spirit AMX V8 at the October 1979

Kevin Bartlett adapted a 1979 FIA Group 1 Camaro Z28 to Australian Group C racing. Sponsorship came from Kerry Packer's Channel 9.
(Courtesy *Street Machine*)

Nürburgring 24 Hour enduro. Once again, those rear drums could overheat.

The premiere sedan race in Australia was the Bathurst round, and Kevin Bartlett was unable to debut Ol' Blue there in 1979. He had sustained an injury in the final F5000 race of his career. This led to John McCormack and Bob Forbes racing the Channel 9 Camaro at Bathurst that year. Unfortunately, the coupe registered a DNF due to gearbox problems. Bartlett did achieve some wins during 1980, plus pole position at 1980's Bathurst. In qualifying, the Camaro reached 170mph on Conrod Straight, a Group C record at the time. However, the coupe just ran out of brakes and came 11th in the final reckoning. In 1981, the Channel 9 Camaro finally got to use four-wheel disk brakes. At that year's Bathurst, Bartlett got pole position once again. The Camaro 350 proved that it had speed, handling and now brakes. However, misfortune struck once again at Mount Panorama, when Bartlett's Camaro was involved in a multiple car crash.

Rolling into 1982, the Channel 9 Camaro was still a fast machine, except for lady luck going out to lunch one more time. Suspension failure in practice caused the coupe to hit a wall, but the car still got rebuilt, and managed to qualify fourth for what would be its final Bathurst. The Camaro was going very well, and Bartlett later said it was developing phenomenal grip through the corners. He had taken

advantage of rule changes to use 14in wide rims that did legally fit under the standard wheelarches and flares. To do this, he purchased a set of new rims. Unfortunately, on lap 27, the left rear wheel rim split! The tire on said rim immediately went flat, flipping the Camaro on its roof when cornering.

It all seemed to play into sponsor Kerry Packer's hands, because the Bathurst telecast aired on rival Channel 7. The repeated showing of footage of the Channel 9 Camaro flipping, with the Channel 9 logo in full view, would have irked Channel 7, but pleased Packer! Kevin Bartlett raced Ol' Blue a few times in 1983, but with Channel 9 sponsorship and Group C coming to an end, it was time to sell the Camaro and race something else. The Channel 9 Camaro has survived as an iconic import of Australian motorsport.

Cheverra – build your own racer!

In early 1975, *Road & Track*'s Tom Lankard noticed on a cross country drive that many were traveling in "open defiance" of the 55mph national speed limit. Perhaps because as a young Homer Simpson said, "People are going to be late!". Lankard felt it was unfortunate that more of the public hadn't written or called their political representatives in the House and Senate, to air their umbridge at the double nickel limit being extended beyond the emergency times of the fuel crisis. Temporary 50mph speed limits and been ended in West Germany and Britain, once the crisis was over. He also noted, the increasing interference of government in the automotive area. Something that would only get worse. [18]

1975 was the big year for the emissions clamp down, but there were a couple of areas Uncle Sam wasn't meddling in, handling and racing. As horsepower went down, interest in scooting around corners picked up. Plus, it was business as usual at the track. One fellow that could help Camaro owners in both areas, was Herb Adams. Adams had a long association with Pontiac. He had been involved with the engineering of the PFST (Pontiac Firebird Sprint Turismo), and was on the development team of the '69 Firebird Trans Am. Along with Skip McCully and Tom Nell, he had provided assistance to the 1970 Titus/Godsall Firebird Trans Am in the SCCA series. Adams was also part of Pontiac Special Projects, the outfit that turned the L75 455 into the Super Duty 455 V8. However, in 1973 Adams left Pontiac to start his own shop, VSE (Very Special Equipment).

VSE lived up to its name, providing parts and kits for improved handling and all-out racing. For the

To cut weight, the Channel 9 Camaro used kevlar spoilers and fender flares. NASCAR origin fiberglass leaf springs and pre '78 aluminum impact bumpers were also part of the Weight Watcher's tricks. (Courtesy *Street Machine*)

most part, limitations imposed by state and federal law meant such hardware had to be installed by the owner. It all overcame the economical, production car nature of the GM F-body, to reach an optimal end in handling and racing. This would have been commercially impossible with a volume-produced factory car. Herb Adams was a SCCA and IMSA road race veteran, so he knew how to achieve such goals.

Adams was also aware of the great interchangeability between the F-body siblings in basic engineering. For example, in SCCA Trans Am racing, many Firebirds were converted into Camaros. The 1971 BF Goodrich Tirebird became a similarly liveried Camaro, and was then purchased by Alfie Reys De Perez for the Mo Carter Camaro team's use between 1972 and 1975. So it was that VSE had a special Firebird package called Fire Am, and a related one for the Camaro known as Cheverra.

Kevin Bartlett used his F5000 racing experience, to get the right parts, and build up a mean 350 V8. (Courtesy *Street Machine*)

The title 'Cheverra' was a joke directed at all those Porsche Carreras that were dominating Trans Am racing by the mid '70s.

Mindful that enthusiast owners would want to daily drive their cars while modifying them, the work could be done in stages. There were copious instructions, that included money saving tips like

Nicknamed Ol' Blue, the Channel 9 Camaro never won Bathurst, but remains an iconic car of Australian sedan racing. (Courtesy *Street Machine*)

spring cutting. Central to Herb Adams' credo was a soft front end and use of an adjustable rear swaybar for fine tuning. Soft front springs, shocks and big front swaybar would prevent bump-steer, while maintaining a cornering line. For good weight distribution, the battery was placed in the right rear part of the trunk. Cheverra's three basic kits involved Street, Auto Cross and Racing.

Street brought a $1^5/_{16}$in front swaybar, plus spherical rod end links. To get the job done for minimal outlay, VSE worked with Appliance Wheel Company for a 15x8in zero offset steel rim set, wrapped in Goodyear GT radials. There were specific wheel alignment specs, a 1in rear swaybar and modified rear spring hangers. V braces tied the front subframe to the monocoque, and stock F-body mounting blocks were removed to lower the coupe one inch. A baffled oil pan and special oil pick-up warded off oil starvation in tight turns.

Auto Cross added brake cooling ducts for the front disks, and custom backing plates. There were cooling holes for the rear drums, plus metallic brake pads and linings. Adjustable shocks – a set of Konis early on – were employed, along with an engine oil cooler and remote filter kit for the wet sump.

Racing was extreme, with addition of solid suspension bushings, HD front hubs and spindles, plus HD Ford rear solid suspension bushings. Big 12in rotors and Hurst/Airheart 4 spot calipers were at all four corners, with a Doug Nash five-speed option and dry sump thrown in for good measure, not forgetting VSE's distinctive nosecone molding.

A built-up THM 400 autobox was often included. Higher front spring hanger location was key to VSE suspension geometry, for less roll oversteer and tail squat.

Stage 3 and VSE's wheelarch flare and fender kit allowed 10in wide rear rims and 1980 Goodyear Wingfoot tires. The higher spring hanger location and 255 section 15in rubber weren't possible on 1st gen F bodies, due to a lack of wheelwell room. California-based VSE had an association with Cars & Concepts Inc of Michigan, concerning race car builds. From 1980, C&C could fit VSE hardware on a turnkey car basis for the public. It informed buyers of the location of the nearest Chevrolet dealer from which the completed coupe could be picked up.

Whether VSE or C&C built a Cheverra, this was a tiny market. Not many Cheverras of any stage were created. Herb Adams built one 427 V8 automatic from a 1977 base car, to enter the 1981 Daytona 24-Hour race, "We set it up to do 180mph on the superspeedway." Yes, there were protests from worried rivals concerning the Cheverra's whale tail spoiler, among other mods. However, a blown tire early in the enduro put the coupe into a wall and out of the race. Post Daytona, it did some racing before being sold. In a way, the Cheverra's strength was its weakness. It was a heavy, modified production car going up against more specialized designs. This made the public identify with the coupe very well, but the excess weight contributed to the overheated tire blowing out.

Nowadays, Herb Adams runs his Passion Motorsports shop in Johnson City. He found the 1981 Daytona racer on eBay, and restored it with a bored-out 460 cube rat motor, Edelbrock pack of heads, cam, intake and carb, plus Borla side exhausts. A THM 400 and Ford 9in diff with 3.00 rear gears make this Cheverra a veritable weapon, "With the changes to it now, and the gearing, it'll probably do a little better than 180mph." No need to doubt Adams' word, and Passion Motorsports can still make and supply Cheverra parts. They still have that nosecone mold!

Camaro on the ovals!
It seemed the pony car equivalent of NASCAR's Grand National ranks was having the same problems as the SCCA's Trans Am series, with which it kind of competed. In the late '60s, NASCAR racing was seen as the sport of the '70s. Bigger attendances, improved facilities, safer racing, and more TV coverage. This held true for the 'big cars,'

The Cheverra was a track-oriented Camaro from Herb Adams' VSE (Very Special Equipment), California-based operation. VSE was associated with Cars & Concepts (C&C). C&C built up this originally '79 Camaro Z28 to Cheverra spec to enter the 1979 24 Hours of Daytona. (Courtesy www.route36.biz)

like Mark Donohue's Flying Brick. However, the junior series that utilized pony cars seemed to have reached its zenith in 1969. It had a name change from Grand Touring to Grand American in 1970, but the series still seemed to have redlined.

Event numbers fell from 35 in 1969, to 27 in 1970, seven in 1971 and just four in 1972. Sponsorship, race attendances and team participation were falling. Like the Trans Am series after 1970, there just wasn't the same money or interest in pony cars, either in the showroom or on the racetrack. So it was that in 1971 there were some invitations for Grand American pony cars to Grand National events that were short on entries.

As part of the major restructuring of NASCAR for 1972, Grand American and ex-Grand National/Winston Cup cars were eligible for the Grand National East Division. This involved smaller tracks with shorter races. Grand American cars had been up-gunned from an earlier 305in^3 limit to 366 cubes, in post 1969 times for better speed and durability. When invited to Grand National events, the pony cars seemed to like the flat tracks. As ever, Tiny Lund did well in Grand Touring/Grand American. Using a 1971 Camaro, he won the Buddy Shuman 276 and Wilkes 400. However, these races weren't counted as Grand National wins, in spite of the pony car invitation.

It took the International Race of Champions (IROC), to get the public interested again in seeing pony cars do speedway racing. This time it was just Camaros. The IROC series had started in 1974 as a best of the best invitational. The world's best

racing drivers took part in a four-race set, driving identical Porsche Carrera RSRs. Cars were shipped from the factory, with Porsche people looking after the cars. Mark Donohue won the final race of 1974's competition, held at Daytona. He took great satisfaction from the championship win, because the cars were identical. No unfair advantage required.

The IROC series was popular, and was broadcast between 1974 and 1980 as a delayed telecast on ABC's *Wide World of Sports*. However, the cost caused a switch to racing Chevrolet Camaros from 1975 to 1980. The racing also changed to an oval format. Originally created by Les Richter, Roger Penske and Mike Phelps, Penske and his organization oversaw the oval-racing Camaro changeover. As President of Penske Racing, Mark Donohue was in charge of a construction crew of 16, which built race-ready Camaros between July and September 1974. Who better than Penske and Donohue to be behind Camaros finely attuned to racing?

According to Donohue, these stock car Camaros were 70 per cent towards the full-on racing Camaros with which Team Penske dominated the SCCA's Trans Am series. Twenty engines came from Traco Engineering, and made a reliable 450 horses each. Roll cage, race seat/harness, full instrumentation, stiffer springs and shocks, plus Minilites were included.

The first 1975 season race took place at Michigan International Speedway, in September 1974. Fifteen coupes were created, for an international invitation list that included F1 stars

C&C fitted a rollcage, fire cutouts, race seat and harness, with this Cheverra featuring a THM 400. Unfortunately, the coupe didn't make the '79 Daytona 24 Hour starting grid. However, it *did* compete in Florida, Michigan and California. (Courtesy www.route36.biz)

With horsepower consigned to history by the EPA and CAFE, interest turned to handling. Herb Adams and Cheverra could help. (Courtesy Herb Adams)

Graham Hill, Ronnie Peterson, Emerson Fittipaldi and Jody Scheckter.

Peterson set the first pole position, only 0.5 seconds slower than the circuit's NASCAR record. Fittipaldi led the series going into the final round. James Hunt joined the IROC series for 1977, following his F1 championship win. However, he wasn't able to emulate his Camaro road racing triumph of 1973. It was generally the case in the IROC series that oval experience proved invaluable. Fortunately for IROC, the Camaro/oval racing format proved seriously popular.

The Riverside rounds of the 1975 IROC series coincided with, and overshadowed, the F5000 season finale. This was in spite of the title decider

Cheverra Big Block V8. Everything you always wanted, but the government wouldn't let you have. (Courtesy Herb Adams)

The Cheverra name was Herb Adams' good-natured take on all those Porsche Carreras dominating Trans Am racing by the mid '70s! (Courtesy Marc Cranswick)

That whale tail spoiler drew protests from race rivals as the Cheverra accelerated to 180mph! (Courtesy Round 2 Models round2corp.com)

involving such illuminaries as Mario Andretti, Brian Redman, James Hunt and Sam Posey. Nevertheless, the nation's attention was on those speedway Camaros. Was it any coincidence that pony car sales, largely involving the GM F-body, were picking up? Jackie Stewart did interview duties for the *Wide World of Sports* coverage of the IROC Riverside rounds. ABC only showed the IROC rounds, not the F5000 finale.

In any case, the IROC series was decided, once again, at Daytona. 1975 IROC champ was Bobby Unser, winning a prize of $30,000. The format was so successful in every way that Emerson Fittipaldi urged IROC organizers to dispatch six Camaros to

In 1975, the IROC (International Race Of Champions) series switched to Camaros. Bobby Unser was IROC champ in 1975, winning 30 grand! (Courtesy *Road & Track*)

Benny Parsons   Brian Redman   James Hunt   Emerson Fittipaldi   Richard Petty   Jody Scheckter   A. J. Foyt   Mario Andretti   Bobby Allison   Al Unser   David Pearson   Bobby Unser *(not shown)*

Gentlemen, start your Camaros.

The third annual International Race of Champions is on.

Once again, in four fascinating events spread widely across the country and the calendar, 12 of the world's winningest drivers are competing in 12 identical cars,

identically prepared. A true test of driving skill.

The cars are Camaros.

That should come as no great surprise. Camaro's aerodynamic shape makes it a natural for these events. The profile is low,

the stance is wide, the size is right—and the feel is terrific. Drivers enjoy driving Camaros, people enjoy watching them.

Camaro has been a particularly popular off-road competition car ever since it was first introduced about 10 years ago.

Chevrolet salutes the 12 distinguished drivers of the third International Race of Champions.

Gentlemen, start your Camaros.   *Chevrolet*

WATCH FOR THE INTERNATIONAL RACE OF CHAMPIONS ON THE ABC TELEVISION NETWORK.

James Hunt joined F1 champions for the 1977 IROC series. However, oval experience won out, with AJ Foyt winning back-to-back titles. (Courtesy GM Archives)

Europe for an equivalent series. 1976 and 1977 IROC titles went to AJ Foyt. Al Unser triumphed in 1978, with Mario Andretti and Bobby Allison claiming the 1979 and 1980 championships respectively. Naturally, Chevrolet used the IROC connection in Camaro ads. A road-going Camaro version would follow with the 3rd gen Camaro.

Roger Penske was very pleased with all this: "It's a big risk, larger than I would normally take in a business venture." Fortunately, it proved a winner for Penske and Chevrolet. Indeed, they were all driving Camaros! [19]

CHAPTER
Six
Surviving & Thriving (1975-81)

Spread your wings

1981 CAMARO Z28. THE HUGGER.

Chevrolet

Extinctus Ponyus?

In 1974, Lee Iacocca told *Fortune* magazine, that a guy wasn't going to buy a car anymore just because it had a long hood. He was posing with the new Ford Granada and Mercury Monarch compacts at the time. Well, it depended who was making the hoods. Between 1969 and 1977, 2,066,205 Monte Carlos were built. Historian Richard Langworth described the Monte Carlo as possessing the " ... longest hood ever bolted onto a Chevrolet." In the pre-downsized GM era of 1970-76, 2,389,860 Impalas were sold, and 932,759 upscale Caprices, Bel Airs and Biscaynes. Over 1974-1980 Chevrolet managed 718,290 Monza subcompacts. However, what of the pony cars? (20)

Motor Trend observed the pony car tale in May

1975, and felt the Mustang II saw Ford taking the Mustang back to its original concept, away from the bloated bolide it had become. Cougar joined Mustang I by becoming obese and traveling to luxo

Based on a 1975 Camaro Type LT, the Legion of Doom wrestling coupe received a complete rebuild. It was the prize at a motorcycle charity benefit.
(Courtesy Ufphen)

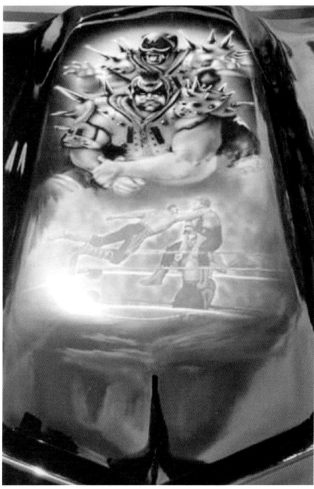

This is the commemorative 25th Anniversary Legion of Doom Camaro.
(Courtesy Ufphen)

land. The Barracuda and Challenger were exponents of the performance car image, only to decline when performance no longer sold. MT judged AMC Javelin as lacking identity and direction, before being supplanted by the new Pacer. The journal felt the GM F-body was still pricey, a pony land trait, but met a contemporary desire for cars of smaller size, improved handling, economy, but with a sporty style.

At Camp Chevrolet, choices went down as sales went up. Yes, the GM F-body was the right kind of car, but it does help when your Big Four rivals vacate the building. The 1975 Camaro started very humbly with the 105-horse six-cylinder Sport Coupe, with a one-barrel 250in³ inline engine. The Z28 was gone, but there were many noteworthy items and accommodations, explaining the sizable 145,770 Camaro total.

Aside from the aforementioned six, an L65 350 two-bbl V8 with 145bhp and 155 horse LM1 four-barrel 350 V8 seemed to provide enough thrust for the masses. In the September 1975 issue of *Road Test*, Don Fuller said Woodward Avenue had become a very quiet place. Any real racing had moved to the dragstrips. Plus, Camaro or Firebird, there was a company in Detroit that would drop a 454 with aluminum heads into your machine for two grand. This was around one half to two thirds a pony's price, and was for the fringe dwellers of 1975 society.

Chevrolet was doing some 1975 engine work,

The Legion of Doom Camaro build involved getting the small block V8 to a dyno-proven 500 ponies! GM's impact bumper expertise originated with early '70s New York taxi trials, as part of Corvette research. Note the new larger rear window of the '75 Camaro. (Courtesy Ufphen)

but not for enthusiasts. It billed its '75s in general as possessing 'Chevrolet's New Efficiency System' of HEI (High Energy Ignition), AIR (Air Injection Reactor) and catalytic converter. So, transistorized ignition, a smog pump and a cat were going to get one through the 1975 emissions apocalypse. Internally the engineer in charge of using cats to get GM emissions ready was nicknamed by colleagues as 'Captain Catalyst.' GM had decided, after earlier decrying the devices, that cats were the way to the future, and was telling everyone it was so.

At the time, enthusiasts knew a few ways around the two-way pellet cats, which had a propensity to burn out if a carb wasn't tuned just so. A hacksaw and hollow insert took care of that. Enterprising souls re-curved the distributor, and had an alternative re-jetted four-barrel Q jet, for outside of smog testing. Milling the heads raised the compression ratio, and was okay on a 49-state basis. It was all a way to reclaim some horsepower and a little liberty. For all 1975 GM F bodies, the coming of a catalytic converter meant a raised floorpan

stamping on the passenger side, to clear said cat. The cat implied no more THM 400, just the THM 350 due to space constraints.

On the comfort, convenience and appearance front, the '75 Camaro was an Alladin's cave, or plush bordello, depending upon your optioning. Power door locks were a new option, so too cruise control, and you could now select a/c on the humble Camaro six. This was in keeping with an international trend towards plusher small cars. They were more frugal, to steer the public through the fuel crisis and past inflation. Deep pile carpet was new, and Birdseye Maple replaced Meridian Walnut interior trim on Camaro Type LT. To slow your pleasure palace, all Camaros now featured finned rear drums.

It was possible to option a four-speed, but just with the top LM1 350 V8. This implied a wide ratio M20 with 10.34in clutch. Showing priorities of the day, 39,843 Camaros were specified with the FE8 radial tuned suspension, which cost $35. Radials had gained a reputation as providing better ride

This 1975 Camaro Sport Coupe included the 145bhp two-barrel 350 V8. It was still peppy, in spite of the forced '75 MY adoption of a catalytic converter. (Courtesy Dusty Old Cars)

116,021 of the 145,770 1975 Camaros sold had V8s. It was a sign of personal car buyers downsizing from the intermediate coupe class. (Courtesy Dusty Old Cars)

All '75 Camaros came with GM's electronic HEI ignition, and a/c was a first-time option on six-cylinder coupes. (Courtesy Dusty Old Cars)

You could specify the top 155bhp LM1 350 four-bbl V8 on any '75 Camaro. The FE8 radial-tuned suspension cost $35, and was fitted to 12,201 cars. (Courtesy Dusty Old Cars)

comfort, improved handling and longer tire life. The last factor loomed large in many buyers' minds. A paltry 422 Camaros carried the F41 handling pack suspension. If you build it, will they option it?! It seemed that, to many, radials meant more about comfort and tire mileage than handling.

There were still a few options available, that allowed enthusiasts to tailor order their Camaro, in the style of Z28s of yore. There was 1975's Z08 Sports Décor option of color-keyed mirrors, inserts on door handles, with appliqué on lower front

and rear bumpers. This was available on any '75 Camaro, with Z08 being superseded mid model year by the returning RS sports appearance pack. This now entailed low gloss black paint on hood, header panel, grille headlamp bezels, fender tops, front roof section, upper part of doors, rear fascia and license plate aperture. An RS tri-color decal existed on fenders and the rear deck lid.

The reinstituted RS pack (Z85) didn't have the

custom bumperless nosecone section of earlier times, and you couldn't get RS with a vinyl roof. To add substance underfoot, the 1975 Z86 Gymkhana Suspension paralleled the contemporary Gymkhana C3 Corvette option, and went beyond FE8 and F41. It consisted of 15x7in rims with bright lugnuts, special center caps/trim rings, white letter E60-15s of a bias-belted nature, special big front and rear swaybars, shocks and steering gear. One could only option Z86, on V8 cars.

The Z08 or Z85 packs when combined with the LM1 350 four-bbl V8, four-speed and Z86 suspension, was a 1975 Camaro Z28in all but RPO code. However, records indicate one genuine 1975 Camaro Z28 was indeed manufactured. What happened to this coupe is uncertain. Some feel it was scrapped and never left GM. Others believe it might have gone to a GM executive as personal transport. Either way, it never went direct to any Chevrolet dealer for sale to the public. Sporty fantasies aside, the key focus of the hour was the downsized luxury coupe called Camaro Type LT. So, that's what *Motor Trend* tested in May 1975. The journal faced off the Type LT, with 8.5:1 top choice LM1 350 V8, standard Camaro suspension, FR78-14s and a/c, against its sibling, or nemesis, a 1975 Pontiac Trans Am automatic with L78 7.6:1 400 V8 and a/c.

These two versions of the GM F-body were seen as the ultimate 1975 examples of the Camaro and Firebird. They reflected their respective companies' brand positions at the time. For Chevrolet, it was middle of the road comfort at any speed, except for Corvette. With PMD, it was performance all the way. The Trans Am was a demon smooth road handler, with no seatback rake adjustment. Camaro Type LT had two-position rake adjustment, for its cloth/velour buckets. The Camaro nearly matched the Trans Am's acceleration, bettered it in fresh air ventilation, and brought more comfort in the ride/handling compromise. However, it did lack the Trans Am's GR70-15 gumballs.

This is a 1975 Camaro Rally Sport. The Z85 RS package returned in mid '75 MY, replacing the Z08 Sports Décor pack. (Courtesy Kevin LeBonte)

No special RS nosecone this time around. However, low gloss black paint did overlay a trim package with tricolor RS decals.
In the absence of the Z28, the Camaro RS was the sportiest Camaro going in 1975 and 1976.
(Courtesy Kevin LeBonte)

Both cars had effective a/c and cold running stumble at low rpm typical of the smog era ... plus radials! They were also expensive, at nearly 6 grand. Even bigger was rearward visibility, because of the 1975 GM F-body's adoption of a wraparound rear window. Basic stats put the LM1-powered Type LT on 155bhp at 3800rpm, with a handy 250lb/ft at 2400rpm. The power steering offered 2.4 turns lock-to-lock. There was a 21-gallon tank for "unleaded gas only," as we soon got used to reading on gas gauges and filler flaps. Front and rear track were a respective 61.6 and 60.3in, with vehicular weight a lofty 3755lb. Man, those options were heavy! Automatic ratios were 2.52, 1.52 and 1.00:1 for a direct top, combined with a 3.08:1 final drive.

Camaro Z28 or no, Camaro sales soared to 182,959 units in 1976. 38,047 buyers selected a six in Bicentennial year. The 105bhp 250in³ six continued, and next up was an econoeight with two-barrel carb and 305 cubes. It made 140 horse. This V8 newbie would be a F-body mainstay through '92 model year. The top dog LM1 350 V8 was upgunned to 165bhp.

The '76 Camaros featured standard power brakes, bigger brake wheel cylinders and improved brake drum linings. Camaro Type LT had a brushed aluminum trunk trim panel, a new Landau roof option that stole Monte Carlo's thunder, plus a new style seat. The plush pew featured squared-off head restraints and new sew lines.

Even 20 years after the first 'Hot One,' Chevrolet's lightweight small block showed reasonable economy during the gas crunch.
Beyond F41, 1975's Gymkhana option provided suspension and tires akin to previous Z28s. Perfect to complement a Camaro RS with the top LM1 V8.
(Courtesy Kevin LeBonte)

With a hot seller you can afford to introduce new stuff. Type LT even had a new faux tan leather trimmed instrument cluster. Optional instrumentation saw an honest to goodness voltmeter that deep sixed the previous idiot light. Still no 70 series tire, nor genuine leather upholstery, but with the finest, glove-soft vinyl to hand … who cares?!

Only the LM1 V8 could have a four-speed, and 56,710 buyers chose this 165 pony, 350 V8 with the 85 buck surcharge. Four-speed devotees numbered 11,396, and paid $242 for the privilege. More popular was the $260 THM 350 automatic, with 160,145 takers. However, the real show was provided by white interior cars, which could have the instrument panel, carpet, cowl kick and rear package shelf in black, blue, green or Firethorn. Little wonder that, in this era, the 3.08 rear end was the 'performance axle'! Next to the 2.73 turnpike

snoozer, it was. However, more worrying was the drop in GM quality.

As recently as the July '74 issue of *Cars*, Joe Oldham mentioned a new Nova SS350, one that typified the quality, materials and workmanship GM was known for. That said, the aforementioned *Motor Trend* May '75 Camaro Type LT vs Trans Am encounter revealed noticeable shortfalls in assembly quality: a poorly put together lower dashboard and glovebox, suspect fit and finish, plus lowball ashtray. A case of a designer supposes, and the UAW disposes? *Motor Trend* suggested buyers give their purchase a good once-over prior to accepting delivery. At this stage quality snafus were visible,

By the mid '70s, Camaro and Firebird were looking very similar, although different V8s and model versions kept them distinct. In 1975-76 PMD continued with the sporty angle relative to Chevrolet. (Courtesy GM Archives)

and relatively easy to fix by an accommodating dealer. However, by 1977 more American cars were recalled than made.

Camaro behind the scenes

By the mid '70s, the GM F-body was a more refined version of the successful coupe first seen in 1970. Front- engined, rear-drive and often V8-powered, they were a familiar sight and a known quantity. However, in 1975, work began on the 3rd gen F-body, and many avenues were considered. That said, the project was soon suspended. As mentioned by designer John Schinella, priority was given to the GM J car, and other pending projects tied to GM's economic survival. Schinella said the staff were in need of inputs concerning weight, size and cost, before the 3rd gen F-body's work could procede.

In the wake of the fuel crisis the Chevette,

This is a 1976 Camaro Sport Coupe with some options. By now Camaro sales were taking off to the tune of 182,959 model year units. (Courtesy Cotton Warehouse Classic Cars)

1976 saw the economy-oriented 140-horse 305 two-bbl V8 debut in the Camaro. This Sport Coupe has the optional C60 factory a/c.
Compared to pre '73 Camaros, the console slap shifter was more user-friendly. However, from 1975 onwards it worked a THM 350 due to space constraints caused by the catalytic converter.
(Courtesy Cotton Warehouse Classic Cars)

downsizing and fuel efficient front-drive cars for the '80s were considered top priorities by GM. The existing 2nd gen F-body and C3 Corvette were traditional cars selling better than ever. So, they would be the final model ranges to get downsized, in 1982 and 1983 respectively. In 1975 Tom Zimmer, chief engineer for Chevrolet B and F-body cars, considered a front-drive Camaro. Chevrolet was doing the front-drive GM J car, and the X car would be front-drive also. In addition, it had purchased a VW Scirocco for evaluation. The new Scirocco had garnered a lot of interest and sales, as a front-drive sporty car.

It was thought a front wheel drive GM F-body, would be a transitional design, moving to the ultimate goal of a mid engined machine. The Fiat X1/9 and Lancia Scorpion were big news at the time. A 2+2 mid engined 3rd gen Camaro and Firebird were certainly looked at closely, at least on a theoretical level. However, Pontiac chief engineer Bob Dorn felt a certain kind of handling, allied to V8 performance, made rear wheel drive essential. Tom Zimmer said by early 1978 that Pontiac had convinced GM brass to stay rear-drive with Camaro and Firebird. That said, the idea of a transaxle, like the Porsche 924/928, was dismissed due to flexible driveshaft problems experienced by the '61 Tempest. That was the last time GM had tried a transaxle.

Even though the 2nd gen Camaro and Firebird

look similar overall, and shared basic chassis and inner body panels, much varied between the two. Doors and body sides were distinct, and there

You are looking at one of the few creatures that can comfortably sit in the back of a GM F body! (Courtesy Cotton Warehouse Classic Cars)

When a car makes you feel good about its looks, that's styling.

When a car makes you feel good about yourself, that's character.

1976 Monte Carlo. Your next look should be at its very affordable price.

Chevrolet

Pony cars like the Camaro were proving popular downsized alternatives to personal sport luxury coupes like this '76 Monte Carlo. (Courtesy GM Archives)

was only 25 per cent parts interchangeability. For commercial viability, it was planned that stat would rise to at least 65 per cent with the 3rd gen F-body. Well, in spite of all of the above blue sky thinking, the 1977 Camaro and Corvette, largely represented business as usual. Sport Coupe, Type LT and Camaro RS: you knew and liked 'em well. However, the range now offered the option of intermittent windshield wiper operation, and the Type LT's base motor was downsized to the 250in³ I6. That said, the 305in³ V8 entry point was now 5 horses stronger at 145bhp. Styling was mostly that from 1974, but front bumperettes were now optional on 49-state Type LTs, and mandatory on all Golden State Camaros.

Camaro sales in 1977 increased to a lofty 218,853, and Camaro had finally toppled Mustang from its position as the number one selling pony. Chevrolet's print ads said: "We're Looking For People Who Love To Drive." With all the cumulative improvements and refinements the GM F-body had amassed, these were coupes for the enthusiast, and those looking for good value in inflationary times. The Sport Coupe came in at $4113.45, with Type LT on $4478.45 and the RS package costing $281. 17,026 buyers chose the Z85 RS pack. You could combine RS with Type LT, and the RS package itself entailed: D35 dual sport mirrors, bright edge headlamp bezels, and 14x7in Argent Rally rims that came with FR78-14 blackwalls. Recommended RS options were a D80 spoiler set, Z21 Style Trim Group and QDW white stripe or QBT white letter FR78-14s.

Camaro RS offered nine color choices, with its tricolor striping color matched to suit. Upper body RS colors were Medium Gray Metallic, Low Gloss Black, Dark Blue and Buckskin Metallic. A four-barrel LM1 350 V8 was available. This unit produced 160bhp at 3800rpm and 260lb/ft at 2400rpm in California. 49-state coupes bumped these stats to a respective 170bhp and 270lb/ft. Sport Coupe, Type LT and Camaro RS could all have the LM1 350 V8. The motor came with a three-speed manual, but a four-speed Saginaw box was an option. Four-speed clutch diameter was 10.34 in, and you couldn't get a stick in California! All LM1 V8s had 8.5:1 CR.

Camaro Z28 - the legend returns
The early 1970s Pontiac Trans Am represented the second coming of the American performance car. First time around the public were barraged with many expensive hardware homologation options,

This is a 1977 Camaro Type LT 305. That year, Camaro sales increased yet again to 218,853. (Courtesy www.2040-cars.com)

for racing that they increasingly didn't attend. Then there was insurance. It was all just too much for the average buyer. Then along came the Firebird Trans Am. It brought a blend of visual excitement, nice V8 sounds and luxury. The public thought this was mighty swell, and, by 1976, one half of all Firebirds sold were Trans Ams. They weren't cheap cars, so the manufacturer, dealers and public were all happy.

Great car, great sales and good business, the Trans Am sparked imitators. The 1976 Mustang II Cobra II, 1976 Dodge Aspen R/T and Plymouth Volare Road Runner, not to mention the Hornet-based 1977 AMC AMX. Yes, it was an opportunity to dust off some hallowed names from the past. So why not Camaro Z28? The 1977 $1/2$ Camaro Z28 made its debut at the Daytona Speedway in February 1977, cost $5170.06 and sold 14,349 units. For all that, the new Zee was different in detail compared to previous editions. The Camaro Z28 had commenced as a late 1967 option code for the hi-po 302 V8, and the coupe always had a special V8. Now, Z28 stood

for a custom suspension appearance package, which employed a warmed-up LM1 350 V8.

The new Z28's LM1 V8 made 185 net ponies at

You couldn't option a four-speed with the L22 250ci six, nor this LG3 305 V8. They were limited to the three-speed manual or THM 350 automatic. (Courtesy www.2040-cars.com)

Intermittent wipers were something new for '77 Camaros. However, that curved command center dash had been a mainstay since the '70 ½ MY. (Courtesy www.2040-cars.com)

4 grand, and 280lb/ft on an unleaded gas friendly 8.5:1 CR. Yes, this motor only had two-bolt mains and a cast-iron crank, but there were good things around. The cam possessed 280 degrees on intake and 288 degrees on the exhaust side, with 58 degrees of valve overlap. There was 0.410in of lift, and an increased diameter a/c pulley, plus a free flow exhaust system; specifically, a single cat, no mufflers and a dual layout into two resonators. It all ended in dual tailpipes. Cost prevented usage of the Nova cop car's dual cats.

The four-speed was the real deal. As with the 1974 Camaro Z28, the BW Super T10 with HD 11in clutch was back, along with 3.73 rear gears. Now, 1st was a 2.64:1 ratio, helping to get 3828lb of coupe moving. The automatic was special, too, with higher shift points than other THM 350s. The change from 1st to 2nd occurred at 4900rpm, and from 2nd to 3rd at 4700rpm. As per 1974, the Z28 automatic had a 3.42 rear axle. This all suited the hydraulic lifter 350 with Rochester Q-jet, which redlined at 5 grand. Positraction cost $54, and 18,095 '77 Camaro buyers added it.

In spite of all of the above, the '77 ½ Camaro Z28's focus was handling. The Z28 had always been a handler, but, times being what they were, handling

If it wasn't for strike action the Camaro would have overtaken Mustang in sales, but in 1977 it finally did happen. (Courtesy www.2040-cars.com)

now took center stage. Indeed, this was the first *Zee* setup for radials. Front spring rates rose from the 1974 Z28's 300lb-in to 365lb-in, and rearward leafs lifted from 89-99lb-in to 127lb-in. The 1974 Camaro Z28 had respective front and rear swaybars of 1in and 0.69in diameter. These measurements now changed to 1.2in front and 0.55in rearwards. There were higher durometer-measured rear shackle rubber bushings, revised rear shackles and revalved shocks. Brakes were the same as in 1974, but steering was faster. There was now a straight ratio of 13.02:1, not 1974's 14.3:1

Wheels were the familiar Z28 stamped steel 15x7in rims, but were now color-keyed and wrapped in Goodyear GR70-15 steel belted radials. The 1977 $^1/_2$ Camaro was available in seven colors, and, befitting the appearance package aspect, had several distinguishing points. There was a multi-colored hoodspear decal, with small 'Z28' decal callouts under the Camaro script on the front fenders and behind the wheelarch. In addition, the D80 spoiler package, inserts for wheelarches/rocker panels/door handles, joined color-keyed impact bumpers. Headlight/tail-light bezels and window trim were in anodized black, plus the rear trunk panel, rocker panel and parking light recesses were blacked out.

Inside, it was standard U14 instrumentation pack and dull finish Vega four-spoke tiller. *Car and Driver* made use of both, as its new-age '77 $^1/_2$ Z28 four-speed hit 60 in 8.6 seconds, and moved onto a 111mph top speed. The latter was achieved by revving beyond the redline, to 5250rpm. First proved good for 40mph, second took one to 60mph and third allowed 79mph to arrive. The four-speed's reverse was now left and down, not far left and up like before. The important $^1/_4$ mile came up in 16.3 seconds at 83.1mph. Gas mileage was between 14.5mpg city and 17mpg highway.

C/D's April '77 report on the 'new' Z28, and W72 400 Trans Am, uncovered the genesis and thinking behind these new-age American GT cars. Head engineer of the returning Z28 was Chevrolet's Jack Turner. He was a chief force behind the F41 suspension option, available on contemporary B-body cars. Turner could make big cars handle, like you thought they couldn't. He explained and demonstrated the Z28 at GM's Mesa Arizona proving grounds. He said they had purchased a Porsche 924 for early Z28 development, and felt the Z28 had the right stuff: "We think this is a pretty special machine," and against the 924 "... I think this machine will run right with it." Jack Turner spoke of the Camaro Z28's

There was no stick shift on Golden State '77 Camaros, but that didn't limit sales. Camaro had the sports/luxo combo the public desired. (Courtesy www.2040-cars.com)

Shoulder portion seatbelt mounting was always a visually-challenging issue on coupes, but color-matched belts could help. (Courtesy www.2040-cars.com)

great linear stability, and good transitions during lane changing and hard cornering. "I've worked with computers and they'll only take you so far." Handling had meant a big baseball bat of a front swaybar and understeer, but Turner liked to feel both ends of the car working, and the '77 $^1/_2$ Z28 delivered on the promise.

Concerning the Z28's shortcomings, like the Vega steering wheel and lack of reclining seats, Jack Turner said: "Don't forget, we're not finished." He promised the 1978 Camaro Z28 would have it all. It sounded similar to what Corvette chief Dave McLellan said about the 1984 Corvette. That is, it's a work in progress, and the good stuff will be on the way soon. In the case of the '77 $^1/_2$ Camaro Z28, omissions were minor. The coupe was virtually

Space savers could boost trunk capacity from 6.6 to 7.3 cubic feet, making them a necessary evil. From 1976, the Type LT had featured a rear brushed aluminum trunk beauty panel. (Courtesy www.2040-cars.com)

there, and 1978 would indeed seal the deal. However, GM seemed to be getting into a pattern, like Jaguar before it. Release first, correct later wasn't going to fly when the foreign competition got it right on the first attempt. Cadillac Allante and Cimarron, plus Pontiac Fiero, needed to get where they were going, sooner. Back in 1977, Tom Zimmer was Camaro chief engineer.

Jack Turner's Porsche 924 comparisons also showed the new trend of benchmark name-dropping. In earlier times, ads would line up an upscale big buck car alongside the promoted hopeful. In AMC's

1967 case, it was its Ambassador with the Rolls-Royce Silver Shadow! Both were the same color in the ad, and mention was made of standard V8 power and a/c included. It was remarked how the Ambassador had an inch more legroom here, and an inch more headroom there. In the end, the idea was to show prospects: "Gee, if it's that good against the finest car in the world, just imagine what it's like compared to Galaxie and Impala?! Well, by the late '70s the consumer was a little too smart for that ol' shell game. So, they handed the spiel to the one guy the public still trusted: the engineer.

The returning Camaro Z28 was one of the quickest cars around in North America, regardless of price. *Car and Driver* tried two other four-speed cars at this time: the $5456 Firebird Trans Am W72 400 and $9187 BMW 530i. Their 0-60mph, $1/4$ mile and top speeds came to a respective 9.3 seconds, 16.9 seconds at 82mph, and 110mph; and 8.7 seconds,

In response to the fuel crisis GM, which had the worst fleet average of the Big 3 at 12mpg, launched the first of its downsized lines as the 1977 fullsize, six-seater family cars. GM had invested a great deal of time and money in the process. The commercially successful result put the heat on Ford and Chrysler, but the new cars lacked the charm and big V8s of their predecessors. (Courtesy GM Archives)

17 seconds at 82mph, and 115mph. Final drive ratios and fuel economy of these two cars came in at a respective 3.23:1, 12.5mpg city/15mpg highway; and 3.64:1, 16.5mpg city/19.5mpg highway. Full throttle decibel readings for Z28, Trans Am and BMW were a respective 78, 80 and 84dBA. Unlike the GM F-body coupes, the BMW was using cheaper leaded regular. The 360 V8-powered Mopar compacts could match the scat of this crowd, and for 1976-77 ... that's all folks! There were no other choices, unless you spent a lot more money, went gray market, or to a specialist like DKM for something that might be 49-state legal. Either way, it was going to cost you.

At this hour, outputs were generally around 180-200 horse at best. BMW and Porsche 3-liter six-cylinders were on a respective 176 and 172 SAE net bhp. Camaro Z28 and base Trans Am 400 punched

It's back! The Camaro Z28 returned as a mid '77 MY entry. No longer an RPO but a specific model in its own right. (Courtesy Richard Budman www.FlemingsUltimateGarage.com)

Now, the Z28 was a handling & appearance special in the mold of contemporary fun to drive, sporty, luxo coupes like Trans Am, Mustang II, Cobra II and Hornet AMX. (Courtesy Richard Budman www.FlemingsUltimateGarage.com)

a respective 185 and 180 horses. The Mercedes 4.5-liter V8 and Corvette L82 350 were on 180 and 205bhp, respectively. More performance saw the Corvette L82 350 do 0-60mph in 7.5 seconds. The Porsche 911SC and Ferrari 308 GTB/GTS sat on

Not a custom job like the previous LT1 and L82 350 V8 Z28 mills, but the 1977 Zee's LM1 was tweaked to 185bhp and 280lb/ft. That was five horses more than Mercedes' most powerful US spec V8 of the day. (Courtesy Richard Budman www. FlemingsUltimateGarage.com)

high sixes. The Jag XJS V12 could accelerate no faster than the Camaro Z28, but could reach nearly 140mph. The fastest car sold in North America was the very expensive, rare and lag prone Porsche 930. Detoxed for smog, 0-60mph was in the low sixes, with a 145mph top end if you could find somewhere to do it. Ralph Nader and his fellow wowser pals wouldn't be your friends if you did ... good!

1978 – the Camaro gets new duds

The 1978 TV commercial said it all – "Chevrolet Camaro – the driver's car." The four coupe range was introduced as Sport Coupe, Type LT, RS with aggressive exterior and legendary Z28. The voiceover said that the Camaro Z28, with its ride and handling components, represented the ultimate Camaro, and "All at a very appealing price." That price was $5603.85. Mention was made of the

Camaro RS' Corvette-style front end and energy absorbing quality. New cast alloy aluminum rims in six matching body colors, the option of removable T-tops, power door locks, power windows and tilt steering wheel ... Camaro had it all on that options list!

Most noticeable were the restyled, color-matched, urethane front and rear fascias. This look had been intended for a '76 MY debut, but production delays spoilt the plan. On a Camaro Z28, the dimension differences – 1977 versus 1978 – were a respective 195.4in/74.4in/49.2in and 197in/74.4in/49.2in for length, width and height. The new bumpers could take more than 5mph taps. The restyle proved very popular, to the tune of 272,631 1978 Camaro sales. Camaro Z28 exploded to 54,907 units. It was the performance car people wanted.

The 1978 Camaro Z28 featured a decorative, Stinger-style faux hood scoop, and functional fender vents. Camaro front fenders had to be redesigned to accommodate the '78 front fascia. 1978 also saw front suspension lower control arm bracing, for chassis stiffness, and reinforced leaf spring shackles. The ad line was now: "His Majesty. The Camaro Z28." And Z28 got an exclusive no. 34 Yellow-Orange color scheme, which was applied to just 2311 coupes. The simulated rope steering wheel was also just for the Zee.

Car and Driver reported on the exalted Camaro Z28 in its March 1978 issue. It discovered the 3560lb four-speed Z28 capable of 0-60mph in 7.3 seconds, 0-100mph in 20.4 seconds, with a 16 second ¼ mile at 91.1mph, and 123mph top speed – this despite a lower 8.2:1 compression ratio. It

could stop from 70mph in only 181ft, idle at 53dBA, record 77dBA at full throttle and get 14.5mpg city and 16mpg highway. Was this enough? President Jimmy Carter thought it wasn't, and he thought you should share his viewpoint. So, the government was going to force automakers to get economical, while at the same time getting them to comply with smog and safety laws. CAFE (Corporate Average Fuel Economy) was to be balanced at 18mpg for 1978, rising to 27.5mpg for 1985, whereupon nirvana would be reached.

If a car didn't meet 18mpg, the buyer would pay a levy for their wanton desires. That is, a gas guzzler tax. However, the chief motivation was an improved national balance of trade, and conservation of finite natural resources. Raising taxation revenue was merely incidental said the government. To comply, there was taller gearing for all, bar the Z28. As *Autocar* magazine stated in its February 25 1978 issue, muscle cars were anathema to Jimmy Carter. However, there were many bright things about the 1978 Camaro, and not solely Z28-related. Removable, Fisher Body-type smoked glass T-tops, coded CC1, were a Trans Am-influenced first time option. LG3 305-powered Camaros gained a standard four-speed. The brake pressure switch was changed to rust-proof nylon, rather than steel, and the RS pack was now a distinct model, not an RPO code. Camaro RS presently possessed D35 sport mirrors, a D80 rear spoiler and ZJ7 Rally rims as standard equipment. Type LT also came with such mirrors and wheels in stock form. In fact, in 1978 only 5696 buyers combined Camaro Type LT with RS.

In 1979, records were set with 282,571 Camaro

Order a Camaro Z28 with four-speed and hold the options. It was a recipe for a relatively light V8 coupe, reminiscent of the good ol' days. (Courtesy Richard Budman www.FlemingsUltimateGarage.com)

The familiar BW Super T10 worked an 11in HD clutch. The four-speed was connected to 3.73 rear gears also. This was all past Z28 practise. (Courtesy Richard Budman www.FlemingsUltimateGarage.com)

The 1977 ½ Camaro Z28 was more than a handling/appearance pack and 185 ponies. It was an automotive enthusiast oasis in an increasingly econobox dominated desert. (Courtesy Richard Budman www.FlemingsUltimateGarage.com)

Since 1974, GM F bodies offered square bumperettes. They looked nice, and warded off the 'park by ear' crowd. You know who you are! (Courtesy Kevin LeBonte)

sales, 84,877 Z28s: 117,108 Trans Ams and 53,807 Corvettes. Big numbers for what were often pricey cars. It was all very profitable for GM, and these cars needed downsizing?! In some respects, the commercial success of such late '70s V8 coupes, was emulated by GM's SUV and truck sales in the 1990s. They were, as the expression goes, cash

cows, or the gifts that kept on giving. The sales achieved in 1979 by Camaro, Camaro Z28, Trans Am and Corvette have never been surpassed.

In many ways, buyers bought such cars due to a question of value. In April 1980, *Motor Trend*'s Fred Stafford wrote a report on the new Porsche 924 Turbo titled "The high price of performance." *Motor Trend's* 1979 0-60mph figures for the GM trio of Camaro Z28, Trans Am W72 400 and L82 Corvette were a respective 7.4, 6.7 and 6.5 seconds. The 1980 BMW 528i and Porsche 924 Turbo that *Motor Trend* tested did a respective 7.9 and 9.3 seconds. The BMW was around the same price as the Corvette, but the Porsche cost 10 grand more! The Stuttgart machine also had the dubious honor of being the slowest car in a group predicated on sporty performance.

Motor Trend said the Datsun 280ZX and Mazda RX7 cost around the same as the Z28 and T/A, but were a second tardier than even the Porsche.

1977 Camaro advertising declared, "We're Looking For People Who Love To Drive." 218,853 heeded the call. (Courtesy Kevin LeBonte)

For 1978, the Camaro received its final 2nd gen restyle. It should have happened in 1976 if not for production delays. (Courtesy Marty Tew & CARtoons)

For Datsuns, Mazdas and Porsches that could boogie with this crowd, it required the 280ZX Turbo, 13B-powered RX7 and Porsche 911SC, all of which cost much more. However, it should be noted that emissions law and CAFE were stricter for 1980, so the Trans Am and Corvette weren't quite the coupes *Motor Trend* had tested in 1979. However, the Camaro Z28 picked up 15 horses for

Color-keyed impact bumpers concealed steel bars, not the aluminum of 1974-76 Camaro. Camaro's bumpers now exceeded the fed's 5mph requirement. (Courtesy www.grautogallery.com)

1980! The 1979 Z28 had been smogged down to 175bhp at 4 grand, with Californian coupes on just 170 ponies. Not that it really bothered buyers, and the cars moved better than mere stats intimated, due to excellent 350 V8 torque. The torque in question for 49-state and Golden State 1979 Z28s were a respective 270lb/ft and 265lb/ft at a mere 2400rpm.

On a cheerier note, the Z28 had received a new three-piece, wraparound front spoiler, standard J50 $76 power front disks, T/A-like fender flares and revised decals on front fenders and lower door sides. It all cost $6115.35, and 81,395 buyers paid extra for the metric footprint QGR P225/70-15s, as opposed to the 3482 souls that accepted the stock QRZ GR70-15s. Suspension and steering on the Z28 were the same as in 1977. The latest ad proclaimed "1979 Z28 Camaro. From people who know what performance is all about." Not forgetting the old tagline "Camaro The Hugger," because it still was!

Compared to the cryptic symbols and unusual controls on imports, the GM F-body's HVAC panel was intuitive. (Courtesy www.grautogallery.com)

127,171 Camaro buyers took the $99 C49 electric defogger. This was new. Previously, owners had to rely on recirculated blower air. 38,604 chose the Eaton made G80 lsd, costing $64. However, the big news in 1979 was the Camaro Berlinetta. Indicated on the VIN, by the second digit 'S.' The luxo Berlinetta replaced the Type LT, and made use of said LT's Amberlite insulation blankets, and the already seen RPO Z54 Interior Décor Quiet Sound package. However, the visuals were revised, with a bright upper and lower grille, brightwork for windshield/rear window moldings, dual pinstripe decoration and color-keyed D35 Sport mirrors. There was argent appliqué on the rear deck, with Polycast PE1 rims as standard and color-keyed alloys optional. U05 dual horns and U14 Special Instrumentation were standard.

Camaro against the odds

The Rally Sport Camaro continued, and all '79 Camaros received the new square style dashboard. This made the a/c vents part of the instrument cluster. Base Camaros and the Camaro RS came with the 250in³ six as stock equipment, but the two-barrel 305 V8 was automatically included with the Berlinetta. 1978 had been a record year for Cadillac, and 1979 broke all records for GM's much loved, old skool performance cars. This was the economic calm before the storm in the auto industry.

The new '79 Foxstang was selling very well, and Jeep sales were buoyant. AMC's Spirit marked the return of a small block V8 option in the company's subcompact, for the first time since the 1976 Gremlin. More than that, American Motors' non-Jeep line, regular passenger cars, the Spirit and Concord, even turned a profit! However, just around the corner lay the second world fuel crisis, with an OPEC-induced overnight doubling of the price of a barrel of oil. This brought recessionary consequences for an industry where the domestic brands weren't having the greatest of times, if one looked in general terms, beyond specific examples of success.

Comparing August 1979 sales with the previous August, the domestic automakers were 20 per cent down. Chrysler Corp had nearly gone bankrupt in 1978. Going into 1980 model year, imports took 30 per cent of the market for the first time. When a 50-day surplus stock was normal, the once hot selling Ford Fairmont and Mercury Zephyr siblings, were on 85 days. The Mustang and Capri Fox based coupes sat on 70 days, and even the successful GM X cars had a 60-day stock surplus. Except for the once much-in-demand Datsun Zee, fuel sipping puddle hoppers were in high demand, with limited stock. It was predicted that 25 per cent of new car dealers

Car and Driver's '78 Camaro Z28 four-speed did 0-60 in 7.3 seconds and 123mph. This was greased lightning for the malaise era. (Courtesy www.grautogallery.com)

It was a time when vinyl looked like leather, not the other way around!
(Courtesy www.grautogallery.com)

would be out of business by the end of 1979.

Acknowledging the troubled state of the Big Four, Washington DC eased up on pending safety regulations, like mandatory airbags. There was even talk of relaxing bumper laws, although you would have to wait until 1987 for that. The government's puritanical tirade against automakers, with post-1967 safety and smog law, had contributed to the weakening of employment in the industry. Over one million auto workers were laid off by the end of 1979. Legislation had diverted resources away from designing the gas misers that the public wanted for the '80s. So, at the eleventh hour, the nation's political representatives were charitable enough to give the Big Three and AMC a little wiggle room, so they could catch up with the imports.

The success of GM's old, standby performance cars and other traditional rear-drive, V8-powered domestics showed two things. Firstly, there was still good demand for the kind of cars Americans used to buy. Secondly, the market was divided between traditional domestic car and truck buyers, think Camaro and C10/K10 Blazer, and those Americans

1979 was a peak sales year for Camaro and Z28. Respective zeniths were 282,571 Camaros, including 84,877 Z28s. They truly were number one! This 1979 Camaro Z28 is a one owner car. (Courtesy Tara Martin)

Blake Bender's restomod 1979 Camaro Sport Coupe was partly inspired by the Camaro featured in the 1982 movie *Fast Times At Ridgemont High*. (Courtesy Blake Bender)

that bought imports. Major magazines would often do comparison tables, showing something like a Camaro Berlinetta and Volvo 242 GL, plus a Japanese coupe. However, in reality such cars had different buyer streams, even within imports.

The second fuel crisis and ensuing recession adversely affected V8 cars, Jeeps and trucks more so, in a market where sales were down across the board. Although, there were examples of rising sales in the econobox crowd, and for some high end sports, luxury imports. The latter being a very small sector, usually impervious to economic fluctuations.

1980 Camaro sales fell to 152,005, with the Z28 on just 41,825. *Car and Driver* had the rhetoric ready in April 1980: "Chevrolet Camaro Z28. A medieval warrior on the path to a rocking chair." Much blame for falling GM F-body sales was attributed to the aging nature of Camaro and Firebird. However, the Corvette and Porsche 911 were even older, and their sales didn't plummet. They were part of that fluctuation compliant, upscale sports, luxury segment. F-body sales were more recession affected, with people forced to shoehorn themselves into some overpriced micro beer can, which turned into a four-wheeled boat anchor the moment you turned on the a/c. But hey, you were getting great gas mileage right?! Beware mild inclines …

The original 305 two-bbl V8 has given way to this very stout four-barrel, 400-horse (rwhp) 377ci small block stroker with aluminum heads.
(Courtesy Blake Bender)

To get some of those now-sacred MPGs, the 250in^3 inline six gave way to the 49-state LCE Chevrolet oddfire 229in^3 V6, and the Californian Buick LD5 evenfire 231in^3 V6. Both had an NVH-scary 90 degrees between the banks, revealing their $3/4$ V8 natures. Smoother and more desirable than either was the new to Camaro, 262 cube, L39 V8. It

The V8 power goes through a THM 350 to a 3.73 rear axle and ten-bolt Positraction lsd, like you would find on a 1971 Z28. (Courtesy Blake Bender)

made the new federally mandated, 85mph, Jimmy Cartified speedometer seem almost comforting. The 1980 Camaro Z28 marched onto 190 horses, thanks to cold air induction on THM 350 cars. It really made a difference. *Car and Driver*'s April '80

Artist Dave 'Big' Deal's take on the classic Chevrolet Blazer. With downsizing, CAFE, front drive and other maladies afoot, the Camaro and Blazer were increasingly some of the few locations where one could find a four-barrel V8 underhood.
(Courtesy Armstrong Tires)

This 1979 Camaro Z28 features Doug Thorley sidepipes connected to shorty headers. (Courtesy Mike Meerdo)

Power comes from a modified LM1 four-barrel 350 V8. It has been overbored 0.030in, with compression ratio increased from a stock 8.2:1 to 10:1. The camshaft is slightly wilder, and valve sizes hail from the 1st gen Z28 302's era, with 2.02in intake and 1.60in exhaust. (Courtesy Mike Meerdo)

report showed the automatic to be swifter than the four-speed. It was a 16.09-second pass at 84.6mph, rather than a 16.4-second result at 86mph.

At full throttle, the cold air injection made its presence heard with 85 decibels. That was quite an induction roar! A rear-pointing hoodscoop aperture opened with the pedal to the metal, courtesy of a solenoid actuated flap. It took cold air from the windshield's base, like 1969's ZL2 hood. Now, the Camaro Z28 was the only Camaro specifiable with the LM1 350.

There had been some powerplant 'musical chairs' parlor games at GM since 1977. Back then the Chevmobile scandal saw annoyed Olds owners discover a Chevrolet, not Rocket, 350 V8 under the hood, so their dealers didn't have the correct belts at service or repair time. A legal case ensued, and by the '80s divisional tags were dropped, in favor of 'GM family engine.'

Then, there was the new Poncho LU8 301 Turbo unit. Originally it was going to be an engine option

for the 1980 Camaro Z28. It was an easy way to reach 210bhp, but was cancelled from the options sheet, lest it put the heat on Corvette. Meanwhile, PMD was offered the LM1 350 V8 for the 1980 Trans Am. However, Pontiac said thanks, but no thanks, and kept it all Pontiac in 1980-81. For now, each division was keeping to its own, but soon we would be living in a small block world. The 1980 Camaro Z28 came with P225/70R-15s standard, with the option of N90 alloys in body matching silver, gold or black.

Camaro Z28 graphics were now triple hue, and black accents ran through the tail-light lenses. Mechanically, Z28 was toned down to match declining firepower, because for the most part things were quiet outside the top LM1 350 V8. In 1980, you could get a Camaro Z28 with LG4 305 four-bbl V8. In California, that's all you got, and it came with ten more horses than a non-Z28 305.

It was a 165bhp mill, with all 305s featuring an 8.6:1 CR, versus the 350's 8.2:1. All Golden State

In place of the stock engine-driven cooling fan comes two 4th gen Camaro electric fans. The usual THM 350 has given way to a GM 700R/4 four-speed automatic. (Courtesy Mike Meerdo)

Camaro Z28s, Trans Ams and Corvettes had the LG4/THM 350 power team in 1980. However, the Corvette rested on 180bhp. This was believed to have been achieved via a freer exhaust system. So, no four-speed in California due to smog law. It was still the mecca for sporty cars, but now it was hard to understand why, given that anything with decent power lay in the other 49 states.

The new Saginaw four-speed for the Camaro Z28 had a 3.42 low gear, 10.34in clutch and 3.08 rear axle. Automatic Z28s retained the 3.42 rear gears. A short 1st gear tried to move *Car and Driver*'s 1980, Z28 four-speed's 3660lb bulk off the line with some alacrity. However, physics dictated a 0-60mph time of 8.5 seconds, with 0-100mph in 23.1 seconds. Maxed out, it was 120mph in top with 4700rpm, and the coupe registered 14mpg overall. Fortunately steering and suspension don't pollute. The 1980 Camaro Z28 sported 13:1 straight ratio steering. Front spring rates were the same as in 1977, but the Zee's front swaybar was reduced in diameter from 1.2in to 1.125in. The F41 came with a 1in bar, when stock Camaros possessed 0.938in. Rear spring rate was 130lb-in, with a 0.594in rear swaybar, with the F41 on 0.562 in. The standard Camaro came with no rear swaybar, and between base and Z28, you could try Camaro RS. 12,015 bought the Z85 1980 Camaro RS, with D80 rear spoiler standard, plus Rally rims, and PE1 or

N90 wheels optional. Add F41 and LG4 305, and the compromise was complete.

Ice age Camaro Z28 during the Cold War
MotorWeek offered a vision of the automotive future in its late 1979 pilot episode. It pitted the family cars of the '80s, a 200in³ Fairmont six against a 2.8-liter V6 Citation. The show predicted that by 1985, these vehicles would be the largest-sized family cars going. In a fall Maryland setting, the *MotorWeek* proving grounds resembled a post-apocalyptic zombie movie. It was 85bhp of Ford versus 115 ponies of Citation. Flesh eating, mutant zombies didn't alight to devour the car testers, but if they did, it would have proved a very great deal more entertaining than driving either the Fairmont or the Citation. There are cars bought from desire, and those purchased out of necessity: these new age family cars were as far removed from desire as Fiat is from reliability. Concerning the pending '80s, enthusiasts could only think "Saints preserve us." Next to this practical pair, the 190-horse Camaro Z28 automatic was greased lightning wearing a spoiler!

Icicles on Floridian oranges, and snow in Miami. Indeed, America struggled through the winter of 1976-77, causing *National Geographic*'s Thomas Y Canby to pose the question: "Is nature on a rampage?" In addition, whether these " ... are

The customized interior features a cherry laminate cut to fit the Z28's gauges. Seating has been recovered in two colors, with Z28 insignia embroidered on the bucket's apex. Sounds come from an aftermarket head unit.
(Courtesy Mike Meerdo)

recognizable long-term patterns of adverse climatic behavior?" [21] At this time scientists believed the world was heading for another ice age, as deer died amid the snow drifts.

To combat all this, the Feds were making smog law stricter, while curbing consumption of finite fossil fuels via CAFE. With all this pending clean air at hand, it was high time for a ragtop, but not from the factory. No, feared federal roll over tests, which never came, had stopped new ragtops in their tire tracks for years. However, have no fear; specialists could oblige.

The company was American Clout of San Jose California. It did conversions for Camaro Z28, Firebird Formula and Trans Ams. It was an offshoot of Autowest, which sold such ragtops to Budget Rent-A-Car. Now, American Clout was a medium or interface, through which Chevrolet and Pontiac dealers across the land, could get a ragtop to buyers. The coachwork and sail cloth top were done by NCE (National Coach Engineering) of Port Sanilac, Michigan.

The roof was removed, and the top handmade. The windshield frame was judged strong enough, and front and rear subframes were joined by steel box section longitudinals. For a convertible, it had a rigid chassis and a loaded nature. So, expect stuff like a/c and $112 Cruise Master K30 cruise

This Camaro Z28 rides on aftermarket American Racing Stics 5 that are no longer in production.
(Courtesy Mike Meerdo)

The Camaro Berlinetta made a 1979 debut as a luxury replacement for the Type LT. It proved popular with personal car buyers wishing to downsize. This is a 1980 ad. (Courtesy GM Archives)

control. American Clout production involved five to ten cars per week, and the spokesman was Chuck Hindmarsh. Autowest President was Chuck Hill. The sail cloth material was Rolls Royce Corniche-like. It was serene at 100mph, with the top down. Buffeting was minimal.

At $16,500, an American Clout convertible was exclusive fun, and suffered only minor problems. Rough roads brought some chassis flex, and the plastic rear window of the top limited rear vision. At this price, a power top would have been nice. Coping with the manual top solo, was heavy going. Yes, it was the price of a Corvette, but with around 150 Camaro Z28 convertibles per annum, as opposed to 40,000 to 50,000 Corvettes, American Clout delivered exclusivity.

Product placement

The American Clout convertibles were showcased on the fifth and final season of TV show *Charlie's Angels*, 1980-81. They were seen in the Hawaiian

In the 1979 Chevrolet range one didn't have to point out the enthusiast cars. In common with domestic rivals 'old V8 gold' was the only way to go! (Courtesy Vereinigte Motor-Verlage)

Rolling into 1980, serious performance ponies were limited to two choices: Camaro Z28 or Pontiac Trans Am. (Courtesy Richard Budman www.FlemingsUltimateGarage.com)

set episodes, where the Angels had gone to the Hawaiian branch of the Townsend Detective Agency. Here, in episodes two (To See an Angel Die) through six (Hula Angels), Cheryl Ladd's character Kris Munroe, drove a dark brown Z28 ragtop. There wasn't much product placement done with the Camaro. This was probably because, early on, GM didn't think the F-body would continue. Later, the cars were selling so well it just didn't matter.

A direct case of Chevrolet being involved was with the TV show The Adventurer. It was a British-made show from ITC Entertainment, the film subsidiary of export-oriented TV company ATV. The Adventurer lasted for one season, 1972-73, and starred Gene Barry. Barry played government agent Gene Bradley, who was masquerading as an American movie star. It was a series very much in the mold of contemporary glamour spy shows, such as The Saint, The Baron, and The Persuaders! Bradley's wheels were a 1972 Camaro SS350. It shared screen time with Maserati Ghiblis and Alfa Spiders in exotic locations. When the show aired in America, it was sponsored by

Chevrolet, hence the choice of the non-RS Camaro with license plate 32 SR 501.

A 1970 $^1/_2$ Camaro SS396, was raced in the 1976 Cannonball Run-inspired movie, The Gumball Rally. Like the real life, 55mph, national speed limit-defying act of civil disobedience, the movie mostly had driver and co-driver piloting speed machines across country. These vehicles included solo bikers and van based teams. The Gumball Rally was the second movie to portray the Cannonball Run. Here, Team Camaro had Gary Busey as Gibson, who spent the entire race annoying his co-driver.

Eventually, near the finish line, Gibson rolls the Hugger on the highway, nearly taking out a red Mustang II Ghia hardtop in the process. The stunt of getting the pale yellow Camaro onto two wheels was performed by Joey Chitwood of the JC Auto Thrill Show. Even though it was a popular movie, Busey's Gibson attempting to relieve himself into a plastic bottle on a snaking backroad wasn't exactly product placement.

In 1977, Henry Winkler starred with Sally Field

In April 1980, *Car and Driver* wasn't too complimentary about Camaro Z28. The journal may have referred to it as a medieval warrior, but sporting car fans loved it.
(Courtesy Richard Budman www.FlemingsUltimateGarage.com)

in the movie *Heroes*. Here, Winkler visits a fellow Vietnam veteran, played by Harrison Ford, who is a stock car racer with a modified '71 Camaro. The coupe gets very trashed in the movie. Once again, it wasn't really beneficial to the Camaro's image.

Another Camaro got pretty beat up in the 1977 movie *In Hot Pursuit* (aka *Polk County Pot Plane*). This movie starred real life stuntmen the Watson brothers, and saw them pull off an armored car bank robbery, using a '68 Camaro 350 as a getaway vehicle. The pair get far enough from the law to switch cars, taking a lady's brand new '77 Ford Maverick four-door sedan from her garage, and replacing it with the trashed Camaro. Naturally, the Ford owner is shocked when she opens the garage door!

Those classic Camaros

You could call the 1981 Camaro largely a carry-over model, with some noteworthy amendments. It proved to be the final year for the 2nd gen F-body. It had 2.84 million sales over 12 production years, mostly for the North American market. Home designed, built and sold, the Camaro and Firebird

Somewhere under all that smog gear and creature feature accessories lay a LM1 350 small block! In 1980, automatic Z28 350s enjoyed a power hike to 190bhp. (Courtesy Richard Budman www.FlemingsUltimateGarage.com)

represented how it was successfully done in Detroit's golden years, moving into the malaise era. Although taking some design influence from overseas, such coupes represented the traditional V8, rear-drive cars that Detroit did so well. The long production run,

1980 saw suspension revisions. Front spring rates stayed at 1977's level, but front swaybar diameter was reduced to 1.125in. Rear leafs were at 130lb/in. Overall, Z28 suspension still had an edge over the regular F41 sports suspension. From 1977, the familiar stamped steel 15 x 7in Z28 rims were color-matched to the body's paint job. (Courtesy Richard Budman www.FlemingsUltimateGarage.com)

once a common occurrence, allowed designs to be refined and improved, until they became a known and trusted quantity.

By 1981, that quantity was 126,139 Camaros sold. 52,004 of such coupes were V6-powered, reflecting the gas mileage seeking, recessionary times. The basic 1981 figures spoke of a 110-horse, 231in³ V6, motorvating a 3325lb two-door, with a 21-gallon tank and an associated EPA rating of 16mpg city and 19mpg highway. To achieve this in 49-state form, you would be working the MM3 wide ratio three-speed, for the LC3 motor. A base Sport Coupe would set you back $6581.23, or you could try the $7356.23 Berlinetta. However, the Camaro Z28 was holding steady on 43,272, at an MSRP of $8025.23. The Zee outsold Berlinetta better than two to one. Your performance choices were simple: a Camaro Z28 with 165bhp stick and 305 V8, or slushbox only LM1 350-powered Z28 with 175 horses.

In February 1981, *Road Test* matched the strongest Camaro Z28 available, almost, against the wildest Trans Am, the LU8 301 Turbo Poncho; 'almost' involved skipping the 3.08 'performance axle' in favor of what was described as the 'EPA Memorial Axle.' That is, 2.73 rear gears, or 'may performance rest in peace' econoaxle. Even so,

for the day, this Z28 did okay. A 16.483-second, manually shifted pass on the third run of six, at 85.63mph, and 0-60mph in 8.9 seconds. It could do all this on 87 octane unleaded. At the time, a Porsche 928 automatic, costing nearly five times the Camaro's price, could not break 8 seconds in North America, smogged down as it was.

In 1981, the most lively Foxstang V8 could only muster a feeble 255in³ V8, with 120 mini ponies for its Cobra. This sedan coupe was the possessor of an 18.2 second ¹/₄ mile, according to *Car and Driver*. Heck, that ain't no Fox Henry, that's roadkill! You could specify a four-speed, but the question was, why?! Concerning *Road Test*'s Camaro Z28, a best highway economy figure of 20.3mpg (US gallon) aligned with an official EPA rating of 15mpg city and 22mpg highway. Not bad for a 3656lb V8 coupe with a/c. The Turbo Trans Am had more of everything on test, including a sizable $8759 asking price. GM corporate policy had witnessed Corvette and Trans Am getting the good stuff since 1972. So the Zee was playing third fiddle, but that would change in the '80s.

The Trans Am F-body sibling had 200bhp, four-wheel disks, 15x8in rims *etc*. Therefore, it came as no surprise that the Camaro Z28's 0.77g skidpad reading should fall short of the T/A's 0.82g

Six C60 factory a/c vents, no waiting! In common with so-equipped 2nd gen Firebirds, the low set two vents for driver and passenger were effective. (Courtesy Richard Budman www. FlemingsUltimateGarage.com)

A 1980 styling revision saw a black accent run through taillight lenses. (Courtesy Richard Budman www.FlemingsUltimateGarage.com)

equivalent. In addition, there was the Chevrolet engineering predilection for understeer, exacerbated by a lack of underhood V8 moxie. However, on that mild December SoCal $^1/_4$ mile day of reckoning, the Trans Am's margin was indeed marginal. Its 3.08 rear axle could have really helped the Z28. The coupes were also similar in their EPA-directed lean carb settings. It caused 'em to overheat, in short order. And yet, some years earlier, one could rip off a

This top of the line 1980 Camaro Z28 automatic has the stock cold air induction and optional N90 15 x 7in alloy rims. '80 MY saw new graphics, hoodscoop and grille, plus flat fender vents. (Courtesy Barry Kluczyk)

succession of passes, sans sweat … but not now.

While these cars represented the last of the old, the 1981 editions did show signs of tomorrow's world. For one, both cars had an electronic Q-jet. This device had been seen on Californian 1980 LG4 305 Corvettes. It adjusted the air/fuel mixture ten times per second. Using the CCC (Computer Command Control) moniker, you had an electronic solenoid linked to a narrow band oxygen sensor. The sensor observed the air/fuel ratio, and adjusted the pulse width of the solenoid accordingly, for optimal emissions/power. Fuel was added, or reduced, in parallel with the Q-jet's primary metering circuit.

CCC took throttle position, coolant temp, and air pressure via the intake manifold; that is, MAP, or manifold absolute pressure. The second element was a familiar bane to many modern motorists: a dashboard engine check light. Yes, the future had indeed arrived, just waiting for those cup holders! The 1981 Camaros also utilized another element

seen since the first fuel crisis: a lock-up torque converter for the automatic gearbox. To maximize mileage, CCC also controlled when the torque converter locked up in 2nd and 3rd. The MX1 slushbox only did top gear.

The option of the G92 3.42 rear axle for four-speed Z28s was overlooked. It cost 18 bucks. The $36 TR4 halogen headlight option was very worthwhile. The GM F-body had been criticized for years, due to its bean counter-dictated stock headlamps. However, only 8715 buyers took the TR4 bait! CCC had permitted the four-speed to return to California, and you could now get the LG4 305 four-speed power team in the Golden State. In Canada, the 1981 Camaro Z28 350 could have a four-speed, and this market didn't have CCC.

From a long term, and not so long term, perspective, the new age electronics were often a concern. Certainly, the computer-controlled torque converter lock-up proved problematic in terms of smooth shifting on 1982 Crossfire coupes. Many

According to the 1980 April issue of *Car and Driver*, the automatic Zee did zero to sixty in 8.5 seconds, and a 16.09 second pass at 84.6mph. It was quicker than its tested four-speed. (Courtesy Barry Kluczyk)

The 1979-81 'square dash' put the a/c vents on the instrument cluster surround. Right to the end of production, the 2nd gen F-body featured a domestic-style park brake and footwell-mounted headlight dipswitch. (Courtesy Barry Kluczyk)

The 1977-80 LM1 350 V8 proved a spirited and reliable performer. Unlike later Crossfire and TPI 350s, the four-barrel LM1 was tweakable for more power with carb and distributor adjustments. Milling the heads to raise compression ratio woke things up also. (Courtesy Barry Kluczyk)

Z28, it was the RPO that became a model, and very quickly, a legend.

You could say *Car and Driver* got 0-100mph in 23.1 seconds, and that *Road Test* registered 0.77g on the skidpad. However, the Z28 had a special quality for car lovers that transcended mere statistics. (Courtesy Barry Kluczyk)

The new Z28 Camaro is for those rare drivers who understand the rush of finely machined road cars. That's the way it should be. The Z28 incorporates lots of special parts that make it capable of spectacular performance. That's the way it's always been. The Z28 is Chevrolet's continuing expression of excellence in engineering and design. That's the way it'll always be. See your Chevrolet dealer about buying or leasing a new Z28. And soon.

Spread your wings

1981 CAMARO Z28. THE HUGGER.

The 1981 Chevrolet Camaro Z28 ... this is where freedom begins! (Courtesy GM Archives)

also prefer the dependability of non-electronic Rochester Quadrajets. On TV in 1980, commercials saw Chevrolet speaking in tongues. Well, it was actually metric, advertising the 5.7-liter Camaro Z28, while a line flashed up on the screen informing (or was that warning?) that California was restricted to the "5.0-liter (305 CID)" motor concerning the Z28. For all the adopted sophistication, the 2nd gen

Camaro Z28 was still a rough and ready racer. So, the final Z28 ad-line was appropriate: "Z28 Parts and parcel, rare road machinery."

In the '80s, there was a move within GM, and outside, to go high tech, world class performance, street sleeper, or adopt any other buzz word or modern industry-speak going. Wild graphics and hood decals fell by the wayside, on the road to refinement. However, the early Camaro F-body's appeal, and that of the Corvette, has always been about raw feel, bucket loads of torque, and frequently manhandling a shift. Then, too, there's the question of value.

With modern safety, emissions and the kind of standard equipment the average buyer now wants, or thinks they want (Cadillac calls it "features to the eyeballs"), you just can't buy an affordable, stripped down car like a 1981 Camaro Z28 four-speed sans a/c. Post hiatus, the Camaro returned as a retro 5th gen. It looked a lot like the 1st gen, but sometimes you just can't beat the real thing.

(Courtesy Elizabeth Cranswick)

Now <u>that's</u> more like it.

The 1977 Caprice Classic Sedan.

Appendix A – Camaro Z28 – Chevrolet's Four Aces

1968 Chevrolet Camaro Z28

Price: $2694 (base Camaro), Z28 package $400.25, fast steering (17:1) $15.80, Positraction lsd $42.15, power front disk brakes $100.10, four-speed $184.35, power steering $84.30

Engine: Solid lifter OHV all cast-iron Z28 small block Chevrolet V8, four-bolt mains, 4.00x3.00in (302ci), 290bhp @ 5800rpm, 370lb/ft @ 4000rpm (SAE gross), 11.0:1 CR, Holley four-bbl carburetion

Dimensions: 184.6in length, 72.3in width, 50.9in height

Weight: 3355lb

Luggage capacity: 8.3ft^3

Front/rear track: 59.6in/59.5in

Gearbox: GM four-speed Muncie Close Ratio M21 1st (2.20) 2nd (1.64) 3rd (1.27) 4th (1.00) 4.10:1 (final drive ratio)

Front suspension: Independent unequal length A arms, coil springs, tube shocks, swaybar (0.6875in)

Rear suspension: Live axle, leaf springs, tube shocks

Wheels & tires: 15x6.0in Rally rims & Goodyear WideTread GT E70-15 bias belted

Brakes: 11in vented disk (front), 9x2.0in drum (rear), swept area 332in^2

0-60mph: 6.9 seconds

$^1/_4$ mile: 14.9 seconds @ 100mph

Top speed: 132mph

Fuel economy: 11mpg (premium gas)

Performance & economy data: *Road & Track*

June 1968

As far as the SCCA's Trans Am series that the Camaro Z28 was intended for, Chevrolet came, saw and Donohue, Penske & Sunoco conquered! The 1st gen Z28 moseyed in with a high winding 302 V8, and became a domestic handling icon. It lasted long after the Trans Am series' early '70s implosion. If you wanted peace and quiet, with no inkling there was a road under you … find another ride!

1970 $^1/_2$ Chevrolet Camaro Z28

Price: $2839 (base Camaro), Z28 package $572.95, power brakes $47.40, 12-bolt Positraction lsd $44.25

Engine: Solid lifter OHV all cast-iron LT1 small block Chevrolet V8, four-bolt mains, 4.00x3.48in (350ci), 360bhp @ 5600rpm, 370lb/ft @ 4000rpm (SAE gross), 11.0:1 CR, Holley four-bbl carburetion

Dimensions: 188in length, 74.4in width, 50.1in height

Weight: 3640lb

Luggage capacity: 6.5ft^3

Front/rear track: 61.3in/60in

Gearbox: GM Turbo Hydra Matic 400 three-speed automatic with 2:1 ratio amplifying torque converter – 1st (2.48) 2nd (1.48) 3rd (1.00) 4.10:1 (final drive ratio)

Front suspension: Independent unequal length A arms, coil springs, tube shocks, swaybar (1.0in)

Rear suspension: Live axle, leaf springs, tube shocks, swaybar (0.69in)

Wheels & tires: 15x7.0in styled steel rims & Goodyear Polyglas GT F60-15 bias belted

Brakes: 11in vented disk (front), 9.5x2.0in drum

(rear), swept area 332.4 sq in

0-60mph: 5.8 seconds

¹/₄ mile: 14.2 seconds @ 100.3mph

Top speed: 118mph

Fuel economy: 11mpg (premium gas)

Performance & economy data: *Car and Driver*, May 1970

The Z28 was back for 1970, bigger and badder than ever, in the peak year of domestic high performance. The Camaro Z28 was no longer a SCCA Trans Am champ, but redefined domestic roadcar handling. And what about that one year only 12-bolt Posi?!

1974 Chevrolet Camaro Z28

Price: $3039.70 (base Camaro), Z28 package $513.45, D80 spoilers $77, D88 four-color stripe decal set $77

Engine: Hydraulic lifter OHV all cast-iron L82 small block Chevrolet V8, four-bolt mains, 4.00x3.48in (350ci), 245bhp @ 5200rpm, 280lb/ft @ 4000rpm (SAE net), 9.0:1 CR, Rochester Quadrajet carburetion

Dimensions: 195.4in length, 74.4in width, 49.2in height

Weight: 3840lb

Luggage capacity: 7.3ft³ (space saver)

Front/rear track: 61.6in/60.3in

Gearbox: GM Turbo Hydra Matic 400 three-speed automatic with 2:1 ratio amplifying torque converter – 1st (2.48) 2nd (1.48) 3rd (1.00) 3.73:1 (final drive ratio)

Front suspension: Independent unequal length A arms, coil springs, tube shocks, swaybar (0.938in)

Rear suspension: Live axle, leaf springs, tube shocks, swaybar (0.69in)

Wheels & tires: 15x7.0in styled steel rims & Goodyear Polyglas GT F60-15 bias belted

Brakes: 11in vented disk (front), 9.5x2.0in drum (rear), swept area 332.4 sq in

0-60mph: 8.1 seconds

¹/₄ mile: 15.415 seconds @ 90.54mph

Top speed: 125mph (estimate)

Fuel economy: 13.3mpg (regular gas)

Performance & economy data: *Motor Trend*, April 1974

The Camaro Z28 was still hanging in there in 1974, courtesy of an hydraulic lifter L82 350, shared with the Corvette. It reached a sales record of 13,802 that year, but Chevrolet still put the *Zee* on hiatus until mid '77 MY. It seemed the public had fallen out of love with high performance.

1981 Chevrolet Camaro Z28

Price: $8025.23 (base Z28), tested with C60 a/c ($560)

Engine: Hydraulic lifter OHV all cast-iron LM1 small block Chevrolet V8, two-bolt mains, 4.00x3.48in (350ci), 175bhp @ 4000rpm, 275lb/ft @ 2400rpm (SAE net), 8.2:1 CR, Rochester Electronic Quadrajet carburetion, Computer Command Control (CCC)

Dimensions: 197in length, 74.4in width, 50.1in height

Weight: 3656lb

Luggage capacity: 7.3ft³

Front/rear track: 61.3in/60in

Gearbox: GM Turbo Hydra Matic 350 three-speed automatic with 2:1 ratio amplifying CCC lock up torque converter on 2nd & 3rd – 1st (2.48) 2nd (1.48) 3rd (1.00) 2.73:1 (final drive ratio)

Front suspension: Independent unequal length A arms, coil springs, tube shocks, swaybar (1.125in)

Rear suspension: Live axle, leaf springs, tube shocks, swaybar (0.594in)

Wheels & tires: 15x7.0in N90 cast aluminum rims (in silver, gold or black – color-keyed to body colors) & Goodyear Polysteel P225/70R-15 radials

Brakes: 11in vented disk (front), 9.5x2.0in drum (rear), swept area 332.4 sq in

0-60mph: 8.9 seconds

$^1\!/_4$ mile: 16.483 seconds @ 85.63mph

Top speed: 120mph (estimate)

Fuel economy: 16mpg (87 octane unleaded gas)

Performance & economy data: *Road Test,* February 1981

It was the swansong for the Super Hugger, with the Camaro Z28 using a tuned version of the LM1 350 V8 in automatic form only. Between 1977 and 1981, the mighty Zee was a standalone model that majored in appearance and newly fashionable handling. However, the Z28 still had good performance for the year, and was no sales slouch. The coupe still garnered 43,272 customers in 1981.

Appendix B – Chevrolet Items of Interest

Websites

camaro5.com
A 5th gen directed site, with forums for earlier Camaros, too.

camaroforums.com
This enthusiast forum covers all Camaro generations. It has regional, Canadian and overseas subsections. There is also an 'Ask GM' sub-forum.

www.camaroz28.com
In spite of its Camaro Z28 forum title, this message board covers all Camaros. It has F-body forum subsections for Pontiac Firebird also.

nastyz28.com
A 2nd gen Camaro owners group and informational resource.

www.customworksperformance.net
A company specializing in performance products, for the 2nd gen Camaro.

www.chevytalk.org
If it wears the Bowtie badge, this website has a forum for it!

ls1tech.com
Many classic Camaro owners have either done, or are contemplating an LS V8 swap. This GM LS performance forum can help.

www.chevyforum.org
A late model Chevrolet forum with a Camaro section.

Bibliography

Autocar, w/e 31 August 1974

Boyce, Terry V, "1967-70 Cadillac Eldorado: Applying a Personal Touch" *Collectible Automobile*, June 2015

Canby, Thomas Y, "The Year the Weather Went Wild" *National Geographic*, December 1977

Car and Driver, September 1969

Grove, Noel, "Swing Low, Sweet Chariot!" *National Geographic*, July 1983

Kelly, Steve, "Sports Car Tournament: Cobra Vs Corvette" *Motor Trend*, March 1968

Knepper, Mike, "Second International Race Of Champions" *Road & Track*, February 1975

Lankard, Tom, "Laws & Your Car" *Road & Track*, February 1975

Motor Sport, August 1973

Mueller, Mike & David, Dennis, *Classic Fifties Cars*, Osceola: MBI, 2006

Myers, Bob, "NASCAR GT And Trans-Am Head Into '68 Season: "Baby Grand" Cars Make Debut on NASCAR Circuits Trans-Am Now in Third Year" *Motor Trend*, March 1968

Road & Track, February 1975

Robson, Graham, *Classic and Sportscar A-Z Of Cars Of The 1970s*, Bay View Books, 1990

Ruszkiewicz, Joe, "1967 Mod Rod" *Rod & Custom*, February 1967

Stone, Matt, *Mustang 5.0 & 4.6 1979-1998*, Osceola: MBI, 1998

Tremayne, David. "Gardner's question time" *Classic & Sports Car*, June 1998

Whipple, Jim (ed), *Popular Mechanics All The 1964 Models*, New York: Popular Mechanics, 1963

Wilson, Quentin, *Great Car*, New York: Dorling Kindersley Publishing Inc, 2001.

Endnotes

[1] Noel Grove, "Swing Low, Sweet Chariot!" *National Geographic* (July 1983): p13

[2] Jim Whipple (ed), *Popular Mechanics All The 1964 Models* (New York: Popular Mechanics, 1963): p11

[3] Quentin Wilson, *Great Car* (New York: Dorling Kindersley Publishing Inc, 2001): p134

[4] Terry V, Boyce, "1967-70 Cadillac Eldorado: Applying a Personal Touch" *Collectible Automobile* (June 2015): p20

[5] "Bridgehampton Trans-Am ... And Then The Stewards Met" *Car and Driver* (September 1969): p63

[6] Matt Stone, *Mustang 5.0 & 4.6 1979-1998* (Osceola: MBI, 1998): p118

[7] Bob Myers, "NASCAR GT And Trans-Am Head Into '68 Season: "Baby Grand" Cars Make Debut on NASCAR Circuits Trans-Am Now in Third Year" *Motor Trend* (March 1968): p61

[8] Mike Mueller & Dennis David, *Classic Fifties Cars* (Osceola: MBI, 2006): p49

[9] Steve Kelly, "Sports Car Tournament: Cobra Vs Corvette" *Motor Trend* (March 1968): p55

[10] Joe Ruszkiewicz, "1967 Mod Rod" *Rod & Custom* (February 1967): p51

[11] "Corvette Sting Ray, 1963-67" *Road & Track* (February 1975): p54

[12] Wilson, op cit. p150

[13] "Worldwide Comment. The worm turns" *Autocar* (w/e 31 August 1974): p16

[14] Ibid. p44

[15] Grove, op cit. p13

[16] David Tremayne, "Gardner's question time" *Classic & Sports Car* (June 1998): p94

[17] "Around and About – Avon Motor Tour of Britain" *Motor Sport* (August 1973): p872

[18] Tom Lankard, "Laws & Your Car" *Road & Track* (February 1975): p16

[19] Mike Knepper, "Second International Race Of Champions" *Road & Track* (February 1975): p106

[20] Robson Graham, *Classic and Sportscar A-Z Of Cars Of The 1970s* (Devon: Bay View Books, 1990): p35

[21] Thomas Y. Canby, "The Year the Weather Went Wild" *National Geographic* (December 1977): p799

Details the evolution of Ford's family car through the golden era of Detroit. It tells how Henry took the no-frills Fairlane, added more zing to create the Torino, and satisfied America's luxury desires with the LTD II; and follows the evolution of Ford's mid-size muscle cars, to the creation of the first car-based pickup – the Ranchero.

ISBN: 978-1-845849-29-0
Hardback • 25x20.7cm • 176 pages • 229 pictures

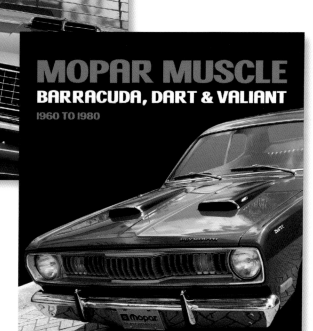

Chrysler Corp's classic rear-drive slant six and V8 compacts of the '60s and '70s. From economy cars to muscle cars, from the street to the strip. The Mopar marvels that challenged rivals and inspired a generation.

ISBN: 978-1-787110-71-7
Hardback • 25x20.7cm • 176 pages • 290 colour and b&w pictures

The history of Ford's first American-designed and built subcompacts. Following the Mustang II and Pinto through a challenging decade, as they competed with domestic and imported rivals in the showroom, and on the racetrack. This book examines icons of the custom car and racing scene, as Ford took Total Performance into a new era.

ISBN: 978-1-787112-67-4
Hardback • 25x20.7cm • 128 pages • 201 pictures

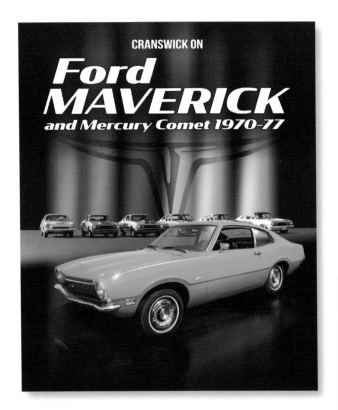

An enthusiast's guide to the commercial and racing history of Ford's Maverick and Comet, charting their development and market battles with domestic and imported rivals, as Ford acknowledged the growing importance of small cars. Covers the sporty Maverick Grabber and Comet GT, and luxury LDO and Custom Option, plus drag racing exploits.

ISBN: 978-1-787116-69-6
Hardback • 25x20.7cm • 160 pages • 241 pictures

A photographic historical study capturing the many Chevrolet Camaro road racing cars in action throughout the world from 1966 to 1984. Includes images of hundreds of Camaros, and uses only period photos, many of which have never been published before.

ISBN: 978-1-787115-12-5
Hardback • 20.7x25cm • 176 pages • 292 pictures

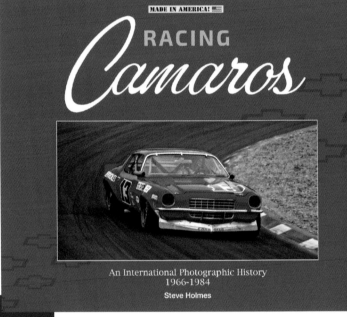

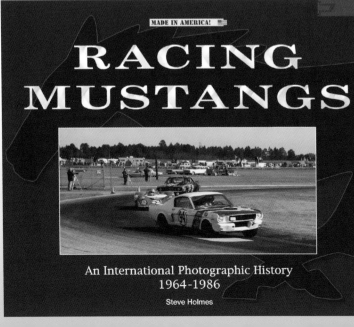

A photographic historical study capturing many Ford Mustang road racing cars in action throughout the world in the period 1964 to 1986. Includes hundreds of period images of Mustangs, many of which have never been published before.

ISBN: 978-1-787117-35-8
Paperback • 20.7x25cm • 176 pages
• 250 pictures

Index